GW00469704

GOD-PRO

DEMO

GOD-PROVOKING DEMOCRAT

The Remarkable Life of Archibald Hamilton Rowan

By Fergus Whelan

NEW ISLAND

GOD-PROVOKING DEMOCRAT
First published in 2015
by
New Island Books
16 Priory Hall Office Park
Stillorgan
County Dublin
Republic of Ireland.

www.newisland.ie

PRINT ISBN: 978-1-84840-460-1
EPUB ISBN: 978-1-84840-461-8
MOBI ISBN: 978-1-84840-462-5

British Library Cataloguing Data.
A CIP catalogue record for this book is available from the British Library.

Typeset by JVR Creative India
Cover design by XXXXX
Printed by ScandBook AB

New Island received financial assistance from The Arts Council (*An Chomhairle Ealaíon*), 70 Merrion Square, Dublin 2, Ireland.

10 9 8 7 6 5 4 3 2 1

For my wife, Sheila.

In memory of Eamon Smullen, 1924–1990

Acknowledgements

Special thanks to Andy Pollock, Padraig Yeates, Theresa Moriarity and Vincent Morley.

Contents

'I have seen many, very many United Irishmen, and with a few exceptions they are … the most God-provoking Democrats on this side of Hell.'

– A New England Federalist Senator
describing his visit to Pennsylvania

1.

Conception at Killyleagh

Says he, 'If ye've laid the pike on the shelf,
Ye'd best go home hot-fut by yerself,
An' once more take it down.'
So by Comber road I trotted the grey
An never cut corn until Killyleagh
Stood plain on the risin' groun'.[1]

Archibald Hamilton Rowan (1751–1834) was born and raised in England. He first saw the light of day at his grandfather's house in Rathbone Place, London, on 12 May 1751. He was educated among the elite of upper-class society at Westminster School and Cambridge University. Arthur Wellesley, the Duke of Wellington, is reputed to have remarked when commenting on his Irish origins, 'If a gentleman happens to be born in a stable, it does not follow that he should be called a horse'.[2] Despite his birth and upbringing, Archibald Hamilton Rowan was not an Englishman; his heart was always in Ireland.[3]

---

1   Wilson (1918), 'The Man From God Knows Where'.
2   He did not say it; Daniel O'Connell later said it of the duke.
3   Campbell (1991), p. 37.

Rowan did not perceive himself as Anglo-Irish, the term sometimes applied to a caste of landed Irish Protestants by those who have imbibed the attitude that to be truly Irish is to be Roman Catholic. Rowan was of Scottish ancestry, but he like his Irish Protestant contemporaries such as Wolfe Tone, William Drennan and Henry Grattan, 'never doubted that they were Irishmen without any qualification'.[4]

Rowan was conceived by his Irish mother at his father's ancestral home, Killyleagh Castle in County Down. This elegant, whimsical castle is still in the possession of the Hamilton Rowan family. Killyleagh's windswept turrets stand perched on a rocky outcrop, dominating the surrounding countryside. To the east lie Strangford Lough and the Ards Peninsula, and yet farther east is the north channel of the Irish Sea. On a clear day the hills of Scotland can be seen on the horizon. The villages of Killyleagh and nearby Comber, Saintfield, Kilkeel, Newtownards and Cloghy feature in Florence Wilson's poem, 'The Man From God Knows Where', which concerns the 1798 rebellion of the United Irishmen and the attempted rebellion of 1803. Although Rowan would take no direct part in the 1798 rebellion, many of the local people of the hinterland of Killyleagh fought at the battles of Saintfield and Ballynahinch. Archibald Hamilton Rowan was conceived in the heartland of enlightened, radical, Presbyterian Ulster.

Rowan was born in London because his mother, Jane Hamilton, had gone there when she knew she was pregnant. Her wish was that her son would have no contact with Ireland during his youth and early manhood.[5] She hoped that Rowan would grow to be a 'cool, foppish'

4   Beckett (1976), p. 10.
5   Nicolson (1943), p. 26.

English aristocrat, loyal to his class and kind, unconcerned about the oppression, poverty and religious divisions of his native country. His mother's stratagems were to no avail. Ironically, it was she who asked Rowan to settle with his family in Ireland many years later. By that time her circumstances, if not her negative attitude towards Ireland, had altered.

Rowan's most illustrious paternal ancestor was James Hamilton, who arrived in Ireland circa 1600. James Hamilton's father was a clergyman, and therefore James was, as they say in Ulster and Scottish parlance, 'a son of the manse'. He graduated from Glasgow University and became a schoolteacher. He came to Ireland as an emissary for James VI of Scotland to serve his interests before the death of Queen Elizabeth I. James Hamilton is said to have negotiated a pardon for the Gaelic chief Conn O'Neill on a charge of treason, and to have conned the feckless Conn out of one third of his property in County Down as a reward for his services,[6] thus becoming a major landowner in east Ulster in the early seventeenth century. He also became a fellow of Trinity College, Dublin. On the death of Queen Elizabeth, James VI of Scotland became James I of England, and James Hamilton was immediately appointed to the Irish Privy Council. He was made Viscount Claneboye in 1622, and was given possession of Killyleagh Castle.

King James had no time for Presbyterianism, which he regarded as incompatible with monarchy, and it is not clear whether he was aware of the new viscount's religious sympathies.[7] While the viscount's 'education and conversation inclined him to be episcopal ... he was in practice Presbyterian'.[8]

---

6   Hanna (2000), p. 22.
7   Holmes (1999), p. 11.
8   Herlihy (1996), p. 20.

Viscount Claneboye is known to have been the patron of at least seven Scottish non-conformist clergymen who settled in Down and Connor, including his own nephew, another James Hamilton.[9] In times of persecution he was willing to shelter non-conformist clergy in his own home.[10]

Hamilton succeeded in wooing Robert Blair, a former teacher of philosophy at Glasgow and one of the most gifted ministers in the contemporary Presbyterian Church of Scotland, to minister at Bangor.[11] Claneboye opened a philosophy school in Killyleagh, which seems an extraordinary project to embark on in a small fishing village in early seventeenth-century Ulster. By the time Archibald Hamilton Rowan penned an account of his ancestry in the late 1790s this school had fallen into decay, but not before it produced at least two world-class scholars: Hans Sloane (1660–1753), founder of the British Museum and inventor of drinking chocolate, as was the great Francis Hutcheson (1694–1746), the father of the Scottish Enlightenment.

Rowan's maternal great-grandfather, William Rowan, had raised a company of men who fought with the Williamite forces at the Boyne in 1690. A letter sent by Queen Anne to the Duke of Ormond on 18 April 1710 suggested that Captain Rowan be rewarded for his many services to 'our late dearest brother and sister, King William and Queen Mary'. Among these services was 'raising a troop of horse in the north of Ireland and arming and subsisting them at his own charge'. Captain Rowan had successfully 'held a pass near Londonderry against the enemy and there lost his lieutenant and many of his men'. He saw military service in Scotland, and when ordered back to Ireland he continued

9   *Ibid.*, p. 19.
10   *Ibid.*, p. 20.
11   Holmes, p. 15.

'his exertions in favour of the [Glorious] Revolution' until the final Williamite victory.[12]

Captain Rowan married Mildred Thompson, who was connected to the Synge family, which had produced a number of bishops and eminent churchmen in the late seventeenth and early eighteenth centuries. The captain hoped that his son, William, would become a clergyman, and with this in mind he sent him to Trinity College, Dublin. However, politics rather than theology seems to have engaged young William Rowan's interest at college. He befriended a fellow student by the name of Markham. Both young men 'were resolute and uncompromising Whigs'. They had adopted a minority, and perhaps unpopular, position in Tory-dominated Trinity. 'Party spirit was so high in those days' that the two chums were 'frequently obliged to appeal to their fists to enforce the reasoning of their heads'.[13]

William Rowan excelled at Trinity, and after graduating he was elected to a fellowship at the college. Such fellowships were reserved for ordained clergymen of the Established Church. As William Rowan 'refused to take the oaths necessary for ordination', the election was declared void. William Rowan must have known the rules before contesting the election, so perhaps the election was a Whig campaign to unsettle the Tory establishment. If it was a campaign to change the rules, it appears to have worked and the rules were soon changed. Having successfully studied law, William became one of the first lay fellows of, as well as legal advisor to, the college.

He prospered at the law, married Elizabeth Eyre of Galway and bought an estate in Donegal. Elizabeth, like so many of the Irish landed gentry of her era, preferred life

---

12 Drummond (1840), p. 13.
13 Rowan manuscript, p. 53.

in the fashionable bustle of London to the remote, rural quietude of Donegal, and hence the move to Rathbone Place.

The Rowans had only one child, a daughter, Jane. She grew to be 'a woman possessed of every amiable quality and perfection of mind and body'.[14] She married Tichborne Aston, a member of the Irish House of Commons for Drogheda in 1746. Aston died two years later, leaving Jane a childless, eligible young widow with 'a good fortune'. She married Gawin Hamilton of Killyleagh in 1750, and the pair moved to Rathbone Place in time for the birth of their son, Archibald Hamilton, the following year.

Rowan spent time living with his grandfather, who planned his education with care, sending him first to a famous school at Marylebone in preparation for entering the upper school at Westminster. The old man would summon the boy every Saturday and assess his progress at school. This was always an ordeal for Rowan, who by his own admission was giddy and negligent, while his grandfather was, to say the least, a hard taskmaster. Rowan said that his grandfather was 'of a choleric habit'.[15] If the old man was pushy about the boy's education, he was more laid back about religion. Mrs Rowan would squabble with her husband about the grandfather's failure to enforce religious principles on his grandson. Although they attended the services of the Established Church, the old man never urged any religious doctrine on the young Rowan. Rowan believed that his grandfather's reason for refusing ordination at Trinity College was that he was, by early manhood, a Unitarian. Unitarians were Protestant Dissenters who rejected the doctrine of the Trinity and the deity of Jesus. Rowan and

14 Drummond, p. 15.
15 *Ibid.*

his father, Gawin (and indeed many of the Presbyterians in Dublin and Ulster who were later leading United Irishmen) espoused Unitarianism. Rowan believed that his grandfather was never shaken from his religious opinions.[16]

The old man's will began with the phrase 'in the name of the One and only self-existent Being', an implicit expression of a Unitarian theology. Unitarianism in the eighteenth century, however, was not solely a matter of theology. Most, if not all, Unitarians in England and Ireland were radical Whigs and enemies of what they viewed as arbitrary power and the corruptions of government, which they believed denied citizens civil and religious liberty. The old man's will concluded as follows:

> From personal affection, and that in the hope that he shall become a learned, sober, honest man, live un-bribed and unpensioned, zealous for the rights of his country, loyal to his King and a true Protestant without bigotry to any sect, I give my property to Archibald Hamilton.[17]

'Un-bribed' and 'unpensioned' referred to the governmental practice of buying support. As Dr Johnson declared, 'In England it is generally understood to mean pay given to a state hireling for treason to his country'.[18] Old Rowan was clearly anxious that the boy should not become a place-chaser or a government hack. Being 'a true Protestant without bigotry to any sect' is a hallmark of Unitarianism.

Archibald Hamilton Rowan lived up to almost all of his grandfather's wishes and Whig principles. He was ever after zealous when it came to the rights of his country, and

---

16   *Ibid.*
17   *Ibid.*
18   Kronenberger (1974), p. 29.

remained a true Protestant and an enemy of religious bigotry. He did not, however, remain loyal to his king. Many radical Whigs of his generation, including the Founding Fathers of the United States of America, found that they could not be loyal both to their Whig principles and to King George III.

When William Rowan died in 1767 his grandson was 16 years old. The terms of the will required the young Archibald to add 'Rowan' to his surname, and thereafter he was known as Archibald Hamilton Rowan. He inherited his grandfather's considerable fortune, receiving an annuity of £584 immediately, a capital sum of £20,000 at the age of 25, and a further annuity of £8,000 upon his mother's death.[19] The will stipulated that he must get his degree at an English university (he choose Cambridge) and not visit Ireland until he was 25 years old.

There is no evidence of antipathy towards Ireland on the part of his grandfather, and it is likely that this condition was the result of pressure from his mother. She apparently blamed the influence of Ireland for turning her husband, Gawin, into 'a muddle-headed raffish sort of a man possessing a taste for low company',[20] and was anxious that her son should be a more polished and urbane aristocrat.

Rowan tells us, however, that 'notwithstanding the injunctions of my grandfather's will I made more than one trip across the channel to see Ireland during my minority'.[21]

---

19 Nicolson, p. 27.
20 *Ibid.*, p. 22.
21 Drummond, p. 50.

2.

Youth Among the Radicals

The time Rowan spent living with his grandfather 'passed heavily enough', but better days were on the way. After his grandfather's death Rowan went to live with his father, Gawin Hamilton, in Cowley Street, London. According to Harold Nicolson, a descendant of the Hamiltons of Killyleagh, Gawin Hamilton 'was more than a Whig, he was a radical'.[22]

Nicolson's comment suggests that Gawin would have been staunchly opposed to aristocracy and court influence on the government, and believed that the Tories were the enemies of civil and religious liberty. Radical Whigs regarded Parliament as corrupt and under the control of the aristocratic landed elite. They supported political reform and opposed the Test Act, which sought to exclude Protestant Dissenters from political and public office. Rowan loved and admired his father, and quickly came to share his father's political outlook. They were to stand by each other through the struggles and vicissitudes of later life.[23]

---

22 Nicolson, p. 2.
23 *Ibid.*, p. 25.

Their Cowley Street home, which they rented from Bonnell Thorton, a well-known wit and an established political writer, was 'a favourite meeting place for English [and Irish] radicals'.[24] Harold Nicolson published a critical biography of Rowan in 1943 in which he displayed vitriolic hostility to his great-great-great-grandfather, Gawin Hamilton, to whom he refers throughout his work as 'Old Baldie'. Despite this disapprobation, Nicolson gives a vivid account of the meetings at Gawin Hamilton's home, which must have made a big impact on the 16-year-old Archibald.

Nicolson writes:

> Gawen [*sic*] Hamilton was known for his advanced opinions, and when the House of Commons rose at night some of the radical members would walk around to Cowley Street, drink large quantities of Mr Hamilton's port and discourse upon the dangers of the 'new monarchy' of young George III and on the iniquities of Bute and Grenville. The poet Churchill would be present at these meetings and speak with passion about his dear friend Wilkes, about corruption in high places, about the coming dawn of English liberties. And there was Dr Charles Lucas, the 'first of Irish patriots', who also modelled himself, even in his manner of conversation, on the genius of the 'North Briton' [John Wilkes]. Dr Lucas [who] was crippled with gout, would be wheeled into the dining room and would shake his silver locks in fury at the ruthlessness of the English administration in Ireland.[25]

---

24 Orr (1998), p. 226.
25 Nicolson, p. 26.

Nicolson's amusing account of a group of port-swilling, bombastic and gout-ridden malcontents portrays a distorted picture of the goings on at Cowley Street. It is clear, even through Nicolson's hyperbole, that Gawin Hamilton's friends were men of intellect – not a few of them were famous for their wit, and some were accomplished politicians and well-known radical personalities. Churchill was a highly intelligent man and one of the most celebrated poets of his time.[26] Wilkes was possessed of a biting wit. The Earl of Sandwich, who was involved in prosecuting Wilkes, once said to him, 'Sir, I do not know whether you will die on the gallows or of the pox'. Wilkes is reported to have replied, 'That depends, my lord, on whether I embrace your lordship's principles or your mistress'.

Yet neither John Wilkes nor Dr Charles Lucas was a figure of fun; they were serious and able radicals who had fought against their respective governments during dangerous times in the cause of democratic reform. Wilkes had been imprisoned more than once. Lucas was outlawed, and might have faced the gallows had he not fled Ireland for the safety of Leiden in 1749. Both men were heroes to their constituents.

The people of Middlesex re-elected Wilkes each time the government deprived him of his seat. The government had sent him to prison and could then deprive him of his Commons seat on the basis that he was a felon. Dr Charles Lucas was alleged by his enemies in Dublin to have risen to prominence by 'cajoling the very scum of the people'.[27] By this they meant the decent common working folk of Dublin, who revered Lucas. Although often referred to as 'the Wilkes of Ireland', and ridiculed by Nicolson for modelling himself

26   Cash (2006), p. 66.
27   Smyth (1992), p. 126.

on Wilkes's manner and conversation, Lucas was twelve years older than Wilkes, and had more claim to be the model than the imitator.

Dr Lucas began his campaign to democratize the governance of Dublin City in 1749. His 'crime' had been to express the opinion that the British Privy Council and the Westminster Parliament had no right to legislate for Ireland. Wilkes's 'crime' twenty years later was to upset the grandson of George II, George III, by using his newspaper, *The North Briton*, to deride the King's ministers, Grenville and Bute, and to attack some of the King's own speeches.

The only way in which it can fairly be said that Wilkes was a model for Lucas was that Wilkes founded *The North Briton* the year before Lucas founded his *Freeman's Journal* in Dublin in 1763. Although *The North Briton* did not survive for long after Wilkes's release from prison, the *Freeman's Journal* was one of Ireland's leading newspapers for more than 160 years, finally closing down in 1924.

Wilkes was the best known and most highly regarded radical in mid-eighteenth-century Britain, and the same can be said of Charles Lucas in relation to Ireland. The fame of these men was not confined to their native countries: both men had substantial international reputations and were admired by some of those who would later be the Founding Fathers of American democracy. If Grenville was a subject of criticism in the discussions at Gawin Hamilton's soirées, it was likely in part the result of his imposition of the Stamp Acts on the American colonists on behalf of George III.

Within a few short years the King declared his American subjects to be in rebellion, and Wilkes became a venerable friend of the American Revolution. Benjamin Franklin visited Dublin to meet with Lucas shortly before the good doctor's death in 1771,[28] and it is said that Thomas Jefferson took inspiration from Lucas as he penned the Declaration of Independence.[29]

Rowan, as a 16-year-old youth who shared his father's radical views, must have been exhilarated by the company of his father's famous and charismatic friends. In masterful understatement, Rowan records that Wilkes and Lucas had 'an influence on my early sentiments'.[30]

It could be said that Rowan was later to benefit from 'the lively lower-class political culture that Lucas developed among the Dublin workers'.[31] The children and grandchildren of those who took to the streets of Dublin in support of Lucas as he fled for his life in 1749, and welcomed his triumphant return from exile in 1760, often cheered Archibald Hamilton Rowan through the same streets in the early 1790s. It would not have been in Rowan's interest to be cheered through Dublin on his return from his own exile in 1805, but the Dublin people showed their support and affection at least once again on a famous occasion in 1829, when their hero was 78 years of age.

Cambridge and John Jebb

In the year 1768 the time had come for Rowan to go to Cambridge. We know little of how he spent his time there, but he did carry on with the boisterous behaviour for which he had become known at Westminster School. One commentator, a Mr Topham, had described Hamilton as 'wasting himself at Westminster', and observed that

---

28 Whelan (2010), p. 111.
29 Aptheker (1960), p. 102.
30 Whelan, p. 155.
31 Herlihy (1997), p. 126.

expecting Rowan to flourish there was like expecting an alpine plant to live in aquatic conditions. Topham had his tongue very firmly in his cheek when he said:

> With more than boyish aptitudes and abilities, he should not thus have been lost amongst boys. His incessant intrepidity, his restless curiosity, his undertaking spirit, all indicated early maturity – all should have led to pursuits, if not better at least of more spirit and moment than the mere mechanism of a dead language … His evenings were set upon … with pranks and gunpowder, [and] in leaping from unusual heights into the Thames.[32]

This 'early maturity' must have manifested itself again at Cambridge. He is alleged to have thrown some furniture out of a high window onto a passing coach, and to have thrown the coachman into the River Cam.[33] He was rusticated for this or some other misbehaviour and was sent down from Cambridge for a year.

He spent that year, possibly 1770, at Warrington Academy, whose guiding spirit was the famous Unitarian clergyman, scientist and political radical Dr Joseph Priestley. In spite of the fact that Rowan and Priestley were friends in later life, the pair are unlikely to have met at Warrington as Priestley had moved on from there three years earlier in 1767.

Rowan met the first love of his life at Warrington. This was Lætitia Aikin, who later became famous as Anna Barbauld. Her father, John Aikin, was teaching at Warrington at this time. This young woman is said to have been 'possessed of great

---

32 Drummond, p. 38.
33 *Ibid.*, p. 41.

beauty, with dark blue eyes that beamed with wit and fancy'.[34] She would later emerge as a successful and highly regarded writer at a time when very few women had managed to break into a profession that was, at the time, male- dominated.

The young Miss Aikin was seven years older than Rowan, and we do not know if his affections were requited. We do know that in the long years ahead Anna Barbauld wielded her considerable talents in favour of many of the liberal and progressive causes that were close to Rowan's heart. She welcomed the American and French Revolutions, she supported her old friend Dr Priestley when he was persecuted and hounded out of England, and she denounced the slave trade, advocated democratic reform and campaigned against the Corporation and Tests. She was the author of several highly regarded hymns, and her 'Hymn for Harvest Time' is sung to this day by Protestant congregations in England and Ireland.

Anna Barbauld had a remarkable public career as a writer and intellectual. We have no way, however, of knowing if Rowan's relationship with her was in any way meaningful or merely a schoolboy crush.

Gawin Hamilton placed his son in the care of the Reverend John Jebb, a Fellow of Peterhouse College, Cambridge. Jebb was a minister of the Church of England who possessed no less than two Established Church 'livings' nearby. It might seem strange for a radical Whig like Gawin Hamilton to place his son in the care of an Anglican clergyman; John Jebb, however, was no ordinary priest. Indeed, within a few years he was to resign his comfortable 'livings' and leave the Church of England. Thereafter he was pressured into leaving Cambridge, a pressure he resisted for some considerable time. Eventually

---

34   *Ibid.*, p. 46.

he was forced out, and in order to make a living he qualified as a doctor of medicine and practised medicine for the rest of his life.

Back in 1774 Jebb had been in close correspondence with Theophilus Lindsey, a fellow Anglican clergyman, who had found it necessary to resign his post in the Church because of his rejection of the doctrine of the Trinity. Jebb, who shared Lindsey's views, would eventually follow suit. Theological disputes, however, are rarely just about theological matters.[35] Even before Rowan arrived in Cambridge, Jebb had been somewhat isolated there due to his reputation as a radical. In 1754 he had infuriated the Earl of Sandwich when he successfully opposed his court-backed bid for the office of High Steward of the University. Sandwich never forgave Jebb, and used all his influence, both in and out of government, in the years that followed to harm Jebb in every way he could.

A decade later, during the 'Wilkes and Liberty' controversy, Jebb refused to sign an address of loyalty to the King. The address read:

> We your majesty's most dutiful and loyal subjects … the scholars of Cambridge we [*sic*] cannot but see with concern and abhorrence the evil designs of bad men who are labouring to seduce the ignorant and unwary from their duty. We will instil in the rising generation true principles of religion and loyalty. We shall add an unfeigned prayer to God to preserve your majesty the beloved sovereign of a united loyal and affectionate people.[36]

---

35 Finlay Holmes, as quoted in Campbell (1991), p. 137.
36 Disney (1787), p. 24.

It took courage for Jebb to refuse to sign. As he was to say later, 'I know I shall feel the vengeance of the Tories as this place [Cambridge] swarms with them'.[37] He was dismayed when many of his colleagues succumbed to the pressure.

Jebb was noted for his 'zealous and active ... exertions to improve the system of education at the university'.[38] Many of Jebb's suggestions for educational reform, for instance his proposals for the yearly public examination of undergraduates, were opposed, not on the merits of the case but on account of Jebb's unpopular religious and political opinions.

Jebb stood his ground for many years, and Rowan would have been conscious that during his time at Cambridge he was under the 'care and patronage' of a Unitarian radical reformer who was unpopular not only with the government and the university establishment, but with most of his fellow scholars as well.

Jebb endured the hostility of Cambridge for twenty-two years, but in 1775, two years after Rowan's graduation, he could stand it no longer, and resigned. He was now without an occupation. Theophilus Lindsey had opened a new Unitarian chapel at Essex Street in London the previous year, and asked Jebb to be his coadjutor there.[39] Jebb, however, had no wish to continue preaching, and instead pursued the study of medicine.

If John Wilkes was the best known reformer of the mid eighteenth century in England, by the 1780s Jebb was the most thoughtful, consistent, radical and democratic of the reformers. In fact, although he was opposed to violence, he was a revolutionary. Other reformers humbly petitioned the Commons for their liberties. Jebb was an early advocate of

---

37 *Ibid.*, p.109.
38 Belsham (1873), p. 49.
39 *Ibid.*, p. 69.

universal suffrage and suggested that people should not ask for this right; they should take it for themselves. He took the old Whig slogan of 'no taxation without representation' to its logical conclusion when he said:

> The people must put themselves in possession of the right [universal suffrage] in the same way as they would abate a nuisance or demolish an enclosure made on a common without legal right. Those who have no representation should tell the government that they will withhold taxes.[40]

Rowan was proud to say that he retained Jebb's friendship and correspondence to the last year of his tutor's life.[41] The two men exchanged letters when Rowan was in Paris at the close of the American war. When Jebb heard that Rowan had met Benjamin Franklin there, he declared:

> I rejoice that you saw that truly great man Dr Franklin. I beg that you will make my acknowledgements to him for his kind enquiries on my health and assure him that for the sake of America, the sake of England, the sake of mankind, I do most cordially congratulate him on the close of the America war. The American cause is the cause of justice and freedom.[42]

In August 1783 Jebb was asked by the Volunteers of Ireland for his advice on their reform programme. He strongly advised them against a petition for reform being submitted to Parliament, feeling that this might all too easily be rejected by the House. A petition, in Jebb's view, 'transfers authority from the senders to

---

40 Disney, p. 171.
41 Drummond, p. 26.
42 Disney, p. 181.

the sent. [...] It calls upon them to reform themselves, which a corrupt body of men never did, nor can do'.[43] Instead, he suggested that they should outline their demands and set a date for their full consideration and implementation by Parliament. They should then adjourn their present assembly to a reasonable time beyond that date, and when the Volunteers reassembled they would know what to do depending on how Parliament had responded. In a second letter of the same month he expanded on why the Volunteers should try to keep the initiative and not rely on the House:

> A new Parliament may contain a greater number of real friends of freedom, but an incurable vice is inherent in its constitution. If it be left to Parliament to form a plan the scheme will inevitably be defeated. The aristocratic interest united with the regal, like a blight from the East, will assuredly blast every hope of harvest. While you retain the matter in your own hands, you cannot fail of effecting, under Providence, the permanent salvation of your country.

When Rowan came to Ireland in 1784, and threw himself enthusiastically into the Volunteer movement, he corresponded with his mentor seeking advice on how he should behave and what stance he should adopt in relation to the question that was causing turmoil within the once great but now declining movement: what were the possibilities of making good citizens of Irish Roman Catholics?

In a letter to Rowan dated 5 March 1785, after expressing his delight that Rowan was settled in Ireland and making a positive contribution to public affairs, Jebb advised him to:

---

43   Letter to the Volunteers of Ireland, 13 August 1783.

Explore with the utmost exercises political truth and having found it avow it with firmness and perseverance. Temporising expedients are always injurious when contrary to natural right and natural feelings. [...] I am of the opinion that there should be one law for Papist and Protestant.

I must declare, I think the Priesthood has ever been the cause of civil dissentions ... The Protestants of the north I much wonder that they should be alarmed with respect to the Roman Catholics much more have they to fear from the intolerant spirit of the Established Church.'[44]

In a follow-up letter in September of that same year he identified the two main issues to be addressed as the rights of Roman Catholics and universal suffrage. Jebb was anticipating Theobald Wolfe Tone and the United Irishmen by more than five years when he wrote, 'No reform can be justly founded that does not admit Roman Catholics and does not restore to the people their full power'.[45]

Jebb was ill when he wrote this final letter to Rowan, and he breathed his last just a few months later on 2 March 1786. Jebb was 50 years old when he died. Rowan was nearly 35 at the time. Jebb had been a friend and mentor for half the younger man's lifetime.

Reverend John Jebb did not live to see just how much Rowan avowed the political principles he had bequeathed. Rowan's firmness of purpose almost brought him to the gallows, and though he avoided paying the ultimate price, he was forced to persevere through a long, lonely and painful exile. Rowan never could temporize, nor did he ever

---

44 Drummond, p. 129.
45 *Ibid.*, p.133.

repudiate the truths or principles he had inherited from John Jebb.

William Drummond and Harold Nicolson, Rowan's previous biographers, utterly failed to understand their subject. They seem bemused by his sometimes rash, risky and courageous actions during the 1790s. Drummond suggested that Rowan had an excess of political testosterone, which resulted in both his youthful pranks and his later actions. A phrenologist who posthumously examined Rowan's skull at Drummond's request concluded that his major characteristic was a 'love of approbation'.[46] Nicolson grasped this theme enthusiastically, giving his work the title *The Desire to Please*. One of the recurring themes of the latter's utterly unpleasant book is that Rowan was mad and/or bad, and that was why he risked his life, family and fortune in a series of pointless escapades, to no serious purpose.

Rowan's youthful hooliganism was on a par with many of his peers, and there is a more convincing explanation for his career as a revolutionary reformer than an infantile desire to please. He once told his wife that he had allowed himself to be led into a more active life than he would have wished, but that his sentiments had nearly always been the same: from education and principle he was led to support the reform of Parliament and equal liberty to all religious sects.[47]

Rowan in early manhood had come under the influence of Jebb, a principled, thoughtful and revolutionary radical. His advice to Rowan to 'explore with the utmost exercises political truth and having found it avow it with firmness and perseverance' had been taken to heart by the younger man.

---

46   Orr, p. 219.
47   Drummond, p. 290.

After Cambridge

From Rowan's memoir, written for his children while in
exile in 1796, we get some details of his travels to Holland,
South Carolina and Portugal. He spent the summer after
Cambridge in South Carolina. He later visited Portugal in a
vain attempt to enlist in the Portuguese Army. Such was his
personal and family wealth on leaving Cambridge in 1773,
however, that he seems to have had little need to pursue a
livelihood, and it is hard to fathom if he had any plan to
make a living, start a family or do anything other than travel
and enjoy the pleasures of easy wealth.

He went to France in 1773 when he was 22 years old,
where he stayed for eleven years. He was by this time a very
tall, good-looking man. Flann Campbell writes:

> Not much is known about these years in France except
> that he met some descendants of the Wild Geese, the
> exiled soldiers who had emigrated from Ireland after
> the Treaty of Limerick in 1691, and he was apparently
> influenced by Jean-Jacques Rousseau and the French
> *philosophes*. He was admired by Marie Antoinette who
> saw him rowing on the Seine and was so taken by his
> appearance that she sent him a ring.[48]

Rowan tells of the French queen noticing him on the Seine,
but makes no mention of the ring. Rather, he tells us that
she remarked to her party that rowing a boat was no proper
activity for an English gentleman.[49]

In 1777, at the height of the American war, Rowan had
the first of several meetings with Benjamin Franklin in Paris.
They would have known a number of people in common

48   Campbell, p. 39.
49   Drummond, p. 78.

since at an earlier period Franklin had spent time in England, much of it in the company of the 'Real Whigs' such as John Jebb, Revd Richard Price and Joseph Priestley, all of whom, like Rowan himself, were Unitarians, and enthusiastic in the American cause.

Rowan petitioned Franklin on behalf of two British officers who wished to get commissions in the Continental Army. Franklin had no authority to issue such commissions, and he suggested that the men concerned should go to America and apply for their commission there. The men in question were not prepared to take that chance, and nothing came of this petition. Rowan recalled, 'I regretted I was not an American but I was determined, if ever I was able, to play the same role in Ireland'.[50]

At around this time, Rowan, against his better judgement, became involved with George Robert Fitzgerald, a 'high player' and notorious Irish duellist. Fitzgerald convinced Rowan to act as his second in a duel with a Major Bragg. Fitzgerald behaved dishonourably in that, having wounded Bragg, he discharged a second shot in an attempt to kill his wounded enemy. His second shot missed, and Bragg succeeded in inflicting a flesh wound on Fitzgerald.

The duel took place at Valenciennes, which was in Austrian territory, and Rowan might have been in serious trouble had not the governor, when he summoned Rowan, noticed that he was wearing a masonic symbol, which he had from the time he was master of the Cambridge Masonic Lodge.

His brother mason allowed him to travel back to Paris unmolested. Fitzgerald continued his high living, and survived many duels. He almost survived a visit to the gallows in Mayo, Ireland, in 1786: the first two attempts

---

50   Wilson (1998), p. 15.

to hang him failed, however it was then a case of third time unlucky.

It is not surprising that a memoir written for his children has little to say about politics and nothing at all about sex. It appears, however, that Rowan earned a reputation for getting 'into various scrapes, especially with married women' before his marriage to Sarah Dawson in Paris in 1781.[51] Thereafter he was reputed to be a reformed man and a good husband.[52] Although we know nothing of scandals directly involving Rowan himself, it was a high-profile scandal involving his sister, Sidney, which indirectly led to his own very happy marriage to Sarah Dawson.

Sarah Dawson was from Lisanisk near Carrickmacross. At the age of 13 her father brought her from Ireland to London, where he placed her in one of the capital's most celebrated schools.[53] She would spend her vacations at Rowan's mother's house in London. Mrs Hamilton became very attached to the girl, and after Sarah finished school at the age of 16 she remained with the family.

The older woman was anxious to find a suitable match for Sarah, and so encouraged visits to their home from, among other suitable men, a clergyman by the name of Beresford. Thus, Rowan's mother facilitated the blossoming of true love, but not as she had hoped. When Rowan's 15-year-old sister, Sidney, eloped with the 35-year-old clergyman, the girl's mother was apoplectic with rage. She summoned Rowan from Lincolnshire and demanded that he pursue the couple, who were thought to be heading for Scotland. It is hard to tell from Rowan's account of the affair if he pursued them with enthusiasm, but he failed to locate them.

---

51   Agnew (1998, 1999), p. 221.
52   *Ibid.*
53   Drummond, p. 82.

Beresford married the girl, but knew that he was in trouble as she was below the age of consent. For a marriage to be legal in the eighteenth century, any person under twenty needed parental consent, which was clearly not forthcoming in this case. As far as Mrs Hamilton was concerned, nothwithstanding her daughter's youth, Sidney's dowry of £30,000 required her to find a husband of more social standing than a mere clergyman.[54]

Sidney then returned to her mother, claiming that Beresford had imposed on her, a claim Rowan felt to be a deception.[55] Rowan was again called from Lincolnshire, his mother insisting that his sister's life depended on him. Rowan tells us:

> As I entered the house I was amazed to find my sister in the full blow of fashionable attire and that Beresford was to take her to the opera. He was in the habit of leaving his wife with her mother in the forenoon and calling for her in the evening but never entering the house himself.[56]

Mrs Hamilton demanded that Rowan bring his sister to France to remove her from Beresford and his influence. Rowan declined to be concerned in this affair, and his refusal greatly offended his mother. He did say that if Beresford mistreated his sister he would 'remove her from his bed without ceremony'.[57] Mrs Hamilton made other arrangements to get the girl to France, and Rowan read in the papers that Beresford had found his wife at Lisle and cited Mrs Hamilton for wife abduction.

---

54 Nicholson, p. 48.
55 Memorials, p. 139.
56 *Ibid.*, p. 140.
57 *Ibid.*

In spite of Rowan's reluctance to become involved, his mother was now in trouble with the French authorities and he felt that he should accompany her to France as she spoke no French and knew little of their customs.[58]

He found lodgings for them in Lisle, and by this time Sidney was in the late stages of pregnancy and about to give birth. Beresford applied to the court that for the safety of the infant, Sidney should be removed from Mrs Hamilton. Rowan spoke to the judges and prevented this, but felt that the judges were prejudiced against his mother. Sidney was removed to the Convent of the Assumption in Paris, a peculiar move for such a determined Protestant family, but Rowan explains that the purpose of the measure was to get Sidney out of the jurisdiction of the court of Flanders.

A mildly amusing incident arose from this very sorry tale. When Rowan visited the convent to see Sidney he signed in as 'Arch. Hamilton Rowan'. He found himself getting treated like royalty by the Abbess, who thought he was an Anglican Archbishop.

This case dragged on for years, and it was a very long time before Sidney was released from convent captivity and the Revd Beresford was allowed to settle down in peace with his wife and daughter.

Rowan finds a wife

Sarah Dawson had accompanied Mrs Hamilton to France, and through all their vicissitudes Rowan observed 'her much good sense and propriety', and he determined to marry her. Much to the delight of his mother, Sarah and Rowan were married in the Dutch legation in Paris (which had a

---

58 *Ibid.*

Protestant chapel) in 1781.[59] Sarah's dowry of £10,000 was paid by Mrs Hamilton.[60]

Choosing Sarah Dawson for his wife was probably the best decision Rowan ever made in his life. Sarah was strong-minded, persistent and loyal.[61] She could be shrewish when she felt that Rowan's revolutionary friends were leading him and the family into danger. When things were going very badly for them during their long separation and exile, she would rebuke and scold him, unfairly blaming him for their troubles, yet she always stood by him 'and battled for him until she wore down the prejudices of the English authorities by sheer persistence'.[62]

Without the tireless efforts of the intrepid Sarah, Rowan would never have set foot in Ireland after 1794. For Rowan's part, he believed Sarah to 'possess great personal beauty and innate elegance of manner', and loved her dearly for as long as she lived.[63]

Initially the newly-weds lived with Mrs Hamilton in a small house, le Petit Hotel de Choisseul in the Rue de Moussean, where their first child, Gawin William, was born. At around this time he saw 'the unfortunate queen', Marie Antoinette, when he accompanied the Duchess of Manchester, the British ambassador's wife, to her presentation. He dined at Versailles with the French Foreign Minister, Comte de Vergennes, when this diplomat was at the height of his career following the Franco–American victory at Yorktown and the subsequent confirmation of that victory by the Treaty of Paris. All that Rowan chose to tell his children about this occasion is a somewhat

---

59 Nicolson, p. 55.
60 Agnew, p. 221.
61 *Ibid.*
62 *Ibid.*, p. 34.
63 Nicolson, p. 34.

incomprehensible anecdote about the hairstyles of the guests and servants.[64]

In 1784, at his mother's request, he brought his wife and family back to Ireland to be near her. What changed Mrs Hamilton's mind and aroused this sudden desire to retire to Ireland, a country for which she appeared to have little affection? Perhaps the wagging tongues, relishing the twists and turns of the ongoing scandal of her young daughter's elopement with a middle-aged clergyman and the younger woman's subsequent incarceration in a French convent made the salons of London less congenial to this proud old lady.

64 *Ibid.*

3.

Brown Bess on his Shoulder

A full eight years after the strictures of his grandfather's will had expired, Rowan and his family finally came to live in Ireland. He first resided at a small house in Kildare, but soon purchased land at Rathcoffey in the same county, and built a fine house incorporating some features of the old Rathcoffey mansion. He also spent a lot of time at his mother's house at 35 Dominick Street, Dublin.

Rowan was 33 years old at the time, and, if anything, his physical appearance and good looks had improved since his early years in Paris. He was now being described as handsome, strong, and of such muscular energy that he could have served as a model for Hercules.[65] He was a very tall and strong man, and turned heads as he walked the streets of Dublin accompanied by his giant Newfoundland dog.

Being of respectable family and large fortune, Rowan, had he wished, could have been welcomed into the arms of

---

65   Barrington (1997), p. 235.

the ruling elite in the capital. However, his radical democratic politics allied to his liberal religious views and his social conscience, were to pull him in a very different direction.

The country to which Rowan returned in 1784 was in the early stages of what was to develop into a severe political hangover. The inebriating revelries had begun with the formation of the Irish Volunteers in 1778, reaching their intoxicating climax on Tuesday 16 April 1782, when the Patriot leader, Henry Grattan, stood up in the Irish House of Commons and told the members and a rapturous multitude in the public gallery, 'I am addressing a free people … Ireland is now a nation'. Two years later the withdrawal symptoms had begun, and the triumph, so vaunted by Grattan, began to appear illusory.

As the American war dragged on, Ireland was left with no regular troops for the defence of the country. In 1776 a Volunteer corps had been founded by Protestants in Tipperary to deal with an outbreak of agrarian disturbances. Those responsible were known as 'Whiteboys', so called because of the white smocks they wore during their attacks on the property and livestock of large landowners.

When France entered the war on the American side in 1781, a Volunteer corps was formed in Belfast to counter any French invasion of Ireland. The idea spread like wildfire, and soon 40,000 men, self-armed and self-arrayed, were marching, drilling and meeting in conventions all over Ireland. There had been voluntary militias before, but nothing on this scale. The soldiers elected their own officers and were not under the control of the government. Protestant Dissenters often had trouble in gaining commissions in the regular army, but not so the Volunteers. While the whole island, or more correctly the whole Protestant male population, was swept by a mania for volunteering, the Dissenters in Ulster flocked to their ranks in their tens of thousands.

Lord Harcourt had warned the British prime minister that the Presbyterians of the north were, in their hearts, Americans.[66] The regular army had been shipped across the Atlantic in a vain attempt to crush the forces of George Washington. Ireland's cities, towns and villages resounded with the marching feet of a new army. Many of these citizen soldiers, particularly the northern Dissenters, regarded George Washington as a hero, and believed that their American cousins were being coerced by their king. As the Volunteers marched, drilled and passed resolutions, they were reading and talking about developments in America with satisfaction. William Steel Dickson, a Presbyterian minister, denounced the British attack on America as a mad crusade, and one historian tells us that 'bonfires lit the Antrim skies to celebrate [the American victory at] the Battle of Bunker Hill'.[67]

Rowan's first biographer, William Drummond, was born in 1778, the year the Volunteers were formed, so he must have relied on the accounts of older men when he wrote:

> The voice of liberty was heard echoing across the Atlantic: it awoke a kindred spirit in the breast of the Irish nation, and having risen in arms to defend her shores, she grasped them more firmly to assert her rights: she felt her power and determined to be free.[68]

The severe economic depression that gripped Ireland in those years was regarded by many Irishmen as arising from the American war and the unfair restrictions placed

---

66 Nicolson, p. 65.
67 Wilson, p. 12.
68 Drummond, p. 114.

on Irish trade by the British Parliament. The exclusively Protestant Patriot opposition in the Irish House of Commons was long renowned for its fine oratory and total ineffectiveness. The rival opposition leaders, Henry Flood and Henry Grattan, now found to their surprise that they had the backing of a large army that was prepared to threaten the government with violent resistance if concessions were not made.

It was events across the Atlantic, however, which finally cracked the British determination to resist concessions to Ireland. In 1781, when Cornwallis surrendered his army of 8,000 men to the American and French forces at Yorktown, everyone knew, though the fighting continued, that the war was over and the great British Empire had been defeated by a citizens' militia of former subjects, albeit with significant help from French regular troops and navy. Lord North's government fell after Yorktown and the Whigs took office. In opposition they had always made sympathetic noises towards Grattan. They now made the concessions that gave him his illusory triumph. Grattan and his supporters had been hoodwinked, for, as Wilson tells us:

> The settlement of 1783 was profoundly ambiguous. The Irish Parliament did not, as it turned out, achieve parity with Westminster under a common allegiance to the Crown; the British government retained significant political and financial control over Irish affairs. Nor was there any broadening of the polity within Ireland; the Irish Parliament remained an exclusive club for wealthy Protestants. The middle-class Protestants who formed the backbone to the Volunteers were kept out; the vast Catholic majority in the country were still beyond the political pale. In

many respects this was an illusory independence for an imaginary people.[69]

Lord Charlemont, the moderate leader of the Volunteers, felt uneasy about the tactic of using military threats to pressurize the government and to win political concessions. He was even more uneasy about the increased clamour, mainly from the northern Presbyterian units of the Volunteers, for reform of Parliament and the extension of political rights to Roman Catholics. Lord Charlemont tried to dampen militancy and discouraged the holding of reviews. He was horrified when some of the northern corps invited Roman Catholics to join. It was illegal for Roman Catholics to bear arms, and Charlemont feared that the recruitment of Catholics might be used by the government as an excuse to suppress the association.

In 1784 Rowan joined his father's corps of the Killyleagh Volunteers as a private. Almost immediately he drew up an address to Lord Charlemont to the effect that Volunteers should continue in existence to press for reform and the end of abuses. His corps elected him to present the address at a review held on the plain of the Falls, near Belfast, in July 1784. Charlemont had reluctantly attended this review, and refused to accept Rowan's address. Charlemont promised that they would shortly meet in a civil capacity and pass an address to Parliament. Rowan replied that 'citizens with Brown Bess on their shoulder were more likely to be attended to'.[70]

In 1785 Rowan and his father were part of a delegation of five from County Down who attended a Volunteer convention held in Dublin. Only 100 delegates were

---

69   Wilson, p. 16.
70   Drummond, p. 117.

present. In the heady days of 1782, some 500 or more would have attended conventions in Dungannon and Dublin. The Volunteer movement had clearly passed its peak.

Some respectable, conservative, Protestant men who were proud to turn out in uniform to defend their country in times of war were not prepared to wear the uniform in peacetime, nor to join armed Roman Catholics to place demands on their government. Henry Flood, who most likely attended the convention to act as a brake on the radicals, made a proposal for reform. Flood's proposal did not include any provision for the alleviation of Roman Catholic grievances, and was rejected. Flood withdrew and retired from the Volunteers. When a motion to the effect that 'the possession of civil rights belonged equally to all Irishmen, whatever religious opinion they might adopt' was placed before the meeting, it received only seventeen votes and the meeting was adjourned, with no date set for a resumption.[71]

Dr William Drennan

In January 1785, when travelling from Dublin to Killyleagh, Rowan stopped off at Newry to be collected by his father's coach. Dr William Drennan, who was at this time practising as a doctor of medicine at Newry, sent him a note asking for an interview. Drennan had recently established his reputation as an eloquent writer in the radical cause. He was the son of Reverend Thomas Drennan (1696–1768), who had been a friend of the notable philosopher Francis Hutcheson in Dublin in the 1720s. William was born in the manse of First

---

71   *Ibid.*

Presbyterian, Rosemary Street, Belfast in 1754, where his father was then minister.

Francis Hutcheson died in 1746, nine years before Drennan was born, but the great philosopher's liberal, progressive and anti-slavery philosophy was to have a significant influence on the radicals of Drennan and Rowan's generation. Hutcheson and his cousin, William Bruce, had left Killyleagh together and entered the University of Glasgow in 1711. After graduating from Glasgow the cousins established a Presbyterian academy in Dublin in 1719, which attempted to emulate the philosophy school founded by Rowan's ancestor at Killyleagh. Hutcheson's Dublin school prepared young men for entry to Glasgow, and ultimately for the Presbyterian ministry. Hutcheson invited Revd Drennan to join him in Dublin. They collaborated in forming a study circle, which between 1720 and 1730 published radical material, including Hutcheson's own works as well as those of controversial republican writers such as Edmund Ludlow, Algernon Sidney and John Toland.

The group published tracts in favour of religious toleration, non-sectarian education and even state payment for Roman Catholic clergy.[72] This was at a time when the Penal Laws introduced at the end of the Williamite Wars were being rigorously enforced. In 1719, the same year that Hutcheson founded his Dublin school, a new penal law had been passed requiring that Catholic priests who had not obeyed the instruction to leave Ireland should be branded in the face.[73] Clearly, Hutcheson and Drennan senior's religious tolerance did not reflect the outlook of all or even most Irish Protestants of that era.

---

72 Stewart (1993), p. 93.
73 Connolly, p. 252.

The members of Hutcheson's group were almost all from Ulster and had become friends at Glasgow University. It is significant, however, that the congregations they associated with in Dublin, based at New Row and Wood Street, were of Cromwellian republican origin. This entire Dublin colony of Glasgow graduates had been associated since their student days with Ireland's, and possibly Britain's, most radical politician, Viscount Robert Molesworth.

Dr Caroline Robins tells us that Hutcheson and Drennan's Dublin circle helped 'to hand to a second generation a patriotic spirit that included all Irishmen in its loyalties, and diffused a liberal philosophy throughout more than one city and country'.[74]

Although Revd Drennan died when William was just 14, his father and his circle of friends had had the most profound influence on William Drennan. He would later write:

> I am the son of an honest man, a Minister of that gospel which breathes peace and goodwill amongst men, a Protestant Dissenting Minister in the town of Belfast. He was a friend and associate of good and may I say great men. Of Abernethy, of Bruce, of Ducal, and Hutcheson.[75]

By the time William Drennan had his first interview with Rowan he was already a committed republican. He was disconsolate as he observed the Volunteer movement fall into decay before the great aims of reform of Parliament and Catholic emancipation had been achieved. In the summer of 1784, a few months before his meeting with Rowan,

---

74 Robbins (1987), p. 163.
75 *Ibid.*, p. 71.

Drennan had established a company of Protestant and Catholic Volunteers that called itself the Newry Union.[76] He produced a declaration on behalf of the new body:

> We shall ever think that an association deserves well of our native land, whose chief object is to unite the different descriptions of religion in the cause of our common country, and although we cannot lay claim to the honour of having first taken up arms, there is still a glorious ambition left not to be among the last in laying them down.[77]

He had published his *Letter of Orellana, an Irish Helot*, voicing his views on the need for constitutional reform and Catholic emancipation. However, he was scornful of the pomp and self-congratulatory displays of the Volunteers, and doubted that the leader, Lord Charlemont, was serious about parliamentary reform, as he was the owner of a number of pocket boroughs himself.

Drennan was fast coming to the conclusion that a secret republican society based on the practices of Freemasonry should be formed by the radicals within the Volunteers. He may even have discussed this possibility with Rowan at their first meeting, because the first impression he formed of Rowan was that he was 'a clever fellow, just the thing for a constitutional conspirator'.[78] Drennan instantly liked Rowan, and observed that he had Cromwellian qualities about him when he said, 'he has something of the Long Parliament in his countenance, some of the republican ferocity'.[79]

---

76 *Ibid.*, p. 129.
77 *Ibid.*, p. 130.
78 Agnew, p. 219.
79 Benn (2008), p. 639.

In temperament, physical appearance and many other ways, the contrast between the two men was very great indeed. Drummond writes:

> The one being of Herculean size, warm, impetuous but highly polished and courteous withal; the other low in stature, cold in manner, slow, deliberative, but lodging in his breast the elements of a lofty and noble spirit.[80]

Rowan was a larger-than-life man of action, while Drennan was a small and rather timid figure. Despite this, they had much in common. Both were Unitarians, and shared the outlook that the penal laws directed at Roman Catholics and Dissenters were a denial of liberty. Both were familiar with the works of three great Unitarian political thinkers of their era: Revd Dr Richard Price, Joseph Priestley and John Jebb. Unlike Rowan, Drennan may have had no direct contact or friendship with Dr Priestley or John Jebb, but he held Priestley in the highest regard and would have very much approved of the letters of advice that Jebb had sent the Volunteers dealing with universal suffrage and the Catholic question. From their first short interview at Newry, Drennan had great admiration for Rowan, and there began an attachment and a political cooperation between them. A few short years later they would both be founding members of the Society of United Irishmen, and later still would stand trial for their lives, but with more luck than some in their circle, both would escape the gallows and great tumult of 1798.

In May 1786 Rowan was unanimously chosen to command the Killyleagh Volunteers. He wrote a letter of

---

80   *Ibid.*, p. 139.

thanks in which he told his men that 'the torpid state of the Volunteers of Ireland distresses me'. He went on:

> Some corps have laid down their arms whilst others have started up. Some new links, then, are now necessary; the reformation of the present state of the representation of the people is the point to which and to which alone the Volunteers should tend ... are the Volunteers to be contented to meet annually in silent mock parade? Are they with the arms of peace in their hands to permit that constitution, which the blood of our ancestors was shed in establishing against open force to be mouldered down to the corrupt practices of a few? Or are they to stand forth [as] the guardians of the rights of mankind, and the determined opposers of every kind of tyranny?[81]

The Killyleagh Volunteers were mainly, if not exclusively, Presbyterians, and Rowan's reference to 'the blood of our ancestors' was obviously intended to be understood as referring to those who fought with King William's forces against James II.

---

81   *Ibid.*, p. 148.

4.

Ruffian Force and Cowardly Calumny

In 1769 the British government had unseated John Wilkes from his House of Commons seat for Middlesex for the fourth time and conferred the seat to the unsuccessful Tory candidate, Henry Luttrell (1743–1829). Luttrell was the son of Baron Irnham of Warwickshire and Luttrellstown, County Dublin. 'Both father and son were notorious womanizers, and they hated each other'.[82] The father once challenged the son to a duel, but the son declined because, he said, his father was not a gentleman.[83] Luttrell was very small in stature though 'strong in body if not in mind'. He had achieved a reputation for bravery as a soldier in Portugal during the Seven Years' War.[84] At the time of his challenge to Wilkes he was a Tory MP for Bossiny in Cornwall.[85]

Wilkes defeated Luttrell's challenge by 1,143 votes to 296. After each of his earlier elections Wilkes was debarred from

---

82 Cash, p. 253.
83 *Ibid.*
84 *Ibid.*
85 *Ibid.*

taking his seat because he was adjudged a felon. The people of Middlesex re-elected him on three separate occasions, and such was Wilkes's popularity that no one before Luttrell was prepared to stand against him.

Luttrell, who hated Wilkes, stood against him with the full support of the ministry and the court. Although he lost the election, he succeeded in denying Wilkes his seat and the people of Middlesex their democratic choice. Luttrell earned the gratitude of the government but the utter contempt of the public for this anti-democratic escapade.

Cash writes:

> For some months [Luttrell] did not dare to appear in the street or scarce quit his lodgings. He was the most unpopular man in the House of Commons; newspapers were full of abuse of him; scores of pamphlets appeared vilifying his character and private life and the most scandalous stories were circulated about him and his family.[86]

The government rewarded Luttrell by appointing him Adjutant General for Ireland in 1770. Luttrell continued to sit in the Commons, however, and would often attack the opposition for their pro-American stance. He described them as being 'the abettors of treason and rebellion combined purposely for the ruin of their country'.[87]

As a student at Cambridge, Rowan and his tutor, Dr Jebb, would have followed Luttrell's conflict with their friend Wilkes with great interest. Rowan would have reason to recall the accusations concerning Luttrell's scandalous

---

86   Namier (1964), p. 65.
87   *Ibid.*

character and private life when their paths crossed following an incident in Dublin many years later.

On the evening of 4 April 1788, Mary Neal, a 12-year-old child, was playing near her home on the corner of Fleet Lane in Dublin. A well-dressed male stranger approached her and said that she could earn herself some pennies if she would deliver a message for him. For poor children in Dublin such opportunities were rare, and always welcome. Mary's father, John Neal, had been a successful hairdresser, but had taken to drink after the death of Mary's mother. Though he had remarried, the family was now in great poverty.

The stranger led the child to a house in Thomas Street. He appeared to hold back a short distance from the house and instructed Mary to approach and to knock on the door. When the door was opened by a woman, Mary was dragged and bundled inside, the stranger pushing her from behind. When the man handed over some gold or silver coin to this woman he was shown into a small room containing only a bed at the back of the house. For two hours Mary Neal was subjected to a brutal and violent rape by Henry Luttrell, who by this time had been elevated to the peerage as the 2nd Earl of Carhampton.

None of the prostitutes in the house reacted to the child's pleas for mercy or screams of terror. Mary was released only when she promised that she would say nothing of her ordeal and would return to meet the man in the future. She went home and wept for the entire night, afraid to tell her father or stepmother. A few days later she confided in a family friend, who informed her parents.

Maria Llewellyn, the owner of the house and a madam of several brothels in Dublin, was arrested and charged with complicity in the rape of Mary Neal. However, John Edgeworth, Llewellyn's dangerous and violent partner in crime, went to great lengths to save her from conviction.

He forced a young prostitute, Mary Molineux, to swear false information under the alias Mary Poole, first against John and Anne Neal for street robbery, and then, a separate charge, under the alias Mary Murray against Mary Neal.

Llewellyn had significant influence with the prison authorities, and constables hauled Anne Neal, who was advanced in pregnancy, and her husband to Newgate in the middle of the night. Edgeworth's plan was that if they could be held in custody until the quarter sessions they could not appear as witnesses and Llewellyn would walk free. Mr Hunt was an apothecary who supervised the House of Industry. He was a kindly man who had first examined Mary after the rape. At John Neal's request, Hunt had hidden Mary away in fear of violence from Edgeworth and his cohorts.

Anne Neal and her baby died in the prison, and John Neal believed that the prison authorities had allowed Llewellyn to 'ill use' his wife, causing the deaths of her and her baby. On the day of Llewellyn's trial, Edgeworth planned to abduct Mary Neal at Church Street on her way to the Four Courts, but his plan misfired. Mary gave her evidence, and Llewellyn was convicted and sentenced to hang.

There then began a campaign to get a pardon for the convict based on a strategy that reveals a great deal about attitudes of the ruling elite to young females of this era. Various informations were sworn to the effect that Mary had been working as a child prostitute. It appears that involvement in the rape of a 12-year-old was not such a serious matter if the child was a prostitute.

Many men of 'high rank' came to the House of Industry to intimidate Mary into making a false confession. These men, while they may have known Llewellyn in the course of her business, are unlikely to have exerted themselves out of concern for the well-being of a brothel-keeper. Mr Hunt did what he could to protect Mary, and probably felt that only a man of considerable social rank could resist these men in their endeavours. It was possibly he who tipped off Archibald Hamilton Rowan about the case. Rowan decided to intervene on the child's behalf.

Rowan took exception to the conduct of these men, whom he said were engaged in 'a species of after-trial unknown to the spirit of our constitution'. Sarah Rowan travelled in her coach to the House of Industry and took Mary to safety at Rathcoffey.[88] Rowan then interviewed her neighbours, who all told the same story: that though Mary and her family were poor, and John Neal 'drank too freely', they were of good character and unquestionable honesty.

In an attempt to clear Mary's name, Rowan brought her to the Castle to see the Lord Lieutenant. Rowan had no wish to see Llewellyn hang, but he was not prepared to let her, or her cronies, save her neck at the expense of her victim's character and reputation.

Llewellyn did not hang, or even serve a sentence. She was pardoned and set at liberty by Westmoreland, the Lord Lieutenant.[89] This was not because of the depraved and ham-fisted antics of Edgeworth, but rather because she had friends in high places, not least the main villain in the affair. Carhampton was never asked to answer for raping this child, and in fact went on to become commander-in-chief of the British forces during the 1798 rebellion. Fitzpatrick tells us:

> The picketings, free quarters, half hangings, floggings, and pitch-cappings ... were directed by Carhampton ... and that thirteen hundred of the King's subjects

---

88 Nicolson, p. 79.
89 Memorials, p. 153.

had been already transported by Lord Carhampton without trial or sentence.[90]

During the rebellion, many of his ill-disciplined troops treated women, young and old, with the same savage brutality as young Mary Neal had been subjected to by their diminutive commander.[91]

Edgeworth was convicted of suborning the jury, sentenced to twelve months in prison and ordered to make two visits to the pillory. The Lord Lieutenant again felt the need to step in, however, and pardon Edgeworth.

Rowan published a pamphlet entitled *A Brief History of the Suffering of John, Anne and Mary Neal*, which he printed on his own printing press and distributed widely. He also confronted the Dublin barristers' dining club to challenge them for their involvement in the smear campaign against Mary Neal. This incident was recorded for posterity in the amusing account left to us by Jonah Barrington, a senior member of the Dublin Bar.[92] For all Barrington's sardonic amusement, even he could not but admire Rowan for his courage and sense of honour on behalf of a poor, abused and violated child.

Without Rowan, Mary Neal would have been left at the mercy of powerful, unscrupulous, privileged men who believed that poor people like the Neals had no right to justice or the protection of the law. Indeed, they were prepared to pervert the law to punish the innocent and protect the guilty. Anne Neal and her baby were denied the very right to life itself by the system presided over by men like Carhampton and Westmoreland. William Todd Jones, a close friend of Rowan, once observed that the clique who

---

90 Fitzpatrick (1865), p. 47.
91 *Loc. cit.*
92 Barrington, p. 234.

ruled Ireland, 'were unique in Europe in that the chief gratification was to be had in the rancorous, indiscriminate and defamatory abuse of the [poor] general inhabitants of their native land'.[93]

The working-class people of Dublin were delighted when Rowan broke ranks with the upper-class elite to bring the case of one of their own to the Castle. At a meeting held in Werburgh Street on 19 December 1788 the Goldsmiths of Dublin framed an address congratulating Rowan for his efforts on behalf of 'indigent and oppressed innocence'. The *Dublin Evening Post* published the address in full, as well as Rowan's reply. Rowan, when thanking the Goldsmiths, took the opportunity to highlight the political implications of the case:

> Virtue and innocence have been the sport of ruffian force and coward[ly] calumny. The guilty instead of being punished have been protected and pardoned. It is become the duty of every citizen to reflect on how this has happened, and if he cannot stop the current of vice at least to declare his abhorrence of the public protection of it.[94]

By championing the cause of Mary Neal, Rowan won a place in the hearts of working-class Dubliners. Ever after they would cheer his carriage in the street, and he retained their affection until the end of his days.

A satirical petition was circulated in Dublin that read as follows:

Petition of the statue of justice on the Castle Gate
Remove me I pray you from this castle gate

---

93 Drummond, p. 146.
94 *Dublin Evening Post*, 3 January 1789.

> Since the rape of an infant and blackest of crimes
> Are objects of mercy in these blessed times
> On the front of their prison or hell let me dwell in
> For pardon is granted to Madam Llewellyn.

William Drummond relates how Rowan gave Mary Neal a job as a servant and then apprenticed her to a dressmaker. Drummond comments rather priggishly, however, that 'her future behaviour was not such as would requite the care of her benefactor or justify the interest she had excited in the public mind'.[95]

Drummond should not have been surprised that this sordid story had no fairy-tale ending. This raped and abused child of an alcoholic father saw her parents unjustly imprisoned, her stepmother and sister murdered, and her own reputation maligned by her so-called social betters. She was forced to accept that those who had harmed her, the brothel-keeper, the pimp and the peer of the realm, could go on their merry way as if nothing of consequence had happened. How unlikely was it that Mary Neal would become an upstanding member of a society that had only utter contempt for her and her family? Her so-called 'betters' regarded people like the Neals as the 'lowest sort', who should have no expectation of justice or dignity from a ruling class that despised them for their poverty.

Rowan and the Murdered Bull-Baiters

At approximately one o'clock in the afternoon on Stephen's Day 1789, Mr Vance, the High Sheriff of Dublin, and Alderman Carlton left the coffee house near the Royal Exchange and rode out with the Castle main guard to the

---

95 *Ibid.*, p. 103.

North Lotts, below the new Custom House, to confront a group of tradesmen who were engaged in the ancient, if cruel, sport of bull-baiting. The tradesmen were not trespassing, nor was bull-baiting illegal at this time. Stephen Wade explains:

> The whole business was done with a mix of ritual and carnival that characterized working-class culture … After a coming bull-baiting was advertised, the bull decorated with flowers or coloured ribbons would be paraded round the streets of the town … The parade ended, the bull with a rope tied round the root of his horns, would be fastened to a stake with an iron ring in it … dogs which had been made ready for attack would be un-leashed; there would follow a series of savage encounters in which lumps of flesh would be torn off the bull and there was a high chance that some dogs might die.[96]

Some of the 'better sort' of citizens obviously felt that the workers were not entitled to enjoy their ancient amusement. The sheriff's repeated warnings to the crowd to desist and disperse were ignored. The crowd were asserting what they believed to be a right of the 'lower orders' of Dublin. The sheriff ordered his men to commence arrests, and eight persons were seized. The sheriff then proceeded to try to remove his prisoners to the new prison. As the soldiers retreated towards the city with the arrested tradesmen they were pelted with stones. The soldiers fired over the heads of the crowd at this point, but one man was mortally wounded opposite the Custom House. The military reached Abbey Street, where the sheriff ordered his men to fire on the

---

96   Wade (2008), p. 58.

crowd, killing two more men. Several others were 'so desperately wounded that their lives were despaired of'.[97] Farrell Reddy, a coach maker, James Mahaffy and Patrick Keegan were killed.[98] Sheriff Vance was arraigned for murder, but the relatives of the dead had no money to pay for the prosecution.

Following the publicity surrounding the Mary Neal case, the families of the dead turned to Rowan and wrote to Rathcoffey pleading for his assistance. Rowan was reluctant to get involved for fear that he would be accused of 'a vain attempt to win popularity', but eventually agreed to attend a public meeting on the matter in Saint Mary's Parish.[99] He raised a public subscription for the legal costs of the bereaved families, but carried most of the expense personally. As he had done in the Mary Neal case, he carried out an investigation of his own.

He wrote to his wife, Sarah:

> I got down at Ellis's about twelve, and from that time I was tracing every step of the military on that fatal day; and the more inquiry I make, the more I am confirmed in the opinion of it being a most diabolical exercise of power. I saw the father and mother of one of the sufferers, whose story is itself a tragedy.[100]

Vance was prosecuted, and the Attorney General argued that the dead men had not been involved in trespass and that bull-baiting was not illegal, citing many 'instances of corporations holding their charter by having public

---

97 *Freeman's Journal*, 28 December 1789.
98 *Ibid.*
99 Drummond, p. 104.
100 *Ibid.*, p. 105.

bull-baits; Chester does so; the Isle of Wight and Naas hold their charters by it'.[101]

This trial was a form of class struggle between the working tradesmen of the city and the city fathers, and there was always only going to be one outcome: Vance was acquitted. He was not even criticized for the unnecessary intervention in the affair that led to the killings and woundings. At the very least Vance should have read the Riot Act before ordering his men to open fire. Judge Richard Power clearly had more empathy for the bull which survived than the citizens who died, and felt compelled to criticize the dead and wounded workers for engaging in the barbarous custom, which he was determined to discountenance.[102]

Rowan argued that English law only allowed the killing of a person as lawful when it was absolutely necessary. He recalled that:

> At Cambridge there was constant bull-baiting under the very eye of the vice-chancellor and all the doctors of divinity ... and in Paris bull-baiting was attended by the first nobility of that kingdom.[103]

As Rowan was commenting after the verdict had been delivered he had to choose his words carefully, and was most likely taking refuge in sarcasm when he wrote:

> The worthy judge who presided at the trial whose clear, concise, and constitutional charge to the jury must create respect and honour; whilst the benevolent manner in which he expressed himself concerning the innocent amusement of the people

---

101 *Ibid.*, p. 106.
102 *Loc. cit.*
103 *Loc. cit.*

and their right to indulgence in them, excited the love and esteem of his audience.[104]

The War between Magee and the Sham Squire

Mary Neal and the unfortunate bull-baiters and Rowan's role in these affairs were much commented on in the Dublin newspapers of the time. The *Dublin Evening Post* lionized Rowan as a hero of the downtrodden and oppressed. Not so the *Freeman's Journal*.

John Magee, the editor of the *Post*, took great delight in exposing the murky past and indeed present activities of his rival editor of the *Freeman's Journal*, Francis Higgins.

The *Freeman's Journal* had been founded by Charles Lucas in 1763, and under his direction took an anti-government stance, but Higgins took control of it in 1784 and brought it into the government camp. At the time of Higgins's battles with Magee he was in receipt of £1,600 a year from the government – money was paid in fees for the various government proclamations published in the *Journal*. Lord Clonmell would sign proclamations on 'every conceivable infraction of the law'. Fitzpatrick claimed that these proclamations were 'a libel on the country', and asked 'was any offender ever taken up in consequence of such publications?'[105] The proclamations were a bribe to Higgins, which he needed badly because of the *Journal's* declining readership.[106]

Almost every issue of the *Post* would print letters from various 'correspondents' giving lurid details of Higgins's career. In 1789 the *Post* reprinted the details of the trial of Higgins in 1766 for faking conversion to Roman Catholicism and forging documents suggesting that he was

---

104 *Ibid.*
105 *Ibid.*, p. 31.
106 Bartlett (2004), p. 25.

a wealthy landowner in order to deceive the daughter of a wealthy Catholic merchant into marriage. Higgins served a term in prison for this, and the judge who sentenced him bestowed on him the nickname the 'Sham Squire', which 'was to dog him for the rest of his life'.[107] Magee delighted in informing his readers that the Sham was very close to the woman the *Evening Post* referred to as 'the virtuous and chaste Madam Llewellyn'. As well as being a newspaper man, the Sham was a judge, a position he owed, according to the *Post*, to the 'virtuous and humane Lord Carhampton'. The *Post* informed its readers that Madam Llewellyn would shortly pose for a portrait with the judge from Kilmainham court (the Sham), who 'deals out justice and substantial justice to the poor, the oppressed and anyone else who cannot stand up for themselves'.[108] Magee claimed that the Sham was the proprietor of a gaming house and brothel, and identified him as being responsible for 'liberating Llewellyn and her obliging friend Edgeworth'.[109]

The Sham had Magee arraigned before his good friend Lord Clonmell. Clonmell ordered Magee to be thrown into prison on a warrant of £7,800, 'at the suit of Francis Higgins'. This amounted to an indefinite prison sentence without trial.

Magee somehow managed to keep the paper going, and in the issue of 30 June 1789 in an open letter to John Scott (Lord Clonmell) he said:

> I again demand at your hands, John Scott ... a trial by peers, by my fellow free and independent Irishmen. Thou hast dragged a citizen by thy officers thrice through the streets of this capital as a felon. Thou hast confined before trial and hast deprived a

---

107 *Ibid.*, p. 24.
108 *Dublin Evening Post*, June 1789.
109 Fitzpatrick, p. 49.

> free subject of his franchise, that franchise for which
> his fathers bled on the walls of Derry, the banks of
> the Boyne and the plains of Aughrim ... I demand
> from thee a trial by jury.[110]

Rowan wrote to Magee criticizing the unconstitutional behaviour of Clonmell and pledging financial support for an appeal. Magee immediately published this letter in the *Post*. The Sham realized that Magee had exposed Rowan to charges of contempt of court. In the next issue of the *Journal* he taunted and threatened Rowan, suggesting that he might soon be joining his friend behind bars. The authorities were not at that time prepared to take on such a formidable opponent, however, and took no action against Rowan.

On 14 July 1789, the day the people of Paris stormed the Bastille, it was business as usual in Dublin as the *Post* continued to do battle with the Sham and Lord Clonmell. That day's issue of the *Post* carried two items of interest. The first was an advertisement from four citizens of Dublin supporting Magee. The four Dublin citizens were Archibald Hamilton Rowan, James Napper Tandy, Henry Jackson and Samuel Gardiner. All four were Presbyterians. James Napper Tandy had an immense reputation as an opponent of the government, and for twenty years had led the opposition in Dublin Corporation. Henry Jackson was a leading industrialist who had been an officer in the Volunteers and an ally of Tandy on the Corporation.[111] Samuel Gardiner has been described as an 'opulent citizen' and had a tailoring business at Fisher's Lane.[112] These men, less than two years later, would form the nucleus of the Dublin Society of United Irishmen. The other interesting item carried in that

---

110 *Ibid.*, p. 61.
111 Binns (1854), p. 23.
112 Bartlett (1998), p.100

issue of the *Post* was a letter more elegantly written than the usual material of the *Post*, signed 'Sidney'. This letter criticized the 'Lawyers of Dublin' for not denouncing the illegal and unconstitutional nature of Clonmell's treatment of Magee. William Drennan was known to use the pen name, Sidney. If this elegant epistle was indeed the work of William Drennan, then the Bastille Day *Evening Post* carried the opinions not only of the later leading lights of the United Irishmen, but also of Drennan, the first person to suggest the need for a secret revolutionary brotherhood.

Magee finally managed to get bail, but could get no constitutional remedy for the injustices inflicted on him. He contrived a bizarre and expensive scheme to get revenge on Clonmell. Clonmell had a beautifully appointed house and gardens at Blackrock and had spent much time and money improving his magnificent 'pleasure grounds'. Magee bought an adjoining field, which he named 'Fiat [as in Warrant] Hill'.

He announced that he was to host an outdoor function to celebrate the birthday of the Prince of Wales, and invited 'all his friends, private and political, known and unknown, washed and unwashed ... with plenty of Sylvester Costigan's whiskey [available] and *table d'hôte* for the ladies and gentlemen'.

Lord Cloncurry was in attendance, and recalls how:

> The entire disposable mob of Dublin of both sexes [were] climbing poles for prizes, running races in sacks, grinning through horse collars [...] A number of active pigs with their tails shaved and soaped were let loose, and it was announced that each pig was to become the property [of] anyone that could catch and hold it by the slippery member.[113]

---

113 Fitzpatrick, p. 88.

The pigs were hemmed in such a way that the only place for them to run was through Clonmell's 'magnificent demesne'. The next day his grounds 'lay uprooted and desolate' and 'exhibited nothing but the ruins of the Olympic pig hunt'.

It is not clear whether Rowan, Magee's best-known political friend, attended the memorable event on Fiat Hill, but he accompanied Magee on his next court appearance when Magee gave a surety that he would cease pestering Clonmell.[114] Rowan's very public support for Magee would have done little to endear him to the lord who would eventually preside at the trials of Rowan and William Drennan for seditious libel in 1794.

---

114 *Ibid.*, p. 90.

5.

From Volunteer to United Irishman

Neither the *Freeman's Journal* nor the *Dublin Evening Post* covered the storming of the Bastille until nearly two weeks after it happened. The Sham Squire described the happenings in Paris as anarchy and murder, while John Magee hailed them as the people's victory over tyranny. In those days important news travelled only as fast as a horseman could gallop or a ship could sail. However, delay in the arrival of the news did nothing to moderate the impact in Ireland of the momentous events in Paris.

Wolfe Tone described the French Revolution as 'a gigantic event', which, he claimed, brought an end to 'the days of apathy and depression' within the radical movement in Ireland. Tone tells us:

> Mr Burke's famous invective appeared; and this in due season produced Paine's reply, which he called *Rights of Man* ... this controversy ... changed in an instant the politics of Ireland ... As the revolution advanced and as events expanded themselves, the

public spirit of Ireland rose with a rapid acceleration. In a little time the French Revolution became the test of every man's political creed and the nation was fairly divided into two great parties, the Aristocrats and the Democrats.[115]

Lord Charlemont, the Volunteer leader, had become gravely concerned at the prevalence of 'wild democratic notions', and urged his friends in Belfast to establish the Northern Whig Club along the lines of the Whig Club he had himself established in Dublin.[116] His hope was that he could curb the enthusiasm of the radicals by 'promoting the cause of constitutional freedom'. His hopes in this regard were somewhat frustrated because the radicals were the most enthusiastic members of the new clubs, and though the Catholic question was evaded or suppressed, the clubs, at least initially, adopted much of the radical language of Paine and the French Revolution.

The first meeting of the northern Whigs was chaired by none other than Gawin Hamilton, Rowan's father. The secretary, Dr Haliday, wrote from Belfast to Rowan in Dublin:

> When we first thought of establishing a Northern Whig Club ... you naturally occurred to our thoughts; your excellent principles were too well known and your exertions on behalf of liberty and of justice not to excite a general wish that we might have you to boast as one of our members. I now write with the pleasing expectation that I shall be

115 Bartlett (1998), p. 39.
116 Drummond, p. 149.

empowered to add your name to our respectable list of original members and in the hope that we may have the satisfaction of seeing you sometimes amongst us.[117]

Rowan had been admitted to the Whig Club of the capital on 19 January 1790 and was begining to be regonised as a popular leader of the Dublin radicals. He recalled how:

I had been elected … major of the Independent Dublin Volunteers, of whom Mr Grattan was colonel. I also became a member of the Whig club, and received the freedom of the [Dublin City] Commons, with addresses from several of the Dublin corporations. I joined 'the society of United Irishmen heart and hand', [which] led to an acquaintance with the popular leaders in Ireland, and transmitted the name of an insignificant individual to posterity.[118]

Rowan had joined the Dublin Society of United Irshman in late 1791, shortly after it was founded. His fellow society members were much impressed by him. William Drennan regarded him as a most valuable revolutionary. Wolfe Tone regarded him as a man of position, good address, influential connections and great personal courage.[119]

Paine's *Rights of Man* appeared, and Rowan and the radical element within the Whig club set up a committee to oversee the distribution of cheap editions. Some 20,000 copies were bought in Ireland by the end of the year.[120]

117 *Ibid.*, p. 150.
118 Drummond, p.159
119 Nicoson, p. 94
120 Mansergh (2005), p. 120.

Throughout England and Ireland people were taking sides in the Burke–Paine debate. In his *Reflections on the Revolution in France,* Edmund Burke had made a blistering attack on Dr Price, a Unitarian minister who had welcomed the early stages of the French Revolution. Burke delighted the British government and the Tories by suggesting that reformers like Dr Price were atheists engaged in sedition who were trying to overthrow the Church and the King. Thomas Paine, a veteran propagandist of the American Revolution, produced his *Rights of Man*, defending not only Dr Price but also the notion that a people could choose the form of government under which they wished to live, and could change that government if they so desired.

Tone believed that Burke won the debate in England but that Paine had the victory in Ireland. The *Dublin Evening Post* often made positive references to 'Mr Paine' and many negative references to Burke and his work. The *Post* quoted Mirabeau against Burke as follows:

> Mr Burke has made an attempt at system without order, demonstration or argument. Emotions, violence and resentment are evident in every page, but it is not the anger of a great and good mind. It is that of Milton's fiend contemplating our first parents; his imagery is incorrect, distorted and often filthy; his language rumbling, noisy and inharmonious. Burke's book is the production of a loquacious impostor who soothes our prejudices but invades our rights.[121]

Rowan was now deeply involved in a secret six-man committee whose aim was to revive volunteering in Dublin. A similar secret committee in Belfast, under the leadership

---

121 *Dublin Evening Post*, 19 July 1791.

of Samuel Neilson, formed a democratic political club among the Green Company of Volunteers and was working towards the same objective.[122] Among Neilson's group were Sam McTier (brother-in-law of William Drennan), William Tennant and Thomas McCabe.

The other members of Rowan's Dublin committee were James Napper Tandy, Edward Newenham, William T. Smyth, John Ashenhurst and Thomas Bacon.[123] All the Belfast and Dublin men, with the exception of Edward Newenham, would shortly join the open and public debating club, the Society of United Irishmen.

Thomas Bacon was a master tailor, and at this point was turning out uniforms for the Volunteers.[124] A few years later, in 1798, Thomas Bacon was hanged from a lamp post on Carlisle Bridge in Dublin, accused of being a rebel officer and a spy.[125]

Rowan's secret committee was not a secret for very long as they printed some of their resolutions for select distribution. Copies soon fell into the hands of the Sham Squire, who forwarded them to Undersecretary Edward Cooke at the Castle.[126] The Sham ran a network of spies and informers throughout the 1790s, and kept Cooke and the Castle informed on the goings on in the Catholic Committee, the Volunteers, and of course the United Irishmen.

There was perhaps a contradiction between the desire for secrecy at the leadership level while the whole point of volunteering was that free citizens with the right to bear arms to defend constitutional freedoms should publicly assert that right by holding parades and reviews.

---

122 Jacob (1937), p. 55.
123 *Ibid.*, p. 123.
124 Bartlett (2004), p. 247
125 O'Donnell (2003), p. 93.
126 Mansergh, p. 123.

John Binns, who was later both a United Irishman and a member of the London Corresponding Society, claims to have been present at a parade of the Dublin Independent Volunteers led by Lieutenant Colonel Archibald Hamilton Rowan on 14 July 1790, held to commemorate the fall of the Bastille the previous year. They carried a transparency depicting, 'a globe which showed America shedding a blaze of light on the old world'.[127] Binns relates how, as Rowan's men marched up a hill close to the upper Castle gate, four sturdy ruffians grabbed the banner and ran to the Castle gatehouse. The Castle guard formed up to protect the banner thieves and Rowan ordered his contingent to load and prime their weapons. In response, the Castle guard, which numbered about 100, and was of equal strength to Rowan's, shouldered their own weapons. The crowd, including Binns himself, who had been following the Volunteers, prudently withdrew. The officers from both sides parleyed, however, and agreed that a detachment drawn from an equal number from each would take the ruffians to prison to be dealt with according to law.[128]

If Binns recalled the date of this incident correctly, Rowan's men were parading regularly, for the *Evening Post* tells us that on 25 July Rowan led a parade of 300 Dublin Volunteers through the streets of the capital.[129] In imitation of the French revolutionary style the men wore a national cockade, which was painted green and emblazoned with the Irish harp and crown. By this time Catholics were joining the Dublin Volunteers in numbers. The recruitment of Catholics and the adoption and adaptation of French iconography and rhetoric alarmed moderate reformers and infuriated the government.

---

127 *loc. cit.*
128 Binns, p. 26.
129 *Dublin Evening Post*, July 1791

Not all of the Volunteers were prepared to follow the radicals, either in their attitudes to the French Revolution or the rights of Roman Catholics. In the autumn of 1791 the Volunteers in Armagh took sides in the bitter sectarian conflict that had broken out there, and announced that they would enforce the laws against Roman Catholics bearing arms.

The *Evening Post* reported on 17 October that Rowan had convened a meeting of the Protestant members of his Dublin corps, which passed a resolution condemning the Armagh corps for upholding a law 'which in our opinion disgraces the statutes of the nation'.[130] The paper also reported that other units in Dublin followed Rowan's lead.

A Brotherhood of Affection

By now Rowan was one of the leading and most high-profile radicals in Ireland, well known and popular in both Dublin and Belfast. Wolfe Tone and Thomas Russell had met with Rowan's friends in Neilson's secret committee in Belfast on 14 October to establish the Society of United Irishmen. The members of the new society adopted a test, pledging themselves to 'Forward a brotherhood of affection, an identity of interests, a communion of rights and a union of power among Irishmen of all religious persuasions....'

Thus, the first meeting of the society adopted just the sort of principles Rowan had long espoused,

The Dublin Society would meet on Friday evenings and ballot new members, compose addresses to the people and correspond with radicals in England and Scotland. Almost from the beginning, Thomas Collins, a member of the society, gave a detailed account of everything that transpired at the meetings to Dublin Castle. However, the informer often

---

130 *loc. cit.*

expressed his frustration: he believed that a secret committee that met elsewhere made all the decisions in advance of the open meetings. Neither Collins nor any other informer ever managed to penetrate such a committee. If this secret committee did exist, it is almost certain that Rowan was its guiding spirit. It is clear from Collins's report that Rowan was a leading, influential and enthusiastic member of the new society.

The Eagle Tavern proved too small for the growing organization, which soon had to move to larger venues. A student, who was apparently free to walk into a meeting held in the Tailors' Guild Hall in Back Lane, near Cornmarket, saw Wolfe Tone, Napper Tandy and Hamilton Rowan sitting together. He was not impressed by Tone or Tandy. Tone was 'a flimsy man in whom there was no harm'. The student claimed that Tandy was the 'ugliest man he had ever gazed on'. He must never have seen the Sham Squire. Rowan, however, was the most handsome and the largest man the student had ever seen. 'Tone and Tandy seemed like pygmies beside him'.[131]

Tone declared that the aim of the Dublin Society was 'to make all Irishmen Citizens and all citizens Irishmen'.[132] In December 1791 they circulated liberal sympathizers all over Ireland, calling on them to form similar societies. The heady enthusiasm of the time ensured that the response was spectacular. Drummond described the exponential growth of the society in these terms:

> Like the circle caused by a pebble caste in [the] middle of the lake, it continued to spread wider and wider ... moving on with swelling strength and accelerating speed ... the union passed through every class of

---

131 Boylan (1981), p. 21.
132 Jacob, p. 79.

society, lighting on the bench and the pulpit, on the
desk and on the anvil, shooting like an electric shock
through the ranks of the militia, animating the breast
of women with heroic daring, and infusing courage
into the hearts and vigour into the arms, even of boys
and children.[133]

If the movement was growing in morale and membership,
the enmity of the government and the ruling classes towards
the United Irishmen was also growing apace.[134]

The Burke–Paine debate inflamed passions all over Ireland,
and indeed in England and Scotland. As the Volunteers and
the common people of Dublin and Belfast celebrated Bastille
Day 1791, a Tory mob in Birmingham rioted for three days.
Having failed to locate and murder Dr Joseph Priestley,
the mob had to be content with burning his house, library
and meeting house, and many other properties in the city
associated with the Protestant Dissenters. The crime of the
Dissenters was that they were perceived to be sympathetic to
the French Revolution. Burke, who was advocating war with
France, was suggesting that Priestley, his friend Dr Price and
the Dissenters were the enemy within.

In many English cities the 'Association for Preserving
Liberty and Property against Republicans and Levellers'
targeted meetings of reformers, burnt copies of *Rights of Man*,
burnt effigies of Paine and Priestley, intimidated democrats
and organized riots, usually involving drunken mobs to
protect the Church and the King and to uphold law and order.

While Dublin Castle could count on the support of the
Freeman's Journal, and spies and informers like the Sham and
Collins, at this juncture the authorities had no possibility of

---

133 Drummond, p. 159.
134 Jacob, p. 29.

mobilizing support from what they called the lower orders in Dublin.

The *Freeman's Journal*, however, ran a propaganda campaign on behalf of the Castle. It had four main pillars. Firstly, the *Journal* preached the absolute necessity for Britain and Ireland to join the Dutch and the Austrians in their counter-revolutionary war against the new French republic. Secondly, the paper attempted to stir up Protestant fears of 'Defender' attacks and arm seizures, which were allegedly escalating in Louth, Cavan, Monaghan and Meath. The Defenders was an armed secret society of Roman Catholics that had emerged in response to the sectarian conflict in Armagh, but was now spreading, not just through the countryside but into the towns, and even into Dublin City itself.

A third pillar of the *Journal's* campaign was to threaten the leadership of the Roman Catholics so as to encourage them to cease flirting with what the paper called 'republicans and levellers, and to desist from seeking reform until the times were more auspicious'. Finally, the *Journal* relentlessly attacked the Society of United Irishmen. In a classic instance of the pot calling the kettle black, the Sham Squire sneered at the social origins of the radicals when he wrote:

The Whigs of the Capital, a junta of sage sapient porter house politicians, who forsook their hand-craft trades to become cobblers of the State and tinkers of the Constitution ... hatched the brood called United Irishmen. Between these and the northern Whigs were generated the Jacobins of Belfast upon those of Paris begat the Defenders, the Dungannon Convention and the National Guard.[135]

---

135 *Freeman's Journal*, March 1793.

Spies, informers and eventually agents provocateurs watched every move made by the new society, but despite this the society had something of a charmed life for the first few months of its existence. Members flocked in and fraternal addresses and messages of support were received from all over the country, and even from overseas from such bodies as the Revolution Society in England and the Friends of the People in Scotland. The Revolution Society was a reform club that looked to the Glorious Revolution of 1688 and the overthrow of James II by William of Orange as the harbinger of British liberties. Rowan's old mentor John Jebb, who had passed away a few years previously, had at one time been its leading light.

Napper Tandy Blunders

The *Freeman's Journal* campaign cut little ice in Dublin, but the honeymoon enjoyed by the United Irishmen came to an end in February 1792. Napper Tandy mishandled the first major confrontation between the society and the government. The Solicitor General, John Toler, later Lord Norbury, launched an attack in Parliament, saying:

> I have seen papers signed by Tobias McKenna, with Simon Butler in the chair and Napper Tandy lending his countenance; I should have thought they could put a better face on it. But sir such fellows are too despicable for notice; therefore I shall not drag them from their obscurity.[136]

Tandy was sensitive about his ill-favoured appearance and took personal offence at Toler's jibe. He demanded an apology, which Toler refused, claiming that Tandy

---

136 Jacob, p. 80.

was trying to subvert parliamentary privilege. Toler also let it be known that he was willing to fight a duel, but Tandy demurred. Instead, he announced his intention of publishing an account of the affair. This was a blatant breach of parliamentary privilege, and Tandy was arrested, but escaped the messenger sent to bring him into custody.

William Drennan observed that Tandy had flinched from facing Toler or going to prison, and had lost ground in the affair.[137] The government added insult to injury by offering a paltry reward of £50 for the apprehension of Tandy. Their spy, Thomas Collins, gleefully informed them that 'poor Napper's sun is set, his declining to fight they say out Herod's Herod'.[138] Collins was quoting Shakespeare's *Hamlet* to suggest that Tandy was seen as an overacting and violent blusterer.

Wolfe Tone felt strongly that the United Irishmen could not let matters rest without conceding 'a total forfeiture of character'. Tone writes:

> I cast my eye on Archibald Hamilton Rowan, a distinguished member of the society, whose many virtues, public and private, had set his name above the reach of even the malevolence of party, whose situation in life was of the most respectable rank, if ranks be indeed respectable, and, above all, whose personal courage was not to be shaken, a circumstance, in the actual situation of affairs, of the last importance.[139]

Rowan agreed to take the chair of the society in the place of the fugitive Tandy, and on 25 February 1792 the society

---

137 Agnew, vol 1, p. 396.
138 McDowell (1940), p. 14.
139 Bartlett (1998), p. 49.

issued a far more blatant attack on what it called 'Undefined Privilege', adding that the society would not:

> Shrink from ... any constitutional enquiry into our Principles and Conduct and reserving for that occasion the Justification of our Actions we resign to merited Contempt the Scorn of official station or the Scoff of unprincipled Venality.[140]

Tone and Rowan were here inviting prosecution, and if Toler or anyone else challenged one of them to fight a duel, they would regard it as a bonus and a means to restore the honour of their society. There was no question whatever of either Tone or Rowan refusing to fight. Tandy came out of hiding on 18 April, the closing day of the parliamentary session, in the full knowledge that he could not be held in custody after the session ended. The whole Dublin Society of United Irishmen escorted him to Newgate, and half an hour later they marched him home in triumphal procession.[141]

Earlier that day Tone and Rowan strutted into the gallery of the House of Commons wearing their gaudy Whig Club uniforms so that any MP who wished to take issue with their breach of privilege and their insults could do so. Much to their amazement they were neither charged nor challenged. Why they were allowed to snatch this victory and rescue some honour from the jaws of defeat must remain a mystery. Tone believed that the government at that time had 'no wish just then to embroil themselves with a man of Rowan's firmness and courage, not to speak of his great and justly merited popularity'.[142]

---

140 Jacob, p. 81.
141 *Ibid.*, p. 82.
142 Bartlett (1998), p. 51.

If it was, indeed, that Rowan was a man the government were afraid to tangle with in the spring of 1792, circumstances would change before that year was out. He was charged with seditious libel in the hope that by bringing its most illustrious, popular and courageous member to the gallows it would put an end for once and for all to the Society of United Irishmen. Even then they were cautious, and did not bring the case to trial for nearly fifteen months.

6.

The Government Crackdown

A secret committee of the Irish House of Lords was established to look into 'the causes of disorder'. This was not with a view to eliminating grievances or alleviating the suffering or distress that lay behind the discontent. Rather, the committee wanted to identify the leaders of discontent and the promoters of sedition with a view to putting a stop to their activities. The Secret Committee was much concerned with the growth of the Defenders, whom it suggested were:

> Poor, ignorant labouring men, sworn to secrecy and impressed with an opinion that they are assisting the Catholic cause … They first appeared in Louth in considerable bodies, several of them were armed … the disorder soon spread to Meath. Cavan and Monaghan … at first they took nothing but arms but afterwards plundered the houses of everything they could find. Their measures appear to have been conducted with the upmost secrecy and a degree of regularity and system not usual in people of such

a mean condition and as if directed by men of superior rank.[143]

While this dismissive attitude towards the abilities of poorer people to mount effective resistance is fairly reflective of the social hierarchy of the day, in the context of the reports of the Secret Committee it was being stated explicitly for a sinister purpose. The committee was very anxious to place the blame for the rise in Defenderism on the Catholic Committee if they could, or better still establish a link between Defender violence and the United Irishmen.

One of the Secret Committee's reports had this to say of Rowan's Dublin corps:

A body of men associated themselves in Dublin under the title of the first National Battalion; their uniform copied from the French, green turned up with white, white waistcoat and striped trousers, gilt buttons impressed with a harp, and letters importing 'First National Battalion'; no crown, but a device over the harp of a Cap of Liberty upon a pike.[144]

The government could not long tolerate public displays of armed men in uniform, including some from the lower classes and even Roman Catholics, marching through the streets of Dublin, modelling their symbols on the National Guard of Paris. When the Dublin Volunteers planned to hold a public parade to celebrate the French victory at the battle of Valmy the government finally put its foot down, proclaiming on 8 December 1792:

143 Fleming (2005), p. 160.
144 *Ibid.*, p. 162.

> Divers, ill-affected persons have entered into illegal
> and seditious associations in the county and city
> of Dublin ... publicly declared their intention
> to appear in arms to avow their approbation to
> tumult and disorder, and to encourage the citizens
> of Dublin to follow their evil example, and have
> also conspired together to raise, levy and muster
> within the county and city of Dublin a number of
> armed men, to parade in military array, with various
> devices and ensigns of disaffection to his Majesty
> and the constitution ... and have raised great alarms
> in the minds of his Majesty's loyal subjects.[145]

Volunteer public gatherings were banned. Failure to obey
the proclamations would lead to military intervention and
bloodshed on the streets. As neither Britain nor Ireland was at
war with France at this time, Rowan and the United Irishmen
believed that this was yet another attack on their civil liberties.
Unwilling to give in to the government on the one hand, but
not wishing to precipitate a bloodbath or invite arrest and
charges of treason on the other, they chose a response that
defied the government but remained within the law.

A meeting of the United Irishmen held on 14 December,
with Rowan in the chair and William Drennan acting as
secretary, endorsed an address of encouragement to the
Volunteers. Drennan wrote:

> Citizen soldiers to arms!
> You first took up arms from foreign enemies and
> domestic disturbance. For the same purpose it
> now becomes necessary that you resume them.
> A proclamation has been issued in England for

---

145 Jacob, p. 149.

embodying the militia; and a proclamation has been issued by the Lord Lieutenant and the council in Ireland for repressing all seditious associations. [...] Citizen Soldiers to arms! Take up the shield of freedom and the pledges of peace – peace the motive end of your virtuous institution. War an occasional duty ought never to become an occupation. Every man should become a soldier in defence of his rights; no man ought to continue a soldier for offending the rights of others.[146]

The address went on to suggest a convention of Protestants to follow the example of the Catholic convention (which was being held between 3 and 10 December in the Tailors' Hall, Dublin). The purpose of such a convention would be 'to establish an intercourse of sentiment, a uniformity of conduct, a united cause and a united nation'.

Tone was acting as secretary to the Catholic Committee, and he and the committee were anxious that no pretext be given for the suppression of the convention by too close an association with the beleaguered Volunteers. The *Freeman's Journal* was already classifying the convention as a seditious gathering attempting to overawe Parliament. The Catholics were inclined to be cautious about too close a link to the radicals.

According to Drennan:

Many in the [Catholic] Convention regard us as republicans and sinners and don't like to have communication with us. Tomorrow will produce something. It is said that the Riot Act will be read to the Volunteers if they assemble.[147]

---

146 *Ibid.*, p. 152.
147 Nicolson, p. 96.

Rowan had wanted to bring the Volunteers onto the streets and defy the ban but disperse peacefully when the Riot Act was read. He could not, however, convince his colleagues.

On 16 December 1792 Rowan and Tandy, in Volunteer uniform and wearing sidearms, mustered several of the Dublin corps to Pardon's fencing academy at Crow Street in central Dublin. There they distributed Drennan's address to the Volunteers assembled, as well as to the many citizens who watched proceedings from the public gallery. Copies of the address were showered out of the windows to the multitude outside who could not gain access to the hall. Several of the Dublin Volunteer corps thanked the United Irishmen for the address and thereby succeeded in giving 'great offence to the government'.[148] William Drummond, Rowan's first biographer, denied that Rowan was present at Pardon's that day and suggested the trial witnesses who later swore he had been present had perjured themselves. However, John Binns, then a young soap boiler's apprentice and later a leading United Irishman, recalled in his memoirs that he was in the gallery and that Colonel Hamilton Rowan, a man Binns admired, was the presiding officer at Pardon's.

Five days later Sheriff Carleton called to Dominick Street and arrested Rowan on the charge of distributing a seditious address. Believing the judge's assurances that the case would quickly come to court, Rowan was prepared to stay in prison 'in pursuance of his opinions'. On his lawyers' advice, however, he accepted bail on a surety of £200, a decision that subsequently proved wise. The government had no intention of moving quickly against Rowan for fear that his popularity in Dublin might lead to an acquittal by a jury of his peers. The government took its time in the hope

---

148 Jacob, p. 152.

that, by a slow process of intimidation and entrapment, they could, at best, get Rowan to flee, and if not, procure perjurers and a packed jury that would bring in a guilty verdict.

The Joe Corbally Affair

Rowan was brought before the courts in December 1792, but his trial proper did not begin until 29 January 1794. In the meantime a succession of visitors came to his house in Dominick Street with suspicious offers of assistance. Rowan tells us that one man called Corbally offered to teach Rowan's manservant how to make artillery ammunition. Rowan, with more prudence than he would later display, refused to have any dealings with these 'visitors', believing that the government was simply baiting traps to bolster its case.

The Corbally referred to is Joe Corbally, a tailor from the Naul in County Dublin, and Rowan's implication that he was an agent provocateur is unjust. Jemmy Hope, the working-class United Irish leader, was 81 years old when he dictated his memoirs to R. R. Madden, fifty years after the events he recalled. Hope often has his facts mixed up, but he also has an ability to capture the mood of the times. Though his grasp of detail is suspect, his analysis is insightful and, perhaps more than any other observer, he knew the United Irish movement from the inside.

Hope says this of Corbally:

> When Defenderism was introduced into the counties of Meath and Dublin [Corbally] was appointed a captain, but a faction sprung up in his neighbourhood ... which began to plunder in the name of the Defenders ... [Corbally] procured a warrant, arrested some of the robbers and delivered them up to the civil authorities. The Volunteers

had not been put down and [he] used to discipline his men as if they were Volunteer recruits on a hill in the neighbourhood. Archibald Hamilton Rowan and James Napper Tandy happened to pass from Drogheda to Dublin ... where the men were mustered and went to tip them and gave them advice to desist telling them that appearing in arms would not serve either themselves or the country: and the parades discontinued. A magistrate named Graham induced two of the robbers whom Corbally had arrested to swear against him as a leader of the Defenders. Graham [then] offered [Corbally] his liberty and a large reward, if he would swear against Rowan and Tandy.[149]

The *Northern Star* reported that Joe Corbally was also offered a place with the Revenue if he would swear that Tandy and Rowan were leaders of the Defenders.[150] This he refused to do, and was sent to jail. He was lodged with another Defender prisoner called Maguire, who was also being pressurized into implicating Rowan. Corbally charged Graham with trying to force him into perjury. However, Graham released Maguire, who promptly vanished, and Corbally could not sustain his case. Graham made a countercharge against Corbally, who was sentenced to two years in jail for perjury.

Jemmy Hope goes on to tell another story about Joe Corbally. While not related to Rowan's vicissitudes at this time, it is worth recounting as an illustration that even if Hope sometimes has his facts wrong regarding individuals, he can portray vivid truths about the cruelty and even barbarism of the authorities' response to disaffection.

---

149 Newsinger (1992), p. 83.
150 Curtin (1998), p. 59.

Hope described how Joe Corbally was transported to Botany Bay. During the voyage he was handcuffed to a fellow prisoner. This man was accused of a plot to murder the captain and turn pirate. The prisoner was flogged to death, and Corbally lay for days handcuffed to the corpse. The details of this story bear a remarkable similarity to a well-documented episode that involved the Reverend Thomas Fyshe Palmer, William Skirving and Thomas Muir, Scottish friends of Rowan, who were transported to the penal colonies in May 1794. They were accused of a similar plot to murder the ship's captain, and a number of their fellow convicts were brutally flogged.

War with France

Rowan had been arrested in December 1792 as part of the government drive to be done with the Volunteers and the United Irishmen. On 21 January 1793 the French brought King Louis to the guillotine. France was now a republic, and the war, which Edmund Burke and the Tory press, including the *Freeman's Journal*, had so long advocated, was now inevitable.

If Rowan and his friends had been feeling the pressure before war was declared in February 1793, the crackdown on the democrats and all the disaffected, including the Defenders, exceeded all that had gone before them in terms of intensity and severity. The war meant that those who had welcomed the French Revolution could now be classified as traitors and treated accordingly. Demands for liberty, democracy and reform of the franchise could be dismissed as French principles.

The Volunteers had been suppressed, a bill prohibiting conventions of any kind had been introduced, and bills banning the importation of gunpowder and embodying a militia were all designed to narrow the democrats' options.

The charging of Rowan, Tandy, and other leading United Irishmen was designed to terrify the timid and isolate the courageous.

The authorities continued to increase the pressure on Rowan. High-ranking government officials such as John Foster, the Speaker of the House of Commons, were trying to goad him into flight by saying, within the hearing of his friends, that 'Hamilton Rowan did not know the risk he ran as they had evidence that touched on his life'.[151] Nor was this an idle threat. Marcus Beresford wrote to his father, John Beresford, stressing the government's determination to hang Rowan.[152] By February 1793 Rowan was said to be 'in high dudgeon' and seemed to have plans 'of quitting Ireland'.[153]

The Society of United Irishmen was also feeling the pressure, and the anti-combination laws, which were designed to suppress agrarian secret societies such as the Whiteboys, were used against the Volunteers. The Volunteers dared not muster in public, and the few who wore their uniforms in groups of two or three experienced military harassment and intimidation.

Throughout March and April the *Freeman's Journal* reported with ill-disguised glee the execution of dozens of Defenders at Dundalk, the flogging of many more, and the transportation of dozens to Botany Bay.

On 1 March 1793 Simon Butler and Oliver Bond were summoned to the House of Lords to answer a charge of signing a statement from the Society of United Irishmen that criticized the Lords' Secret Committee. They were fined £500 each, sentenced to six months' imprisonment and were taken to Newgate under heavy guard. The Chancellor, Lord

---

151 *loc. cit.*
152 *loc. cit.*
153 Agnew, vol i, p. 495.

Fitzgibbon, later the Earl of Clare, addressed the convicted men as follows when passing sentence:

> You, Simon Butler and Oliver Bond, are called to the bar [of the House] to answer for a libel on this high court of Parliament ... You, Simon Butler, cannot plead ignorance in extenuation; your noble birth, your education, the honourable profession to which you belong, his Majesty's gown, which you wear and to which you now stand a disgrace, gave you the advantage of knowledge, and are strong circumstances of aggravation of your guilt.[154]

The Honourable Simon Butler was an aristocrat and the brother of Lord Mountgarret. Butler took great umbrage at the chancellor's words, and six months later asked Rowan to become his messenger when challenging Fitzgibbon to a duel over the affair.

---

154 Fleming and Malcomson, p. 172.

7.

Banquets Amidst Starvation

Oliver Bond, sometimes referred to by his enemies as Oliver 'Cromwell' Bond, the son of a Dissenting minister, was a very wealthy draper of woollens who had made a fortune since coming to Dublin from his native town of St Johnston, a few miles from Derry, in 1783. Such was the social status and wealth of Butler and Bond that their conditions of confinement were a great deal less harsh than those of their fellow inmates at Newgate. From the outset the two prisoners partook in lavish dinners with much drinking and conviviality involved, and Martha McTier worried lest the ill-behaved aristocrat Simon Butler was corrupting the 'virtuous Presbyterian' Oliver Bond at Newgate.[155]

Maura Maher writes:

Friends were allowed to visit them and give them presents and they were given as much food as they

---

155 Agnew, vol i, p. 536.

fancied ... In the six months of their captivity the
two friends had a wine bill of £500.

Nicolson suggests that the figure of £500 refers to a wine bill
for only two months.[156] This must be an exaggeration for it
equates to more than three times William Drennan's annual
income at the time, and it would have required a large
number of hard-drinking men to consume that amount of
wine in such a short space of time. However, seventy-one
United Irishmen entered into a lottery, which obliged them,
when their ticket was pulled, to host a dinner for the two
prisoners in the jail, along with eight companions.

Drennan, who mentions a more credible, yet still
extraordinary, figure of £100 for wine, was outraged at the
expense at a time when unemployed workers were starving
in Dublin and elsewhere.

The gentlemen of the United Irishmen were very
popular with the Dublin working class. If any member of
the society was more popular with the workers than Rowan,
it was Oliver Bond. He was said by government informers to
'enjoy great dominion over the smiths and other desperate
fellows'. Yet there was no mob violence in protest against his
imprisonment. This was most likely because during Bond's
comfortable confinement the working people of Dublin had
more serious problems to contend with. Drennan described
how:

The Liberty weavers in the silk, worsted and cotton
lines are in great ferment, and the women are in a
rage. Some of them this morning attacked some of
the bakers' shops, and where there was no bacon to
be sold, and in a panic, most of the shops in the city

156 Nicolson, p. 115.

were closed for a half an hour, but the guards were ordered and I believe are still parading through the Liberty. More danger is apprehended on Saturday night or Sunday when they will become sensible to the extent of the evil.[157]

As Butler and Bond commenced their sentence, Wolfe Tone published an address to the workers of Dublin, signing himself 'a Liberty Weaver'. In it he foretells of the distress in Dublin that would be brought on by the war with France. He asked, 'What quarrel have we with France? Why did the French cut off the King's head? [...] but will our going to war put it on again?' The 'Liberty Weaver' went on to explain how the dumping of British goods would bring starvation within a month and reduce the workers of Dublin to beggary.

Tone's stylish prose and insightful analysis has one major flaw. He forecast distress in the future whilst the Dublin workers were already experiencing it in the present. Tone was, at this time, heavily involved in his duties with the respectable gentlemen of the Catholic Committee. He clearly saw little, and knew little, of the realities of the daily lives of the men, women and children of no property.

Rowan, on the other hand, must have immersed himself in activity to relieve the workers' distress. John Philpot Curran, his counsel at his trial the following year, reminded the jury:

There is not a man in this nation more known than [Rowan for his] extraordinary sympathy for human affliction. There is not a day when you hear the cries of your starving manufacturers in your streets, that

---

157 Agnew, vol i, p. 542.

you do not also see the advocate of their suffering
– that you do not see his honest and manly figure,
with uncovered head, soliciting for their relief ...
you may trace his steps to the abode of disease,
famine and despair ... bearing with him food,
medicine and consolation.[158]

The war with France had led to a collapse in trade in England
and Ireland. The English merchants responded to the crisis
by dumping their surplus goods on the Irish market, making
the problems for Irish workers even worse. Martha McTier
watched starving tradesmen from the Liberties of Dublin
march through the streets of the capital.[159] In response to
the deteriorating conditions of the unemployed workers,
Drennan and Rowan placed a notice in the *Dublin Post* on
28 March on behalf of the United Irishmen, recommending
the non-importation of British goods and suggesting that
purchasing Irish goods was:

> The only means of diffusing comfort and
> independence in the place of idleness and indigence
> through the great manufacturing classes of our
> fellow citizens.

Rowan and Drennan were very conscious that the profligacy
of the Newgate prisoners could undermine United Irish
efforts to develop and harness anti-war sentiment among
the starving working class. Rowan had a printing press
at Rathcoffey. The government recovered a pamphlet
circulating in the Rathcoffey area in which the author,
claiming to be a poor manufacturer, concluded: 'We do

158 Drummond, p. 193.
159 Agnew, vol 1, p. 541.

not want charity, we do want work, and we are starving for what? A war.'[160]

The Sham Squire poured scorn on the suggestion of a non-importation policy, which he said would 'take profit from fair traders in Dublin and transfer it to smugglers in the north'. However, he was at his most splenetic when he jeered:

> Most benevolent Society – why not check the vagrancy of your table? If your subsidies to the carousals of the Green Street [Newgate] Saturnalia have left you anything besides words for the cause of benevolence, devote a little cash for the relief of the miseries you effect to pity. Words, my masters, are a windy diet.[161]

The Sham also rejected the idea that the collapse of Irish manufacturing had anything to do with the war or the commercial relationship with Britain. If the workers wanted to know the source of their miseries, 'they will find it in the rebellious manifestos of their worthy friends the United Irishmen and the Levellers in the north'. Alternatively, the workers should blame 'Tom Paine's productions and the activities of the National Guard and the Defenders'.[162]

By May, starving people from the Liberties were reported as stealing three carloads of bacon and a canal barge filled with flour. This time the Sham, rather than denouncing the United Irishmen for their lack of benevolence, called the hungry people 'the idle, dissolute and abandoned vagrants of the Earl of Meath's Liberty', and demanded that 'the hand of every man must be raised against this banditti of miscreants'.[163]

---

160 Chambers (1998), p. 28.
161 *Freeman's Journal*, May 1793.
162 *Ibid.*, May, 1793.
163 *loc. cit.*

Oliver Bond kept his name in the public eye by publishing a series of advertisements in the *Evening Post* assuring his friends and customers that his business was running as usual during his incarceration. He also, rather provocatively, published an advertisement informing the gentlemen of Dublin who wished to read the *Northern Star*, the paper of the Belfast United Irishmen, that copies could be had on request from his home in Bridge Street, Dublin.

Rowan may have pulled a Newgate lottery ticket early, for we know that in the company of his father, Gawin, Napper Tandy and eight companions, he entertained the prisoners on 8 March as they commenced their second week of confinement. Present among these dozen democrats was a young man whom Rowan had met less than a month earlier. Lord Edward Fitzgerald was newly arrived from Paris, bringing with him his beautiful young wife, Pamela, the daughter of Philip Egalité.

Fitzgerald had left France on 26 January, just days after the execution of the King, and before war was declared between France and England. Fitzgerald brought with him greetings from Tom Paine, who was thinking of coming to Ireland. He had informed Rowan already of his certainty of war, and now hinted to his fellow diners of a French landing in Ireland. Was Fitzgerald sent as an emissary by the French? William Drennan certainly thought so.[164]

Butler, Bond and their company must have enjoyed listening to what Citizen Edward had to say as they quaffed expensive wine in the insalubrious surroundings of Newgate Prison.

Perhaps it was the reputation Oliver Bond gained for mixing good food, good wine and revolution in Newgate that led the Sham Squire, a few years later, to refer to Oliver

---

164 Nicolson, p. 104.

Bond's United Irish Committee, based at Pill Lane, Dublin, as 'the Society of Eating and Drinking Democratic Citizens'.

The Abuse of Belfast

On the day after the Rowans' banquet at Newgate on 9 March, the citizens of Belfast experienced civil disorder on a considerable scale. Four troops of dragoons had been sent to the city from Dundalk, where they had been used to put down the Defenders. The Lords' Secret Committee had issued a proclamation accusing the Presbyterian clergy of Belfast of 'praying from the pulpit for the victory of French arms and in the presence of military associations which have been newly levied and arrayed in that town'.[165] Before leaving Dundalk the officers of the 17th Dragoons were inciting their men, urging that 'when they came to Belfast not to spare leg, arm or life'.[166]

The Belfast Volunteers had a hint of what was coming, and by keeping a low profile denied the troops obvious targets for attack. George Benn tells us:

> The troops who had just arrived in the town, seeing no living enemies, attacked the harmless images. They succeeded in pulling down the sign of Dumouriez which was above the door of a publican in North Street; they sallied then to Mr McCabe's and destroyed all his windows; then did the same to the house of a milliner, Mrs Wills in the Main Street [High Street], where some Volunteer hats and cockades were displayed; they tore down the sign of Dr Franklin at Watson's in

165 Benn, p. 648.
166 Agnew, vol i, p. 502.

Forest Lane and attacked in a reckless manner several inhabitants.[167]

The *Evening Post* reported that among the wounded was Charles Rankin, a Justice of the Peace who was stabbed by a dragoon and slightly wounded. Rankin was a leading United Irishman and had chaired a meeting of the society in Belfast in December 1792.

This was no spontaneous riot. The dragoons had the help of at least one local, who 'pointed out the fit places to attack, which were marked on paper'.[168] The rioters claimed that their behaviour was provoked by a blind fiddler playing a pro-French air; an excuse the *Evening Post* remarked was 'too trifling a cause to be seriously mentioned'.

On hearing of the events in Belfast, about 1,000 armed countrymen came into the city and met at the Third Presbyterian Meeting House in Rosemary Street. The dragoons then withdrew from the town. Martha McTier told her brother:

> Now the criminals are gone they departed in triumph with General Dumouriez's wooden head and while there was a huzza of women and children at their departure, one of these sign-slaying heroes slashed his sword on a lad near him, cut him desperately and rode off unmolested. In any other town they would have been stoned to death, but there never was a Belfast mob.[169]

Two days after the riot on 11 March, the Secret Committee issued yet another proclamation, which had obviously been

---

167 Benn, p. 651.
168 Agnew, vol i, p. 502.
169 *Ibid.*

in preparation before their soldiers had reached Belfast. This proclamation denounced and suppressed the Belfast Volunteers with as much vehemence as Rowan's Dublin corps had been denounced the previous December:

> Assemblages of men in military form are prejudicial to the public peace and good government; that such bodies were levied and arrayed in the town of Belfast and drilled and exercised there by day and by night … the obvious intent is to overawe Parliament and the government and dictate to both that arms and gunpowder to a very large extent had been sent to Belfast.[170]

In July, William Drennan complained that the Lord Chancellor, Fitzgibbon, continued his 'particular abuse' of Belfast. He was also dismayed at the daily ongoing executions of the Defenders at Dundalk. He scolded his brother-in-law, telling him:

> You are all cowed by this bouncy bully of the law … [Belfast continues to] persevere in a pettish silence, while every remaining right is thus insolently torn from you and your miserable countrymen, every day murdered before your eyes.[171]

Napper Tandy was charged with distributing his pamphlet, *Common Sense*, to some Defenders in Louth, but skipped bail and left the country when warned that more serious charges were in preparation.

Dr James Reynolds, a young physician from Tyrone and a United Irishman, was called before the Secret Committee

---

170 Benn, p. 650.
171 Agnew, vol i, p. 555.

but refused to answer their questions until they explained whether they were a legislative or a judicial body. Lord Clonmell replied with a scurrilous attack on the United Irish Society and told Reynolds that he was mad. He remanded him in the custody of the Black Rod, then after dithering for a few days remanded him to Kilmainham Gaol.[172] They chose the county jail rather than the city jail of Newgate to keep him away from Butler and Bond.

Rowan paid a visit to London in late March on some 'private business'. The 'newspapers in the pay of government' chose to believe that he had gone on the run, and proclaimed that Rowan and Tandy were both now *dishonoured fugitives from justice*. Many of Rowan's friends had advised him to stay away from Ireland. The government, however, was probably disappointed when he returned just before Easter to answer his bail.

Rowan had written to Drennan from London to the effect that the English radicals, with whom he discussed his own pending prosecution and the committal of Bond and Butler, were of one mind that the government in Ireland had acted illegally. Rowan had hoped to discuss his case with Thomas Erskine, the eminent defence lawyer, but Erskine was out of London at the time of Rowan's visit.

William Godwin, the political philosopher, records in his diary that he had dinner with Rowan, John Horn Tooke and John Thelwall in London on 24 March 1793. Tooke and Thelwall, both of whom were leaders of the reform movement in Britain, would be defendants in the infamous treason trials of October 1794. Thomas Erskine was given much credit for the collapse of those trials and the acquittal of Tooke and Thelwall. It was Godwin, though, who made the incisive intervention that helped Erskine to formulate

---

172 *loc. cit.*

his line of defence. Another defendant, Thomas Holcroft, who was a friend of Godwin's, had begged him to intervene. Godwin wrote in the *Morning Chronicle* that if opinion could be classed as treason, no one was safe. He went on to say:

> If men can be convicted of High Treason upon such constructions and implications as are contained in this charge, we may look with conscious superiority upon the republican speculations of France, but we shall certainly have reason to envy the milder tyrannies of Turkey and Ispahan.[173]

It is very likely that one of the many well-known English radicals Rowan would have met on his London visit was the beleaguered Dr Joseph Priestley, at this point the subject of scathing attacks and abuse in the Tory press. Rowan ensured that the London radicals were well informed on what was happening in Ireland. After he returned home they continued to follow developments there with great interest, particularly the vicissitudes of Rowan and the United Irishmen. A very large public meeting in London toasted Rowan as a martyr for liberty following his imprisonment the following year.

Challenging the Chancellor

Back in Ireland it seemed that almost everyone but Rowan and a stalwart few were keeping their heads down. Rowan would not be cowed by the bouncing bully Fitzgibbon. On 15 August 1793, Butler and Bond were liberated, having finished their sentence. Butler originally intended to ask John Sheares, a fellow lawyer and United Irishman, to act

---

173 Goodwin (1979), p. 341.

for him in challenging Fitzgibbon concerning the remarks he made when passing sentence. Sheares was out of the country, however, so the task fell to Rowan. Simon Butler could have found someone else to be his messenger rather than asking a man who was on bail on a very serious charge and the target of so much intimidation and entrapment.

Once asked, Rowan would never demur, therefore Rowan approached the Lord Chancellor on this mission of dubious legality. Butler should not have put Rowan in this position. On the other hand, perhaps Rowan was grateful for the opportunity to let the public know that he, for one, was not afraid.

On 12 October 1793, Rowan met Fitzgibbon at his house and informed him that Butler required an explanation as to why the chancellor had, when sentencing him, 'made use of expressions towards him which must have been offensive to the feelings of any gentleman'.[174] Fitzgibbon informed Rowan that he thought his words were called for in the circumstances of the case, and that if the matter were to be done again he 'would (perhaps) use the same terms'.

Fitzgibbon, who believed lawyers to be members of an elite profession, added that he was 'concerned to see Mr Butler playing the fool so much, as he belongs to a profession to which I am very much attached'.[175] Rowan felt that he had no option but to report the chancellor's response to Butler, and prepared a note of the meeting, which he furnished to the chancellor two days later. He informed the chancellor that Butler intended to publish the note 'to preserve the truth from misrepresentation'.[176] Fitzgibbon, when acknowledging Rowan's note, observed that it would be 'highly unbecoming to state his opinion on the steps Mr

---

174 Fleming and Malcomson, p. 174.
175 *loc. cit.*
176 *loc. cit.*

Butler is about to take'.[177] The exchange ended in stalemate, but the public knew that Rowan and Butler had stood up to the chancellor.

The exchange also gave rise to an opportunity for Rowan and the government to settle their differences. An old friend of Rowan, one Captain Murray, was sent by Fitzgibbon to warn Rowan about pushing his luck too far. Murray greeted his friend with, 'So a pretty piece of work you have made, Hamilton, taking a challenge to the chancellor'. The pressure must have been getting to Rowan, for he informed Murray that he regretted having come to Ireland, where 'party ran so high', and told him that he intended to leave Ireland as soon as the present prosecution was over.

Murray reported back and Fitzgibbon immediately let it be known that if Rowan left the country and agreed to stay away for a few years the case against him would be dropped. However, Fitzgibbon added a stipulation that subverted the chances of a deal, and was probably designed to do so. Rowan was informed that he must remove his name from the membership list of the United Irish Society. The government not only wanted Rowan out of Ireland; it wanted him to be seen to have deserted his comrades in their hour of need. Rowan's sense of personal honour prevented him from taking advantage of this opportunity.

In one way it was a timely offer; Rowan's mother, who first invited him to Ireland, had just died, leaving him an added fortune of £8,000 a year. He could, if he chose, have walked away from his troubles to live a life of ease with his wife and family.[178] Choosing to stay in Ireland in these circumstances, on a point of principle, caused some friction between him and his wife, Sarah. Sarah felt that a few words

---

177 *Ibid.*, p. 176.
178 Nicolson, p. 102.

of apology from Rowan could help him to avoid a sentence and a heavy fine.[179]

There was no way for Rowan, either to apologize or to withdraw from Ireland, without betraying his sense of himself as a man of courage and principle. Ironically, the prospect of inheriting his mother's money probably made it harder for him to leave. The idea of selfless public virtue, which he had inherited from John Jebb, had always been his way of validating himself and salving his conscience regarding his unearned personal wealth. His increased wealth may have implied a corresponding increase in his obligations to the cause of reform, above his personal or familial well-being. His best option, therefore, was to tread carefully until his trial came, taking his chances with a hostile prosecutor and what was likely to be a rigged jury.

Even now, however, he allowed his sense of honour and his determination not to bend before intimidation to cloud his judgement and drag him further into the maelstrom of personal and political affront, and possible governmental retribution. Rather than keep a low profile at home, he embarked on a high-profile mission to Scotland to uphold his honour and the honour of the Society of the United Irishmen.

179 Agnew, vol i, p. 533.

8.

Challenge at Edinburgh

Thomas Muir, a Scottish radical, had founded a branch of the Society of the Friends of the People in Glasgow in October 1792. He has been described as 'the most gifted Scottish leader' and was sentenced to fourteen years' transportation after a scandalous mock trial at Edinburgh in August 1793. Earlier Muir had gone to France, trying to convince the authorities there that the execution of the King would be a disaster for the reform movements in Scotland, England and Ireland. On his way home from the failed mission he had stopped in Dublin and was feted by the United Irishmen and sworn into their society.

William Drennan dined with Muir in Dublin and described him as a 'sensible, honest and intelligent man'.[180] When Muir left Dublin for Belfast en route to Scotland, Drennan gave him a letter of introduction to Samuel Neilson and the Belfast United Irishmen.[181] Before heading north, Muir spent a few weeks with Rowan at Rathcoffey. Muir's father wrote to him advising him that he had been outlawed

---

180 Agnew, i, p. 556.
181 *loc. cit.*

94

and to stay away from Scotland to avoid arrest.[182] Rowan had urged him to return to face his accusers and defend his actions. Rowan was conscious that when Tandy fled 'justice' the enemies of reform portrayed his flight as dishonourable and a stain on the character of the United Irish organization. Muir took Rowan's advice and disregarded his father.

Taking Rowan's advice cost Muir his freedom, and would eventually cost him his life.

Muir exposed himself to a vindictive prosecution in Scotland. The trial was a travesty, and the judge is reputed to have whispered to a juror 'come awa o[h] master Horner and help us hang ane o[f] these damn scoundrels'.[183] The judge was particularly scathing about Muir's propaganda among the working class, and suggested that the rabble had no right to representation.[184]

The authorities had seized Muir's papers, among them an address from the United Irishmen signed by Rowan and Drennan. At the trial the Lord Advocate of Scotland, Dundas, referred to Rowan as 'a ferocious person' and the address as being from 'one of those wretches who had fled from the justice of their own country'.[185] Dundas, in error or by design, described the seal of the United Irishmen as representing 'a human heart pierced by a spear'. In fact it was 'a pole supported by two hands, that of the Protestant and Catholic united in the grasp of friendship with a Bonnet of Liberty on top'.[186]

Muir defended the reputation of his Dublin friends, telling the court:

---

182 Thompson (1964), p. 136.
183 *loc. cit.*
184 *loc. cit.*
185 Nicolson, p. 107.
186 Drummond, p. 172.

The gentlemen whose names are prefixed to that address are both in Ireland and have honoured me with their friendship; the first, Dr Drennan, is a physician not more distinguished by his genius and abilities than by his philanthropy and benevolence. A. H. Rowan is no less eminent for his excellent qualities. He, it is true, is indicted to stand trial, he has not fled.[187]

Muir was mistaken when referring to Dr Drennan's philanthropy, for he could barely make ends meet at this time, and rather it was the much wealthier Rowan who had the reputation for philanthropy.

Rowan was not happy to leave it to Muir to vindicate his reputation, and he wrote to Dundas seeking a retraction. When he received no reply, he and Simon Butler crossed to Scotland in October. They crossed to Portpatrick in a sloop with three horses on board and arrived at Edinburgh on 4 November.[188]

The two friends went immediately to the Tollbooth to see Muir, who was preparing for his removal to the penal colonies. Rowan presented Muir with a finely crafted pair of pistols, both as a memento and a precaution against the perils that Muir was destined to encounter in his travels.[189] Later, when the authorities became aware that Muir was in possession of the weapons, they were of course confiscated.

---

187 *loc. cit.*
188 Nicolson, p. 107.
189 Kay's Originals, p. 168. Kay's portraits were collected by Hugh Paton and published under the title 'A series of original portraits and caricature etchings by the late John Kay, with biographical sketches and illustrative anecdotes'. These are unique records of the social life and popular habits of the Edinburgh of the time.

Rowan was arrested in Muir's chamber by the messenger-at-arms under a warrant from the sheriff. Sarah Rowan believed that her husband had been lured to Scotland so that he could be implicated in Muir's sedition, convicted by an amenable Scottish jury and sent to Botany Bay.[190] Sarah's worst fears were not realized, however, and Colonel Norman McLeod, a member of the British Parliament and 'a fellow labourer in the cause of reform', bailed Rowan for the sum of £165.[191]

McLeod organized a dinner at the Hunter's Tavern for the two Irish visitors, which was attended by a select group of about sixty 'Friends of the People'.[192] The sheriffs noted the names of all who attended, including William Skirving, Maurice Margarot and Reverend Thomas Fyshe Palmer. Palmer was a Unitarian minister and an old friend of Rowan's from Cambridge, where they both studied under John Jebb.[193] A few weeks after their celebration with Rowan and Butler these three men were charged with sedition and, following rigged trials, were sent to the penal colonies along with Muir. This was akin to a death sentence in slow motion, and only Margarot was to see his native land again. The trials and savage sentences were seen as 'the blackest page in the recent annals of the Criminal Court of Scotland'. An anonymous writer in 1837 observed:

> Botany Bay is now a comparative Paradise to the penal colony then in its miserable infancy ... then the harbour of the off-scourings of British society ... The sentences handed down to the martyrs was the most shocking species of transportation;

---

190 Nicolson, p. 108.
191 Drummond, p. 172.
192 Kay's Originals, p. 168.
193 *Ibid.*, p. 179.

transportation not to America, not to a cultivated
society, to an easy master and to kind treatment,
but to an inhospitable desert in the extremity of
the earth – condemned to live with ruffians whom
the gibbet alone had spared and under a system of
despotism rendered necessary for the government of
such a tribe.[194]

The four became known to history as the 'Scottish Martyrs'
and are commemorated in Edinburgh by a fine monument
erected by the Chartists more than half a century later.

The main purpose of Rowan's visit to Edinburgh was so
that he could challenge Dundas to a duel. However, Dundas
gave Butler a note telling Rowan:

I do not hold myself accountable to you or to any
person for any observations which in the course of
my official duty I felt it proper for me to make with
respect to the publication alluded by you. I have
only to add that my opinion on this subject remains
perfectly the same.[195]

Colonel McLeod admonished Rowan, telling him that the
cause of liberty could not be advanced by duelling anywhere
in Great Britain. Rowan's descendant and biographer, the
vitriolic Nicolson, wonders why his ancestor embarked on
this 'pointless and ineffective expedition' and suggests, on
the evidence of an amusing but benign portrait of Rowan
produced by the famous caricaturist Kay of Edinburgh,
that 'my great-great-grandfather was not at this period at
his best'.[196] While most thoughtful democrats of that era

---

194 Davis (2004–2007), p. 149.
195 *Ibid.*, p. 178.
196 Nicolson, p. 108.

would have agreed with McLeod, Nicolson's observation, like the rest of his book, is both unfair to Rowan and totally lacks empathy or insight into his motives.

The war with France was being used as an excuse to crush the reformers in England, Scotland and Ireland. The Volunteers had been suppressed. The town of Belfast was under the control of a hostile soldiery. The Defenders were going to the gallows by the dozen or being flogged through the streets of Dundalk. Tandy had fled, and the newspapers and government officials were lying to the effect that Rowan had also cut and run.

Butler, Bond and Reynolds had gone to jail and many of their friends feared that they would be next. Muir was to be transported because Rowan had encouraged him to return home. The Sham Squire's newspapers in Dublin were congratulating the administration for the vigilance, patriotism and spirit they displayed when resisting and effectively repressing the United Irishmen.[197]

Challenging Dundas was one way for Rowan to assert that he had not fled and that Muir had friends in Ireland who would stand by him. Most importantly of all, Rowan could show that he and the Society of United Irishmen had not been intimated. Unlike Nicolson, the Dublin newspapers of the day fully understood the significance of what was happening. They were full of the events at Edinburgh.[198] While the Sham Squire ridiculed 'the renowned political knight errant Don Archibald', he fully understood his motive. The Sham saw 'the crusade to the land of the Bannocks … as a sort of antidote to oblivion'.[199]

On Rowan's return, the Belfast United Irishmen held a dinner to celebrate his 'triumph' as he passed through the

---

197 *Freeman's Journal*, May 1793.
198 Nicolson, p. 108.
199 *Freeman's Journal*, November 1793.

city. Rowan's father, Gawin, was present that evening, which was spent 'with that conviviality and heartfelt pleasure which the patriotic and the virtuous alone experience'. They drank the health of Rowan with the words: 'May the friends of liberty ever be found virtuous and brave'.[200] Thomas Russell and Thomas McCabe got very drunk at the event and had an altercation with some army officers on their way home, which nearly resulted in Russell fighting a duel. He sobered up overnight, however, and apologized to the officers the next morning. No duel took place at Edinburgh, but Rowan took great pleasure in declaring to the newspapers and the world that the Lord Advocate's assertion that Rowan was a fugitive was a 'falsehood'.

The venture into Scotland was a sorely needed boost for the United Irishmen. However, the Sham Squire advised the government that they could learn something from their Scottish counterparts when dealing with Rowan's friends, for the *Freeman's Journal* observed:

> If a few of his associates should speedily experience the fate of the Scottish patriot Mr Muir, it would tend admirably to teach them better manners.[201]

200 Drummond, p. 177.
201 *Freeman's Journal*, November 1793.

9.

From Trial to Newgate

The year 1794 opened ominously for Rowan. Besides all the pressure under which he had laboured since his arrest, three separate but related circumstances conspired to convince his friends that his trial and punishment would not be further delayed. Firstly, the pulpits of the Established Church in Dublin had been ringing with denunciations of 'a society which they say has been established for abolishing the Christian religion'.[202] While the Christian churchmen did not name the society, everyone knew that they meant the United Irishmen.

Westmorland, the Lord Lieutenant and the House of Commons joined in the war of religion.[203] This was an attempt by the government, with the help of its allies in the Established Church, to convince the Protestants of Dublin that the United Irishmen was the atheist enemy within. In such an atmosphere it would be somewhat easier to get an exclusively Protestant jury to convict Rowan. Nor would Rowan's well-known Unitarianism protect him from

---

202 Agnew, ii, p. 5.
203 *Ibid.*

charges of atheism. Drennan complained that in Dublin 'a Unitarian and a Deist here ranks as the self same character, and if you deny the Trinity, you will be set down to deny there is a God'.[204]

The second circumstance, which did not augur well for Rowan, was that in early January Joe Corbally, the Defender, was convicted of perjury. Corbally had accused Justice Graham of suborning witnesses against Rowan and Tandy. The lawyers were surprised that the prosecution was prepared to bring this case to trial, 'given the [poor quality of the] evidence adduced'.[205] William Drennan saw the trial of Corbally as a touchstone for the Rowan case and became convinced that the authorities would 'condemn and punish Rowan as severely as they can'.[206]

The third reason Rowan and his friends feared the worst was that Jack Gifford, a newspaper editor in the pay of the Castle and the government's choice for sheriff, was to empanel the jury. He could be relied on, not just to secure witnesses to swear perjury against Rowan, but also to pack the jury.[207] Gifford was a profoundly unpleasant individual. In later life Henry Grattan summed up Gifford's character with eloquent virulence when he dubbed him:

The hired traducer of his country – the excommunicated of his fellow citizens – the regal rebel – the unpunished ruffian – the bigoted agitator, in the city a firebrand, in the court a liar, in the streets a bully – in the field a coward.[208]

204 *loc. cit.*
205 Agnew, ii, p. 2.
206 *loc. cit.*
207 Hill (1997), p. 243.
208 Barrington, p. 155.

Grattan attacked Gifford nearly a decade after the trial of Rowan, but his references to 'the traducer of his country' and 'a liar in the courts' may well refer to his role in the affair. It is likely that Grattan's reference to 'the unpunished ruffian' and 'in the streets a bully' refers to the armed attack led by Gifford on the crowds celebrating the acquittal of William Drennan in May 1794. Almost certainly the reference to 'a coward in the field' recalls an event in 1798 when Gifford revelled in his involvement in the murder of 350 to 500 unarmed men who had surrendered at Gibbet Rath, near the town of Kildare. Gifford boasted that 'the Curragh was strewed with the vile carcasses of popish rebels and the accursed town of Kildare has been reduced to a heap of ashes'.[209] Giffard was indeed an unscrupulous adversary.

On a day leading up to the trial, Drennan called to Rowan's house to discuss the case and found his friend in low spirits. He was conscious that there was a sense of domestic disharmony in the air. Drennan came to the conclusion that Rowan had personal, but not political, courage.[210] Perhaps it was not the lack of political courage or fear of the authorities that was getting to Rowan as much as the 'outrageously violent' disputes he was having with his wife, Sarah. She was a most obstinate woman who wanted Rowan to do a deal to save himself and their family from destruction.[211] Such was Rowan's determination to stand his ground that the couple were thought to be on the brink of separation.[212] Those who thought the couple might separate knew little of Sarah's true nature. She would often chide Rowan for getting himself and the family into difficult and dangerous situations. However,

---

209 Hill, p. 256.
210 Agnew, ii, p. 2.
211 *loc. cit.*
212 *loc. cit.*

once she understood that Rowan was not for turning, she would support and stand by him to the very edge of doom. Rowan was fortunate to have Dr Reynolds, who had been released from Kilmainham, staying at Dominick Street at this time as 'his mild firmness' served to divert some of Sarah's anger.[213]

Sarah got her way on one important matter. Rowan wanted Simon Butler and Thomas Addis Emmet, fellow United Irishmen, to defend him at his trial. Sarah insisted that John Philpot Curran, one of the greatest advocates of his day, was given the brief.

Trial, January 1794

On 29 January Rowan's trial finally got underway. That morning Rowan had met many of his supporters for breakfast at the Exchange and they went together to the Court of King's Bench. Rowan sat between his friends Hampton Evans and John Byrne. Evans was a Protestant and Byrne was a Catholic. Both were very wealthy United Irishmen. If this was an attempt by Rowan to set the scene, Jack Gifford went much further in terms of choreography. Dressed in military uniform, he lined his soldiers up in the hall to intimidate the defence lawyers and to militarize the proceedings to imply that the defendant was a very dangerous conspirator. He ordered his platoon to file into the court, distributing them at key points in the public gallery.[214] As far as Giffard was concerned, this was to be no ordinary civil trial.

John Magee's old nemesis, Lord Clonmell, he of the famous pig hunt at Blackrock, took the bench. He was

---

213 *loc. cit.*
214 Nicolson, p. 110.

assisted by William Downes and Robert Boyd, justices of the King's Bench.[215]

Rowan objected to two members of the jury on the basis that he could bring forward proof that they had declared that 'Ireland would never be quiet until Hamilton Rowan and Napper Tandy are hanged'.[216] Clonmell did not allow this challenge.

The Attorney General, Arthur Wolfe, led for the prosecution. He began by accusing the United Irishmen of using the Volunteers for the purposes of terrorizing the administration, telling the court that the National Guard had used the Volunteers as 'a cloak for creating an armed banditti'. He then read from Drennan's address to the Volunteers, commenting now and then on the seditious nature of the document. William Drennan sat listening as his address was denounced as a 'libel', allegedly produced 'to incite tumult and anarchy'. However, Drennan seems to have been dismayed more by the Attorney General's 'miserable' performance and poor delivery when reading the address than by any apprehension of danger.[217] Drennan was not to know then that a few weeks later he would stand in the same courtroom accused of the same seditious libel.

The Attorney General denounced the address for seeking to 'give the right to vote to every man in the community'. He warned that the 'Constitution would be buried in the anarchy of republican power formed by the very dregs of the people' and he asked the question 'when government is guided by the people … Where will be the House of Peers?'[218]

Gifford had procured two witnesses: John Lyster, who held an ensign's commission in the militia, and William

---

215 Agnew, ii, p. 9.
216 Drummond, p. 189.
217 Agnew, ii, p. 8.
218 Trial Report, p. 14.

Morton, an apprentice goldbeater. Both swore that they had seen Rowan distribute the address at Pardon's academy. The defence produced witnesses to say that Lyster was untrustworthy. Morton was a nephew by marriage of Giffard. Under cross-examination Morton could not remember whether he had kept the address for a day or a week, or to whom he had given his copy. Gifford helpfully shouted from the body of the court that Morton had given it to him. The witness then confirmed that his uncle was right. When asked why he had given the paper to Gifford, he replied, 'No reason, I gave it by accident, he was the first person I met whom I knew'. No wonder William Drennan thought 'the evidence sworn as to the distribution' was as miserable as the earlier performance of the Attorney General.[219]

When the prosecution had concluded its case, Curran rose for the defence. He began by highlighting Gifford's intimidation tactics, describing Gifford's rise to office as being like 'a corpse floating up to the surface from putrefaction'. He told the court:

> When I consider the period at which this prosecution
> is brought forward; when I behold the extraordinary
> safeguard of armed soldiers, resorted to … I never
> rose in a court of law with more embarrassment.[220]

He begged the jury to consider whether Rowan was being hunted as a criminal or a victim.[221] Curran delivered what was to become a universally famous and much-quoted trial speech. His line of defence had three main aspects. He argued firstly that the address was no seditious libel, secondly that the prosecution witnesses were not credible, and finally

219 *Ibid.*, p. 8.
220 Trial Report, p. 36.
221 Nicolson, p. 110.

that Rowan's character and station in life were such that he would never incite tumult and anarchy to overthrow the constitution as the prosecution had alleged.

Curran concluded:

> Let me tell you, gentlemen of the jury, if you agree with his prosecutors in thinking there ought to be a sacrifice of such a man, on such an occasion, and upon the credit of such evidence you are to convict him, never did you, never can you, give a sentence consigning any man to public punishment with less danger to his person or to his fame; for where could the hireling be found to fling contumely or ingratitude at his head whose private distress he had not laboured to alleviate, or whose public condition he had not laboured to improve?

The speech was interrupted many times with outbursts of applause. It ranks as one of the best of Curran's many fine speeches of his long career. However, as John Binns observed, as far as the judges and jury were concerned it was 'a case of casting pearl before swine'. Following Clonmell's charge to the jury, which has been described as 'the most bare-faced piece of partiality ever heard in a court', the jury took just ten minutes to convict.[222]

Curran's concluding remarks were a reference to the possibility that Rowan might be sentenced to the pillory, a sentence usually reserved for the lower orders and for the most shameful of crimes. Usually the pilloried victim would be pelted with rubbish and showered with abuse from the populace. Curran was implying that it would not happen in this case, such was Rowan's popularity in Dublin. When

---

222 Agnew, ii, p. 9.

it was suggested to Rowan that he might have to go to the pillory, he observed that he would have no objection to appear in any place before the public.[223]

The judge adjourned the proceedings for four days, after which the sentence would be pronounced. The court was cleared by the military, and Curran was paraded home in triumph by the crowd. Sheriff Jenkin escorted Rowan to Newgate in a carriage with a file of soldiers on each side and a troop of horses at the rear.[224]

Rowan spent his first night of confinement in a cell with two other prisoners. These unfortunates had to share a prison bed, but Rowan had arranged for a bed to be taken in to him from his Dominick Street home. When Drennan called to see him the next morning he met Sarah Rowan on her way out and walked her to her carriage. She was 'highly indignant at the judge', but by no means crestfallen.[225]

Two days later, as Rowan began his first Sunday behind bars, Sarah attended a religious service at the Great Strand Street Meeting House in Dublin. She was accompanied by her son, who was described as 'one of the handsomest boys in the city'.[226] Most of the congregation 'ogled Sarah'. One elderly lady, Mrs Rose Bruce, 'praised her much'. Sarah was the centre of attention as her husband was now an imprisoned martyr for civil and religious liberty.

Sarah may have been conducting some business on behalf of her husband on that day. The minister's ledger contains four subscriptions attributed to A. H. Rowan dated February 1794.[227] He donated over £100 to the Great Strand Street ministers during that month.

223 Agnew, ii, p. 11.
224 *Ibid.*, p. 10.
225 *Ibid.*
226 Agnew, vol ii, p. 13.
227 See Royal Irish Academy, 'Dublin Unitarian Collection' STR 3, final page.

Sarah would have expected the mostly positive reception she received from this congregation, for they were Unitarians and traced their origins in the city of Dublin back to the republicans and commonwealth men who came to Dublin during the Cromwellian period.[228] The ministers at Strand Street preached freedom of conscience, religious toleration and civil and religious liberty for all. Many members of the Dublin Society of United Irishmen, including Rowan and Drennan, were long-standing members of the congregation.

Another elderly female, Mrs Dunn, the widow of Reverend Dunn, late of the Cook Street congregation, approached Sarah and said that she was sorry for her husband's imprudence.[229] William Drennan thought that Mrs Dunne was being rude to Sarah because she hoped her lawyer son would be appointed as a judge by the administration. In spite of the rudeness of the old lady, Sarah Rowan knew that she was among friends at Strand Street.

Rowan's first biographer, Reverend William Drummond, who himself had flirted with United Irish radicalism in his youth, was minister to the Strand Street congregation when he edited Rowan's memoir and published his *Autobiography of Archibald Hamilton Rowan* in Dublin in 1840.

As Sarah courted the support of the Dublin Dissenters, Rowan was busy at Newgate. Over the next few days he submitted affidavits seeking a retrial on the basis that he had further information on the unreliability of the witnesses and that Gifford had a record of public antagonism towards Rowan ever since the latter had come to Ireland. He alleged that Gifford was 'a writer in the government pay [*sic*], author of a government paper, and to have endeavoured to get such a jury as would bring

---

228 See Whelan (2010).
229 *loc. cit.*

him in guilty'.[230] When the court reconvened to consider this new evidence all three judges 'were very severe in delivering their opinions' against Rowan.[231] Clonmell took an hour, and his two fellow judges took ten minutes each, to uphold the conviction. Rowan took the opportunity for the first time to speak in his own defence, telling the court that he 'avowed himself an United Irishman and gloried in the name'.[232] He stood by the terms 'Universal emancipation and representative legislature' as used in the address, and denied the meaning imputed to those words by the prosecution.[233]

Sentence of the Court

Rowan's friends expected the sentence to be severe, potentially involving either pillory or transportation. In the months leading up to the trial the *Freeman's Journal* had been advocating such measures for those the paper referred to as 'Archibald firebrand's friends'.[234] Butler suggested that it might be a £2,000 fine and four years in prison.[235]

It fell to Justice Boyd to deliver formally the sentence of the court:

> The sentence of the court is that you, Archibald Hamilton Rowan, do pay his Majesty a sum of five hundred pounds, and to be imprisoned for two years, to be computed from the 29th January, 1794, and until that fine is paid; and to find security for

---

230 *Ibid.*, p. 13.
231 *Ibid.*, p. 15.
232 Drummond, p. 196.
233 *loc. cit.*
234 *Freeman's Journal*, November 1793.
235 Agnew, ii, p. 10.

your good behaviour for seven years – yourself in
the sum of two thousand pounds, and two sureties
of one thousand pounds each.[236]

Rowan's friends must have breathed a sigh of relief that the
sentence had not been more severe. There had been many
hints from government sources of hanging, and his friends
in Scotland had been sent to the penal colonies. There had
also been much talk of the pillory. Richard Kirwan, a famous
chemist and one of Rowan's Unitarian friends, went to
Dublin Castle to tell the secretary that 'the people of Dublin
will not allow this, and weak as I am [he was 61 years old]
I will draw my sword and head the mob and break your
pillory to atoms'.[237] As an eminent chemist he was probably
one of the few men in Ireland at this point who understood
that a pillory was composed of atoms.

The secretary assured Kirwan that such a punishment
was not intended by the government. Rowan tells us that
Kirwan was in 'political principle a high conservative
aristocrat', but this seems unlikely. Kirwan was a Unitarian
in theology, and it would be unusual, if not unheard of,
for a Unitarian to be conservative in politics. The basic
premise of Unitarianism is that no authority, whether civil
or religious, has authority over a man's conscience. Openly
avowing Unitarian belief could lead to prosecution. The
government, the bishops of the Church of England and the
Tories were steadfast in their opposition to Unitarianism
and Unitarians. Why would Kirwan be disposed to support
such conservative elements?

Dr McNeven claims that he had sworn Richard Kirwan
into the United Irishmen, but this may have happened later

---

236 Drummond, p. 197.
237 *Ibid.*, p. 199.

as at the time of the trial the United Irishmen was not yet a secret society.[238]

In giving Kirwan the assurance that the pillory was not intended, the secretary was 'letting the cat out of the bag', showing that the sentence was a political, and not a judicial, decision. So why did the government not hang Rowan, as many of them had indicated was their wish?

Clonmell and his fellow judges were biased. Gifford, his witnesses, and at least some of his jury were corrupt. The adulation of the crowd for Curran and his efforts showed that the accused and his cause remained popular in Dublin. Rowan's crime was the distribution of words on a piece of paper. Nobody had been injured; there had been no disturbance. To hang a man for handing out pieces of paper at an event that was not illegal and which passed off peacefully would have been draconian, even by the standards of the Secret Committee.

Rowan asked to be allowed to serve his time in Naas Gaol, but this was refused. With his bed from Dominick Street he was reasonably comfortable in prison. He was determined not to emulate the high-living antics of Butler and Bond. His wife and two of his children would bring his dinner each evening and dine with him. On Sundays he would host a dinner for some of his fellow inmates 'who were of the better order'. He wanted no wine, but as the Newgate water was reputed to be bad he ordered 'Bristol water and good beer'.[239]

Rowan's fame and popularity as 'a patriot martyr' was in the ascent. The trial was regarded by many as a travesty in which the witnesses had been suborned. Archibald Hamilton Rowan was now the toast of democratic and radical societies throughout Britain and Ireland.

---

238 See: http://www.igp-web.com/IGPArchive (accessed 6 May 2012).
239 Drummond, p. 201.

On 2 May 1794, 300 democrats met in the Crown and Anchor tavern in the Strand, London. Among the toasts that were given to 'unbounded applause' were 'the rights of man, the swine of England, the rabble of Scotland, the wretches of Ireland, Archibald Hamilton Rowan, the patriots of Ireland and the persecuted patriots of England'.[240]

Letters of support came to Newgate 'from all quarters, from public societies and private individuals, at home and abroad'. The workers of Dublin, styling themselves the 'working manufacturers', drew up a petition that they 'were signing by many hundreds'.[241] This was just one of the many addresses to Rowan, but as it gives a rare insight into what working people had to say about their own hardships, the character and punishment of Rowan and the general political situation at the time, it is worth quoting in full. Rowan's reply also deserves consideration.

> Address of the Working Manufacturers:
> We as part of the community, whose distresses for want of employment found a way to your philanthropic breast, have beheld with the pride of honest hearts your exertions in our cause, and that of our suffering brethren now unemployed. We sympathize as men, when we are told that you are sentenced to two years' imprisonment; yet look around with satisfaction, when we hear the universal regret expressed by all ranks of society at your confinement.
>
> Permit us, Sir, to give the only return now in our power, for your attention to our famishing fellow-tradesmen: and to assure you that no period of our lives can to us be more grateful than that when you

240 Bartel (1965), p. 91.
241 Agnew, ii, p. 18.

will return to your family, your country and your numerous friends. In our humble situation of life, we think nothing more dear to a man than liberty, and we are proud to say, that to none will we yield in gratitude.

Rowan's reply:

When the Almighty permitted the natural equality of man to be broken down into ranks and orders of society, he at once granted it as a favour, and imposed it as a duty upon those who possess untoiled-for affluence to devote from their abundance a portion to the relief of the wants and miseries of their less favoured fellow-creatures. My endeavours to discharge that duty are over-rated by your partiality, and over-paid by the approbation you express. I can assure you in return, that it is not the circumstances of my confinement which least affects me, that I am thereby, for the present, debarred of the gratification I have felt, in contributing my limited services to relieve the necessities, and alleviate the distresses of so useful, so numerous a body, as the working manufacturers of this country.

The workers' petition can be read as the obsequious gratitude of the self-pitying to their philanthropic benefactor. Rowan's reply can be read as expressing the smug self-satisfaction of a social do-gooder. However, both are open to very different interpretations. The workers refer to the suffering unemployed as 'brethren'. They sympathize 'as men' with Rowan's plight and highlight the extensive support of all ranks of the community for him. To Edmund Burke, these workers and their brethren in Britain were the 'swinish multitude'. To the prosecutor at Rowan's trial they were 'the very dregs of the people'. They were constantly referred to by their rulers as the rabble. The *Freeman's Journal* had referred to unemployed workers who would seize food to feed their starving children as 'a banditti of miscreants'. When the workers asserted that 'we think nothing more dear than liberty' and 'to none will we yield in gratitude', they were taking the opportunity of telling Rowan and the world that the rights of man applied to them, and if anyone had a mind to deprive them of their liberty they would not take it lying down.

Rowan's reply, while obviously drafted for purposes of public consumption, is nonetheless revealing. His reference to the natural equality of man was a revolutionary notion in an age where one's station in life was dictated by birth and bloodline. However, his reference to 'untoiled-for wealth' and the responsibilities it brings with it is the key to understanding his actions at this point. Rowan was now facing two years in prison because he believed he had a duty, due to his position in society and possession of untoiled-for wealth, to assert the right of all disenfranchised citizens to universal emancipation and a representative legislature.

Thomas Muir wrote to Rowan just before the prison ship *Surprise* sailed out of the Thames, bound for the penal colonies of New South Wales. Muir told Rowan that he was confident the United Irishmen would triumph over despotism and achieve the emancipation of Ireland.[242]

Of course the Dublin United Irishmen were very quick to make a formal address to their imprisoned leader. In their typically florid address they compared the suffering of Rowan to that of Hampden, Russell and Sydney, the Protestant Whig martyrs. Rowan replied that his sufferings were slight

---

242 Davis, p. 151.

and they should not tarnish the illustrious dead by a hasty comparison with the living.[243] John Hampden had been killed fighting on the parliamentary side of the English Civil War in 1643. William, Lord Russell and Algernon Sydney were executed in 1683 for their alleged part in a plot to murder James Stuart, Duke of York, to prevent him from becoming the King of England. Rowan and his United Irish friends clearly saw themselves as being part of traditional British Protestant Whiggery. The Founding Fathers of the United States of America had also seen themselves in that tradition. Irish nationalists from the nineteenth century onwards either forgot, or chose to ignore, the very Protestant and very British aspect of the United Irish leaders' world view.

Rowan arranged to have his portrait painted in miniature by John Cullen and attempted to commission a painting of himself, his wife, his father and his son at Newgate by Hugh Douglas Hamilton. This painting would have been fascinating had it been completed. It is not known whether Hamilton even commenced it.

Meanwhile, for a few weeks Rowan settled into a comfortable incarceration, meeting almost daily with a succession of visitors and well-wishers. William Drennan was a daily visitor. On one occasion when he called, the Duke of Leinster was already there. The duke was Ireland's premier peer, though out of favour with the government because of his suspected liberal sympathies. However, here he was in the common jail paying a complimentary visit to a convicted 'firebrand'. This must have been a source of great irritation to the administration.

The duke's brother, Lord Edward Fitzgerald, was another regular visitor. Rowan and he had become good friends in the year since Fitzgerald had returned from France. Theobald

---

243 Nicolson, p. 115.

Wolfe Tone was also in the habit of visiting Rowan every day.

On one occasion William Drennan called to the prison and found Rowan and Sarah having tea with a fellow prisoner, John Fay, and his wife, a woman Drennan considered a 'beauty in distress'. Drennan observed that 'her fine eyes [were] nearly melted out of her head by weeping'.[244] Her husband, who was a wealthy Roman Catholic, had been remanded to Newgate for a number of months on charges of conspiring to murder Reverend Butler, who had been murdered by Defenders at Clongill, County Meath on 24 October 1793.[245] The charges against Fay had been manufactured as part of an attempt to link the well-to-do Catholics with Defenderism. The *Freeman's Journal* had carried a government proclamation offering a £300 reward for information leading to the apprehension of Butler's murderer. A sum of this magnitude was almost certain to attract unscrupulous witnesses who would tell the prosecutors anything they wanted to hear. When Fay finally went to trial at Trim on 13 March he was acquitted when the evidence against him was shown to be false.

On 2 May, William Drennan and Moses Dawson, a Belfast United Irishman, were on their way to Newgate when they heard the astonishing news that Rowan had escaped. They were informed, incorrectly, that when seeing his wife and children out of the prison to their carriage at nine or ten the previous evening, Rowan had darted off, mounted a horse that was ready, and escaped.[246] Drennan called around to Dominick Street to see Sarah Rowan. When he was there, Gregg, the head jailer, arrived with orders to search the house. Sarah handed over all the keys and every room

---

244 Agnew, vol ii, p. 30.
245 *loc. cit.*
246 Agnew, ii, p. 43.

was examined, but 'no Rowan was found'.[247] The council posted a reward of £1,000 for his capture. Rowan's new life as a fugitive had begun. No one could have foretold that it would be eleven years before Rowan would set foot in Dominick Street again.

---

247 *Ibid.*

10.

Dr Viper Comes to Town

From December 1792 the government had wanted to see the back of Rowan. He had resisted all their pressure, threats and attempts at entrapment, and stood his ground. He had been prepared to fight a duel and to go to jail rather than be branded a fugitive. The news now rang out all over Ireland and Britain that the great patriot Archibald Hamilton Rowan had fled the prison, and possibly the kingdom.

Drennan was mystified, and felt that Rowan's flight would bring 'disgrace, suspicion and ignominy on the United Irishmen'.[248] His mystification turned to anger when he began to hear rumours that Rowan had fled because he had 'implicated himself with Jackson, a man who is closely confined at Newgate on charges of High Treason'.[249] This time the rumours were accurate, for Reverend William Jackson was nothing less than a secret emissary from the Committee of Public Safety in Paris.

The British government had become aware of Jackson's mission to Britain and Ireland, and turned it into a trap

---

248 Agnew, ii, p. 44.
249 *Ibid.*, p. 43.

directed at the leadership of the United Irishmen. Rowan had fallen headlong into the trap, and the United Irishmen were now implicated in treason. The government had all the justification it needed to bring Rowan to the gallows. His exposure also confirmed what the government had long argued: the Society of United Irishmen were not, as they styled themselves, a group of gentlemen reformers; they were conspirators and traitors.

The Jackson mission had its origins among a group of British and Irish radicals in Paris. John Hurtford Stone, an English Unitarian and a political exile in France, was a central figure in the affair. Stone had been a member of Dr Richard Price's London congregation and was a close friend of Dr Joseph Priestley. We can be certain that Stone and a group of Irish and British friends had been urging the French to invade Britain or Ireland since early 1792.[250] This group had included Lord Edward Fitzgerald, Thomas Paine and Thomas Muir. It was Stone who had introduced Fitzgerald to Pamela in Paris.

Nicolas Madgett, an Irishman in the French Foreign Service, had taken over intelligence operations directed at England and Ireland. Madgett recruited Reverend William Jackson, an Anglican clergyman of Irish extraction. His mission was to assess attitudes, in both countries, to the prospect of a French invasion.

Jackson was an enigmatic figure. As well as being a devout clergyman, he had been a scandal-sheet journalist and 'a notorious spreader of salacious gossip'.[251] He became involved in a long-running dispute with the dramatist Samuel Foote. Foote lampooned him in one of his plays as the sinister Doctor Viper. Jackson responded by circulating scurrilous

250 O'Toole (2001), p. 288.
251 *Ibid.*, p. 287.

stories about Foote and encouraged a former servant to accuse the playwright of sodomy. Jackson had worked for a string of different newspapers before going to Paris in the pay of William Pitt.[252] However, the 'intoxicants of the French Revolution' induced him to offer his services to undertake a secret mission on behalf of the Committee of Public Safety.

Almost everybody with whom Jackson came into contact in Dublin, with the exception of Rowan, did not trust him. Ironically, it took Jackson's death by his own hand to convince people that, despite all outward appearances and his dubious history, he had been a genuine, if naïve, secret agent in the service of the French republic.

Jackson began his mission armed with a letter of introduction from John Hurtford Stone and a list of radical and opposition figures in England and Ireland to consult regarding the attitudes of the people of both countries to a possible French invasion. His list of people to see in London included Dr Joseph Priestley, Benjamin Vaughan, a Member of Parliament, John Horne Tooke, Lord Lauderdale and Richard Brinsley Sheridan, the Irish actor and playwright, and at the time of Jackson's desired meeting, an opposition politician. In Ireland Jackson was to seek out Lord Edward Fitzgerald and Archibald Hamilton Rowan.

Hurtford Stone's brother, William, helped Jackson to make contact with some of the British opposition, all of whom stressed that a French invasion of England would unite the whole nation in defence of the country. It may not be without significance that the Stone brothers, Priestley, Vaughan and Rowan were Unitarians and that John Stone, Vaughan and Rowan were all known to, and under the influence of, Priestley. The first leg of the mission to England went well, and William Stone convinced Benjamin Vaughan

---

252 Nicolson, p. 118.

to write a memorandum that sought to convince the French that an invasion of England would be a big mistake.

Jackson destroyed his chances of success when he called to see an old friend, a lawyer called Cockayne, and 'with amazing indiscretion he confided the purpose of his mission'.[253] Cockayne immediately called to Downing Street to see Pitt and to sell his information and his friend.

Pitt ordered Cockayne to accompany Jackson to Ireland 'in order to render abortive his wicked purposes'.[254] Of course, Pitt could have had Jackson arrested before letting him set foot in Ireland, and as William Tone, Wolfe Tone's son, observed:

> Before his arrival in Ireland the life of Jackson was completely in the power of the British government. His evil genius [Cockayne] was already pinned upon him; his mission from France his every thought and his views were known. He was allowed to proceed, not in order to detect an existing conspiracy in Ireland, but to form one, and thus increase the number of victims. A more atrocious instance of perfidious and gratuitous cruelty is scarcely to be found in the history of any country but Ireland.[255]

Jackson and Cockayne landed in Ireland, appropriately enough, on Fools' Day, 1 April 1794. They took lodgings at Hyde's Coffee House in Palace Row.[256] Hyde's had opened that year and offered, beside coffee, a saloon where clients could read papers and discuss business or gossip. They also provided accommodation for travellers and private rooms

253 Nicolson, p. 119.
254 Bartlett (1998), p. xxvii.
255 *Ibid.*, p. 101.
256 *Ibid.*, p. xxvii.

for meeting and dining. Hyde's was the perfect base from which the two companions could start to test the political temperature of Dublin.

Their initial overture met with a firm rebuff. Despite Jackson's letter of introduction from John Hurtford Stone, Lord Edward refused to see him.[257] However, Jackson was an old acquaintance of Leonard McNally, a lawyer, then a trusted United Irishman. McNally was already secretly in the pay of the Castle. He would later 'defend' many of the leaders of the 1798 rebellion and, most treacherously, young Robert Emmet in 1803. All the while he was 'in the pay of the unscrupulous Tory government of that day and basely betrayed the secrets of his confiding clients'.[258]

McNally held a dinner at his home where Jackson and Cockayne met some of the leading United Irishmen. They discussed 'whether the people would be ready to rise in the event of a French invasion'.[259] Cockayne feigned sleep and a total lack of interest during this discussion, but McNally's butler warned him 'to be careful of that man in the corner as his eyes were glinting through his fingers'.[260] The butler need not have worried, and not just because his employer was the most accomplished informer and deceiver in the room, but because no one present trusted either of the visitors, and all made sure that the pair could report only that the suggestion of an invasion or a rising was laughed at by Simon Butler.[261]

It was agreed that Jackson should visit Rowan at Newgate. Whatever Rowan heard from Jackson he reacted very enthusiastically and immediately sent for Wolfe Tone, suggesting that he meet Jackson and his colleague. At first

---

257 Tillyard (1997), p. 143.
258 Fitzpatrick, p. 248.
259 Bartlett (1998), p. xxvii.
260 Nicolson, p. 121.
261 Agnew, ii, p. 47.

Tone was eager to talk to anyone who had reliable news from France, so he made his way to Hyde's. Their conversation, however, which lasted about half an hour, was very general. As Tone rose to go they agreed to meet on Wednesday the following week. When Tone called to visit Rowan on the following Monday the two visitors were there. Tone was suspicious of Jackson and thought he might be a spy for the British government. Being a lawyer, Tone was aware that for a successful prosecution for treason it was necessary for two witnesses to give evidence, and he determined never to have any dangerous conversation with Jackson within the hearing of his friend. He said to Jackson, 'This business is one thing for us Irishmen; but an Englishman who engaged in it must be a traitor one way or another'.[262]

Rowan beckoned Jackson to one end of the room, and Tone and Cockayne withdrew to the other end to discuss banalities. After a few minutes Rowan called Tone over and showed him a paper which suggested that a French invasion of England would serve to unite all parties there to resist it.[263] Tone thought this paper 'admirably drawn up', (Benjamin Vaughan MP was most likely the author). Tone believed that the situation in Ireland was very different and agreed to draw up a paper to that effect.

He went home and wrote a paper that had the potential, if it fell into the wrong hands, to put a noose around his neck. His memorandum began by pointing out that the situations in England and Ireland were fundamentally different:

> The government of England is national; the government of Ireland provincial ... The people of Ireland are divided into three sects, the Established

262 Bartlett, p. 94.
263 *Ibid.*, p. 98.

Church, the Dissenters and the Catholics ... [The Established Church sect, which is] infinitely the smallest, have engrossed all the profits and honours of the country, and a very great share of the landed property. They are, of course, all aristocrats, adverse to change, and decided enemies to the French Revolution. The Dissenters, who are much more numerous, are the enlightened body of the nation. They are devoted to liberty, and through all its changes, enthusiastically attached to the French Revolution. ... The Catholics, the great body of the nation, are in the lowest degree of ignorance and want; ready for any change, because no change can make them worse ... In Ireland the Dissenters are enemies to the English power from reason and reflection; the Catholics from hatred of the English name.[264]

Tone finished by advising the French that they should land 7,000 to 10,000 troops in the west of the country, and that 3,000 should be sent to capture Dublin. He suggested 'that the north would rise to a man' and the country would be theirs.

Tone says that he gave this document to Jackson, who put it into his pocket without reading it. Almost immediately he changed his mind and asked for it back. Jackson handed it over and Tone gave it to Rowan with alleged instructions to burn it, but he also said that Rowan could copy it if he wished. Tone claimed that Rowan did burn the original but Rowan, in his memoir, says that he returned it to Tone, who most likely burnt it himself. Tone went down to Drogheda for a few days to attend the assizes. On the following Wednesday

---

264 Bartlett (1998), p. 230.

morning Drennan had breakfast with Rowan and found his friend in high spirits. Rowan read out the paper and asked Drennan what he thought. Drennan thought it was very well drawn up but very dangerous to keep. Rowan hinted that he was expecting important visitors and asked him if Drennan preferred to be in the cabinet or in the hall. Drennan laughed as he understood that he was being given the option of getting involved in something dangerous or remaining aloof. Drennan waited around for about a minute before departing.[265] He later realized that Rowan was about to have a conference with Jackson, Cockayne, Tone and Reynolds. No other accounts of the meetings with Jackson make any mention of Reynolds being present, but he disappeared on the same day as Rowan escaped, and some thought that he had gone with Rowan. In fact, he believed that he had been compromised and had fled to America.

One way or another, the copy in Tone's handwriting was destroyed, but Tone claims that he was 'unspeakably astonished' when, a few days later, Rowan informed him that he had first made three copies, which he had given to Jackson. Cockayne was given a copy to send to an address in Hamburg, which he sent to the post office. He was arrested and brought before the Privy Council, a procedure he had previously agreed with Pitt.[266]

Jackson, who was preparing to leave Dublin, was surprised at Hyde's and hauled off to solitary confinement at Newgate. Cockayne believed that his mission in Dublin was to entrap United Irishmen such as Rowan, Tone or Drennan. He had no wish to hang his old friend Jackson. He went to see Rowan, and requested him to use his good offices with the prison authorities to secure an interview with Jackson. As

---

265 Agnew, ii, p. 46.
266 Drummond, p. 212.

soon as the sentry was withdrawn from Jackson's cell, Rowan, Cockayne and Jackson held a crisis consultation. Cockayne had been closely questioned by the Privy Council, and had admitted that he had addressed the envelope to Hamburg, but maintained that he knew nothing of its contents. It must have chilled Rowan to the bone when Cockayne informed him that the council seemed to be inveterately against him and were anxious to know if the document they now had in their possession was in Rowan's handwriting. Rowan knew instantly that his neck was on the line and that his only hope of survival was to escape. Astonishingly, Rowan appears still to have trusted Cockayne, for he told him his intentions and asked if his escape would injure Jackson's defence. Cockayne assured him that it could not.

Rowan continued to trust Jackson and remained concerned for him. Months later, when he was in France, Rowan pleaded with the government there to intervene to try to save Jackson's life. Rowan had much experience of eluding attempts at entrapment, and had even suspected the loyal and honourable Joe Corbally, who was prepared to suffer great hardship rather than betray Rowan.

So why was he prepared to hand three copies of a treasonable document written in his own hand to a man he had just met and hardly knew? Perhaps he had dropped his guard since his trial and conviction and believed that the government had no more reason to pursue him. Perhaps the fact that Jackson came recommended by John Hurtford Stone led Rowan to trust him. Jackson probably told Rowan that the English document he had in his possession had been written by Rowan's old school friend Benjamin Vaughan. As we have seen, he and the Stone brothers, like Rowan, were Unitarians. All were friends and admirers of Priestley. Nicolson suggests that Stone's business partner in Paris was Rowan's brother-in-law, Reverend Benjamin Beresford, who had eloped with Sidney Hamilton many years previously, and was still married to her. Drennan also mentions Beresford as being somehow involved.[267] Marianne Elliot suggests that Benjamin Beresford was a brother-in-law of John Hurtford Stone. If Beresford's involvement is simply coincidence, it seems extraordinary.[268] Many years later, during Rowan's exile in London between 1803 and 1806, he and Beresford had a great deal of contact with each other. The Beresford connection might be another reason why Rowan might have been prepared to place his trust in Jackson. Jackson was, as far as we know, a stranger to Rowan, but came well recommended by certain people, almost all of whom he knew well, and some of whom he trusted, respected and admired. Given the role of his brother-in-law in this affair, perhaps historians have been naïve in assuming that the first that Rowan knew of the mission was when he was approached by Jackson in his cell at Newgate. Perhaps the web of contacts had been spun by Rowan himself at an earlier date.

Escape on May Day

In the event, Rowan's escape was not quite as simple or as dashing as Drennan had been led to believe. He offered Mr Dewell, his under-jailer, £100 to let him go to his home in Dominick Street to sign a legal document, allegedly necessary for a business transaction. Dewell, with his sabre and his pistols in his girdle, accompanied Rowan to his house. Rowan asked for permission to enter his bedroom to speak with his wife, and slipped out of the window and descended to the ground on a knotted rope. When Rowan seemed to be dallying, Dewell called out to him, but he got

---

267 Agnew, ii, p. 47.
268 *loc. cit.*

only a muffled response. Eventually he lost patience and burst into the room to find only Sarah and her 11-year-old son, Gawin, inside. Sarah tried to delay the pursuit further by offering a bribe to Dewell, but he said that 'he would far rather see Hamilton Rowan hanged'.[269]

Rowan's friends had recommended that he bring a pair of pistols, but his only weapon was a razor. He was determined not to be taken alive.[270] He made his way to Sackville Street dressed in clothes he had borrowed from his cowman. There he met Mat Dowling, who brought two horses, and they rode through the darkness to the house of John Sweetman, a Catholic United Irishman, at Sutton, a coastal village near Howth in County Dublin. Sweetman's servants were reluctant to open the door to the constant rapping in the early morning darkness, and when they finally did so they thought the man in a cowherd's clothing was a robber. Sweetman was a dedicated United Irishman who later took part in the 1798 rebellion and would spend sixteen years in exile as a result.[271] He was not at this point a known associate of Rowan, yet he received the fugitive with 'the utmost kindnesses'.[272]

By dawn on 2 May the word was all over Dublin that Archibald Hamilton Rowan was at large. Soon the Sham Squire was recounting how the escape was effected. He described how a crowd had lit a May Day bonfire on the green outside the prison, and as Rowan waved his wife to her carriage a few squibs cracked and startled her. Rowan ran, as if to his wife's aid, but disappeared into the crowd and mounted a horse and dashed away. Sarah's coach took off towards Dominick Street, which was just a few hundred

---

269 Nicolson, p. 123.
270 Drummond, p. 216.
271 Nicolson, p. 132.
272 *loc. cit.*

yards distant, with the jailers in hot pursuit, but when they reached the house there was no sign of Rowan. The Sham informed his readers that the fugitive had galloped to Rush, a coastal area of north County Dublin that was renowned as a haunt for smugglers. Rush also had a reputation of pro-American and pro-French privateering during the American war.[273] The Sham claimed that there Rowan 'boarded an American vessel, which was waiting for him which instantly set sail'.[274]

The Sham did make one observation about his own version of events that made him suspicious. 'Why one wonders was no report made to either the head jailer Gregg or the magistrate until the morning after the escape?'[275]

Of course, the escape was never going to be as easy as the Sham suggested. It was one thing to flee the relatively relaxed custody at Newgate; it was quite another to escape from his pursuers, who had the country swamped with informers. The government had called on 'all justices of the peace, mayors, sheriffs, bailiffs, constables [and] all his Majesty's other loving subjects to use their utmost diligence to apprehend the fugitive'.[276] The revenue officers and the military were watching all the ports and embarkation points, and a huge wartime fleet was patrolling the Irish Sea and the English Channel on high alert for suspicious craft.

Sweetman had, in fact, gone to Rush, just a few miles north of his home, in the hope of finding a vessel to take Rowan to France. Even before he arrived there, Dewell, the under-jailer, was searching many of the houses with a military party. The searchers paid particular attention to two houses whose inhabitants had recently spent some time in

273 Morley, pp. 192-196, 2002.
274 *Freeman's Journal*, May 1794.
275 *loc. cit.*
276 *loc. cit.*

Newgate for 'a revenue matter' and had sometimes dined with Rowan.

Sweetman could find no suitable boat, and returned, asking Rowan to consider hiding out in Ireland for a while. Rowan insisted on getting to France, both on his own account and in order to alert the French about Jackson's arrest. Sweetman offered Rowan the use of his small pleasure vessel, and when this was gratefully accepted, Sweetman had to procure maps, instruments and a crew. When purchasing the equipment at a ship's chandler on George's Quay in the city, Sweetman had to feign indifference when a captain of a revenue cruiser told him he had orders to be on the lookout for Archibald Hamilton Rowan.[277]

Sweetman found two brothers, Christopher and Denis Sheridan, who were prepared to smuggle an 'embarrassed gentlemen' to France. They enlisted another man called Murray who had a smuggler's knowledge of the small ports on the French coast. When the Sheridan brothers were introduced to their passenger they produced a proclamation offering a reward of £1,000 for Archibald Hamilton Rowan and asked was this the man they were to take to France. When Sweetman confirmed Rowan's identity the older Sheridan said, 'never mind it, by Jesus we will land him safe'.[278]

On 4 May 1794 at 4 a.m. Rowan and his crew climbed the wall of Kilbarrack graveyard and put to sea in a fair wind.[279] One of the Sheridans said to Rowan, 'our boat is small, but God looks after those like you who have the blessings of the poor'.[280] As they tacked around Howth Head and out of Dublin Bay into the open sea, perhaps Rowan felt

---

277 Nicolson, p. 133.
278 Drummond, p. 218.
279 Nicolson, p. 135.
280 McMillan (1997), p. 87.

that he was beginning a relatively short if perilous voyage. He was actually starting out on what proved to be a long and dangerous journey. He could not know that twelve years of a lonely, frustrating and painful exile lay before him. Nor could he have foreseen that within a few short years some of the dearest comrades he left behind would die brutally, some on the gallows. His friends Edward Fitzgerald, Theobald Wolfe Tone, Thomas Russell, Oliver Bond and Thomas Bacon fell victim to the vicious reaction unleashed on the people of Ireland in 1798. Simon Butler would die of natural causes within a year of Rowan's departure. Samuel Neilson, after years of imprisonment, died of yellow fever in America. Emmet also went to prison, but was destined to spend a long life in America, mourning the loss of a much-loved younger brother, Robert, who was executed when he and Russell led the last stand of the United Irishmen in 1803.

The exposure of the Jackson plot and Rowan's flight was a disaster for the United Irishmen. The city abounded with rumours. Reynolds and Tone were missing and nobody was sure why, but all suspected that they too had been entrapped by Jackson, who was wrongly presumed to be cooperating with the authorities.

The Sham Squire was engaged in what in modern times would be recognized as sophisticated psychological warfare. The *Freeman's Journal* pointed out that the escape was well organized and that Rowan must have had considerable help. In a piece of brazen fiction, the *Journal* informed its readers:

> The business of the escape was a concerted one. The post-chaise on which he travelled to Rush changed horses at The Man of War[281] and he reached Rush at three in the morning, where everything was

---

281 This inn still exists in north County Dublin.

prepared for his reception and conveyance on an American vessel, *The Hope,* which lay anchored at the place to receive him and instantly set sail.

In an attempt to terrify Rowan's friends, the *Journal* carried another piece of fiction, which, like all good propaganda, had the merit of having some basis in fact:

> On the morning on which Mr Rowan escaped his room was crowded with his cronies, Dr R[eynol]ds, Dr D[rennan], Councillors McN[evan], E[mme]t, and S[imon Butler] and three engineers from Rush who were recently tried for abetting the Defenders.[282]

Drennan was not alarmed, but he was disappointed that his friend Emmet was 'panic-struck and talking about [his duties to] his mother and wife' and was on the cusp of withdrawing from the society. When Moses Dawson accompanied Drennan to the next scheduled meeting of the Dublin United Irishmen, they found the room in darkness. The woman in waiting told them that Leonard McNally and Nicholas Butler and another gentleman had been there earlier and had told her that no meeting would take place. Drennan was furious and ordered her to light the candles, and he and Dawson began to compose a resolution condemning the unauthorized actions of McNally and Butler. Eventually a few more drifted in. Drennan felt that Rowan, Tone and Reynolds were already implicated, and the rest of the society would appear to be in a panic if no meeting had taken place. He knew that it was vital that he himself should behave as if he had nothing to be alarmed about. When Simon Butler turned up Drennan was

---

282 *Freeman's Journal*, May 1794.

delighted at his manly spirit and declared, 'he is a man'.[283] Drennan gave himself credit for ensuring that the meeting of the United Irishmen took place because he believed it 'saved the society from an acknowledgement of having implicated itself with Rowan'.[284] Sheriff Gifford led a raiding party to Henry Jackson's place looking for Reynolds, but Reynolds had already left the country. Tone was known to be staying at home, and many wondered why he had not been arrested. In fact he was negotiating a way out for himself with the authorities. The case against him was weak as Cockayne could not, in truth, implicate him, and the document seized was not in his handwriting. He therefore told the government, through Marcus Beresford, that he would make a statement disclosing his role in the affair, but he would not give evidence against Rowan or Jackson. In return, he would not be charged and would be allowed to go to America. The bargain was agreed and honoured by both parties.

Drennan may have saved the society's reputation, but he did not save the society. Indeed, that meeting was the last he ever attended. Before the next scheduled meeting he was arrested and charged, not with aiding the escape of Rowan but with being the author of the seditious address that had been distributed at Pardon's fifteen months earlier. He felt he owed it to the society not to attend any more meetings until he had cleared his name.

Before Drennan stood trial, Sheriff Gifford raided the scheduled meeting of the Dublin United Irishmen on 23 May, seized its books and funds and dispersed the society. Dublin's first open, democratic, non-sectarian political reform club was no more. Less than three years previously the Eagle Tavern

---

283 Agnew, ii, p. 47.
284 *loc. cit.*

and the Tailors' Hall had been filled with respectable citizens
of every religious persuasion urging religious toleration,
reform of Parliament and universal suffrage. The society's
most illustrious member was now an outlaw and branded a
traitor, and Gifford had put an end to the United Irishmen.
The hopes of the reformers were dashed. However, political
movements that capture the imagination of the best and most
enlightened of any generation cannot be suppressed by thugs
and petty tyrants. It would take more than Gifford and a few
armed constables to stop Oliver Bond, Henry Jackson, Samuel
Neilson and Lord Edward Fitzgerald. Perhaps Rowan would
make it to France. Perhaps he would return to Ireland at the
head of a French republican army. If so, his friends in Dublin
and Belfast would be ready to greet him. Almost immediately,
the more determined among them set about organizing an
underground mass revolutionary movement that would be
ready to rise when the first French soldier set foot on Irish soil.

11.

The Glorious First of June

Jean Bon St San André was the boy
Who fought and saved the French convoy
John Bull rang his church bells all for joy
Which caused the French great laughter.[285]

The small vessel made good time as far as Wexford, but was then blown back by contrary winds to shelter once again under Howth Head. By dawn the next day the weather had cleared and they set sail once more in a fair wind. Just over one day later, Rowan and his companions sailed into the English Channel, which was fast becoming a dangerous war zone. A deadly game of cat and mouse was being played out between the British Channel fleet and the French Atlantic fleet. Jean Bon St André, a former Protestant clergyman, had been radicalized by the French Revolution and had risen to become a powerful member of the Committee of

---

285 'La Carmagnole', a French revolutionary song.

Public Safety. St André was now in Brest re-equipping and reorganizing the French naval forces.

Admiral Howe was in command of the British fleet, and he was endeavouring to lure the French out of port and into battle. A food convoy from America was expected in France, which was threatened with famine. If the British could intercept the convoy the French would be forced to deploy their entire fleet to protect the much-needed supplies. Meanwhile, both sides were engaged in small-scale skirmishing and capturing individual vessels. As Rowan's small craft crossed the Channel, he was still nearer to the English than the French coast, and they were suddenly enveloped by the British fleet. Howe was searching for the American food convoy, but also escorting some British merchantmen through the Channel. The merchantmen stayed between the British warships and the coast, however, and Rowan and his crew passed by unobserved.[286]

When they caught sight of the little port of Roscoff they got their first indication of the tensions, suspicions and xenophobia of the French coastal forces. One of the many small batteries on the shore fired a warning shot in their direction. In times such as these, a mysterious stranger landing on their coast claiming to be a friend might not be welcomed with open arms. It was common in the run-up to a major battle for each side to send spies to observe the enemy's preparations. Unfortunately for Rowan, he and his crew had appeared at just such a time. He borrowed Sheridan's red sleeping cap to serve as a bonnet of liberty. He lashed it to the helm with a boathook and sailed unmolested under the fort of St Pol de Leon. They pulled alongside a fishing boat and Rowan stepped on board, having first divided all his remaining cash among himself and his crew.

---

286 Drummond, p. 218.

He told the Sheridans and Murray to head for England and asked the French fishermen to bring him ashore.

A crowd of curious onlookers who had watched the strange goings-on immediately took their visitor to the *hôtel de ville* and awaited the arrival of someone in authority. The commandant of the fort arrived and searched and questioned Rowan. When Rowan showed him the proclamation in the *Dublin Evening Post*, the commandant remarked, 'by your own account you have escaped prison in your own country. I shall take care you shall not escape from me'.[287]

The commandant confined Rowan to an upper room of the building with a sentry on the door. He did agree to Rowan's request that a letter be immediately sent to the Committee of Public Safety. Rowan's 'spirit was agitated' and he was physically exhausted from all his exertions since his escape, and he lay down on some straw in the room and fell into a deep sleep.

At midnight he was roused by the mayor who proceeded to interrogate him aggressively and accused him of being an English spy. The mayor grabbed Rowan's hat and tore out the national cockade that one of the onlookers had pinned to it and proceeded to berate Rowan for profaning the sacred symbol of liberty. However, when the mayor told him that Jean Bon St André was, at that moment, at Brest getting ready to confront the British fleet, Rowan thought all his troubles were over. As a leading member of the Committee of Public Safety, St André had spoken to Jackson prior to the mission to England and Ireland and may even have heard Rowan's name mentioned during the planning stages. St André had assured Jackson that he favoured an invasion of Ireland, and it is possible that Jackson had told this to Rowan.[288]

---

287 *Ibid.*, p. 220.
288 Elliott (1982), p. 63.

The mayor agreed to Rowan's request to send a message to Brest. When St André received the letter he dispatched three officers to bring Rowan to his residence. They duly arrived to take Rowan to see St André and provided a 'rascally nag' as transport. As they rode out of town Rowan was shocked to see Sweetman's boat tied up at the quay wall. Clearly his companions had been pursued and taken. He made many attempts to find out what had happened to them, but could get no straight answers, and it was to be a few weeks before he could intercede on their behalf.

The three officers were veterans of the vicious civil war that had been fought in the Vendée the previous year. They passed the time on their journey by recounting details of many of the acts they had committed during the conflict. Rowan records that he thought their deeds were most atrocious.[289] It is not clear if he shared his views with his companions, but given what we know of the strength of Rowan's feelings about right and wrong it is highly unlikely that he held his tongue. It might have been better to woo his new acquaintances rather than admonish them, particularly in the light of what happened next.

Amongst the Galley Slaves

His escort, either by neglect or design, instead of ensuring his safe transfer to a senior government official, dumped him into the abyss that was the French prison system in wartime. It had taken them two days to get to Brest, and when they arrived at St André's house they found he had gone on board the fleet. The three officers told Rowan that they were anxious to get out of the town before the gates were closed and suggested to him that he stay at the military hospital. This sounded like a reasonable request if you did not know that the hospital was in

---

289 *loc. cit.*

fact a pretty unpleasant prison. Rowan agreed, not realizing that once the door closed behind him he would be in the custody of galley slaves lodged with Frenchmen who were perceived to be enemies of the revolution and British prisoners who were too ill to move to the interior. It was obvious to Rowan that the warders were galley slaves as they wore a wire around their left ankle. They registered his name and gave him a pewter plate and cup. When dinner time came his fellow prisoners objected to his presence in their midst. The galley slaves insisted that he stayed where he had been put. As far as his fellow prisoners and his galley slave warders were concerned, Rowan was to be singled out for particularly hard treatment as a spy.

In these circumstances, even if St André had returned quickly, it would have been extremely difficult for Rowan to communicate with him. St André did not return soon. He was preoccupied with many matters more important than an interview with a mysterious visitor from Dublin. The skirmishing was over and the great battle was about to begin. As the American convoy neared its destination, the British and French fleets clashed in a great maritime slaughter that became known on the British side as the 'Glorious First of June'. James's naval history records:

> The French fleet fought gallantly; but though superior to the British in the size of the ships, and in the numbers of both guns and men, England justly claimed the victory. Six of the noblest warships of France were captured, and a seventh after striking her colours went to the bottom. The loss of English was 290 killed and 858 wounded and that of the French in killed, wounded and prisoners [was] 7,000.[290]

---

290 *Ibid.*, p. 228.

The British had clearly got the better of the French. St André was wounded on board the 121-gun ship *La Montagne*. His reputation was badly damaged when he transferred onto a frigate, leaving more than 300 dead and wounded behind on the severely damaged flagship. He had, however, saved the American convoy. Admiral Howe did not follow through and take full advantage of his victory, and Horatio Nelson coined the disparaging phrase 'a Howe victory'.

News of the battle was slow to reach London and Dublin because many of Howe's ships could not make it back to England for some considerable time. Those that were not badly damaged were held up by contrary winds, and it took them some time to secure their prizes. The French maintained a fiction, which was believed by their people and their international supporters, that they had won the battle. Neither side could conceal that their fleets had been mangled and that thousands of seamen had been killed or wounded. The Dublin newspapers suggested that Rowan was with St André on the *Montagne*. This caused Sarah 'no small anxiety' until she realized it was a fabrication.

Rowan, however, was very far from safe. Although he was allowed to write as many letters as he liked to the Committee for Public Safety, he subsequently believed that none of his letters went any further than the head jailer's office. Rowan had been lodged among French prisoners who regarded themselves as good sans-culottes, and objected to the presence in their midst of an English spy. The English spy theory gained credence among his fellow prisoners and the authorities when Rowan displayed his characteristic human decency. He recalled:

> The idea of my being an English spy had obtained a greater currency from the arrival of six poor priests who were brought in from the hold of a prison ship,

in a miserable condition, covered in sores from lying in the cable tier without any bedding. One of these was placed in the bed next to mine, and I constantly assisted him when obliged to leave his bed on different occasions. This in the opinion of my companions was a decided proof of my being an English spy; for who but such a person would pay any attention to a refractory priest?[291]

He waited in vain for answers to his letters to St André and the Committee of Public Safety. He did not learn until some time later that only the letters he had sent from Roscoff had reached their destination; all the rest were piling up in the head jailer's office. The initial letter, sent when he landed, was received by the Committee of Public Safety, which had instructed that he be conveyed immediately to Paris in a coach and four, with a tricolour to indicate that he was a representative of the nation. By the time the Roscoff authorities received these orders they believed that he was safely with St André, so the message was sent no further.

Therefore, through a series of mishaps and unfortunate events, Rowan became a prisoner and a witness to the Terror, literally, from the inside. He was clearly disturbed and perhaps alarmed by what he saw. He wrote:

One side of the building, in which I was confined, was occupied by the revolutionary tribunals, and we daily saw from our windows on the opposite side, wagon-loads of prisoners brought for trial. Those who were condemned returned immediately in the same vehicle to the guillotine, with their arms

291 Drummond, p. 226.

pinioned and their necks bare, while the crowds were shouting '*Vive la Republique*'.[292]

Given the hostility of his fellows and the prison authorities, one wonders if it crossed Rowan's mind that he might soon be standing in a cart with his arms pinioned and his neck bare on his way to execution. In fact, the desire of his jailer to be rid of him by the guillotine or otherwise led to the end of his harsh captivity, which had lasted more than a month. His luck suddenly changed for the better. The inspector of prisoners of war happened to be an Irishman, Mr Sullivan. When the inspector visited Brest, the head jailer threw one of Rowan's letters at him and said, 'for god's sake rid me of this man, either send him to the guillotine or send him away'.[293] Sullivan, of course, knew the name of Ireland's best known pro-French radical and went to where Rowan was confined to make sure the prisoner was indeed who he said he was.

When the Committee of Public Safety was informed, there was a great deal of embarrassment that a friend and well-known patriot had been so badly treated. It ordered Sullivan to bring Rowan to Paris in the style befitting so distinguished a visitor. This time the coach and four with the appropriate tricolour were procured, and Rowan and Sullivan left Brest in triumph, bound for Paris.

They reached Orleans on 7 June, and on the next day they witnessed a great fête which the deist Robespierre had decreed in honour of the 'Supreme Being'. Rowan described how all the public functionaries assembled in the main church while a banner proclaiming the loyalty of the French people to the 'Supreme Being' was unfurled among the

292 *Ibid.*, p. 229.
293 Nicolson, p. 145.

firing of canon and muskets, while the vast crowd shouted '*Viva* Robespierre'.

While Rowan describes the event, he gives us no clue to what he thought of Robespierre's attempt to create a secular patriotic religion. Robespierre was attempting to combat the atheism that was in the ascendant following the fall of Roman Catholicism in the revolution. As a Unitarian, Rowan no doubt would have approved of the reference to a singular 'Supreme Being'. He would also have approved of the rejection of the old superstitions associated with Catholicism. However, he most likely would have been very uneasy with the State meddling in religious affairs. For Rowan, religion or irreligion was a matter of individual conscience that should not be influenced or controlled by any civil authority.

From the time they left Brest, Rowan was feeling ill. He could eat nothing, and all the water he drank could not quench his thirst. From Orleans, their coach, with its tricolour fluttering in the wind, headed at great speed for Paris. They were waved through security barriers and given fresh horses at post offices along the way. They covered the last seventy miles of their journey in less than ten hours. By the time they arrived in the capital, however, Rowan was in the grip of a prison fever that was so severe he could neither think nor talk.

On arrival he was immediately ushered into the presence of Robespierre. The Jacobin leader was most anxious to apologize to Rowan for all that had happened since his arrival in France. He also tried to question him on the situation in Ireland. What might have been, if Rowan were at his charismatic, enthusiastic best? However, Rowan was in such a miserably sick condition that he could not even answer Robespierre's questions. Robespierre suggested they adjourn their discussion until the following day. Rowan never saw Robespierre again.

The next morning Rowan's condition had worsened and he could not even rise from his bed. Monsieur Colon, the chief surgeon of the army, was ordered to attend the patient. Rowan was given an apartment in the magnificent Palais Royal, which had once been home to his friend Pamela Fitzgerald, the daughter of Philippé Égalité. Some say that Égalité had refurbished this magnificent palace to annoy his cousin, the King. Rowan's needs were to be met at the expense of the nation. It was six weeks before he had recovered sufficiently to meet the Committee of Public Safety. By this time the committee was too preoccupied to pay much attention to what he had to say.

While lying ill he had a visitor to his sickbed whom he identifies only as an old friend from his Warrington and Cambridge schooldays who was now an MP and had been caught up in the Jackson affair. This was most likely Benjamin Vaughan. Vaughan told Rowan that he had been introduced to Jackson in London and 'he thought it best to absent himself although he was quite ignorant of Irish affairs'.[294] Of course, we know that it was not Vaughan's knowledge of Irish affairs that had been useful to Jackson, rather it was the paper he had drawn up on the situation in England that had been so admired by Wolfe Tone. We shall never know if Rowan knew that Vaughan was the author of the paper, or of the English dimension to the Jackson affair. It is clear that his memoir is written in such a way as not to implicate his old friend.

When Rowan recovered he met the Committee of Public Safety, but he chose not to be very specific about the nature of the discussions he had with them. He asked them to intervene to save Jackson. They told him that the British had been informed that if they executed Jackson then General O'Hara,

---

294 Drummond, p. 235.

who had been captured at Toulon, would undergo the same fate.[295] Rowan doubted that this strategy would work and recommended bribing Cockayne. He was assured that this had already been done. We shall see later that Jackson was not protected; if any measures were taken on his behalf, they were not effective.

The Committee of Public Safety had assigned Citizen Herman, intendant of finance, to look after Rowan's financial needs. However, Rowan had managed to make contact with Sarah, who sent him some money from home. This allowed him, as soon as he had recovered, to move out of his government-provided accommodation.

Rowan's second biographer, Nicolson, claims that in an unsigned and undated document uncovered in the French National Archive, Rowan had told his hosts:

> That the whole population except the Episcopalians were discontented with English rule and that the Catholics and the Dissenters would rise if assured of French support. He added that the Irish had no wish to exchange English tyranny for French protection, that they were frightened of being turned into a French province, and that the invading army should for this reason not be too large and should from the outset issue a proclamation guaranteeing Irish independence. Three quarters of the militia ... would leave their flag for the flag of liberty ... [and] two thirds of the English fleet was manned by Irish sailors who would not fail to fly to the aid of their native country.[296]

---

295 *loc. cit.*
296 Nicolson, p. 151.

These are very interesting observations for a number of reasons. Firstly, the clear statement that the French were welcome in Ireland as invited allies only, and not as foreign invaders, was to remain a central plank of United Irish diplomacy for the next decade. This sentiment was clearly spelt out nearly ten years later in Robert Emmet's speech from the dock in September 1803, when he asserted that he would have immolated the French in their ships had they come as invaders.

Secondly, Rowan appears to have been privy to information about a high level of Defender infiltration of the militia, and possibly of the fleet. When the seamen victors of the Glorious First of June staged their mutiny on the Nore two years later, there was much Irish involvement. There was talk of sailing the fleet to France, and much circumstantial evidence of contact between the seamen and agents of the United Irishmen. Of course, when the rebellion broke out in Ireland in 1798 and some militia soldiers defected to the rebels, most did not. However, no French help arrived until the rebellion was over, so Rowan's thesis of how the militia would react if French help arrived was never properly tested.

Rowan's information to the French appears realistic and well informed and was of course based on much of what Tone had written earlier. The comments of the person who wrote the report for the committee suggests that he fully understood how important a role Rowan could play in the event of a French landing in Ireland. The anonymous official suggested that Rowan should be at the head of an army that could land at Wexford and advance on Dublin. 'If Hamilton Rowan, that illustrious martyr to Liberty, should lead the Wexford army, his manifesto would stir the people of Dublin whose idol he is'.[297]

---

297 *Ibid.*, p. 152.

The Fall of Robespierre

We do not know, however, if this report was even considered by the Committee of Public Safety. Given the major crisis that engulfed the committee at this time, it is highly unlikely that it was. Rowan's illness began in early June and he tells us it lasted for six weeks, which means that he was not fully recovered until mid to late July. During that time serious divisions developed within the committee regarding the progress of the war and the Terror. For four weeks Robespierre stayed away from committee meetings. His sister claimed that a subterranean intrigue led by those who wished to prolong the Terror was directed at her brother, who, she claims, had wanted to substitute leniency for harshness.[298] When Robespierre returned to the committee on 26 July he spoke against the intriguers, and said that the next day names would be named. The next day, however, Robespierre and his followers were shouted down and arrested. Rowan explained what happened:

> Callot, D'Herbois, Barrere and their partisans, industriously heaped all the odium for measures of severity on Robespierre, hoping to screen themselves from the enormities which were common to all such governments. In this they were seconded by all the enemies of the revolution … Their united efforts brought Robespierre, Couthan, and St Just to the scaffold … under the pretence of public good.[299]

Sixty of Robespierre's supporters, including Rowan's benefactor, Citizen Herman, were brought to the guillotine at Place de la Révolution two days later. It took just one

---

298 Tannahill (1966), p. 104.
299 Drummond, p. 237.

Killyleagh Volunteers drilling in the courtyard of the castle, 1913.

Archibald Hamilton Rowan with his mother and sister.
Courtesy of Rowan Hamilton family.

Archibald Hamilton Rowan as a younger man.
Courtesy of National Gallery of Ireland.

Reverend Jackson.
Courtesy of National Library of Ireland.

Leonard McNally.
Courtesy of National Library of Ireland.

MAY—EVENING SPORTS; or, ROWAN lost in the SMOKE.

Jail break. *Faulkners* weekly magazine, May 1794.
Courtesy of National Library of Ireland.

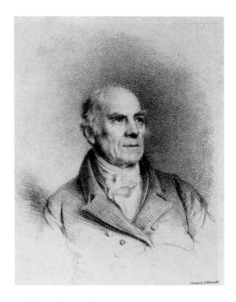

Archibald Hamilton Rowan as an old man.
Courtesy of National Gallery of Ireland.

Archibald Hamilton Rowan with Simon Butler at Edinburgh.
Courtesy of National Portrait Gallery, London.

and a half hours for all of them to die, which suggests one execution every ninety seconds. Rowan was some distance from the scaffold, yet the blood of the victims streamed under his feet. He was greatly surprised at the reactions of the crowd, who cheered as each severed head hit the basket, apparently blaming Robespierre for the abuses that had arisen from his efforts to control food prices so that the poor could eat.

The fall of Robespierre spelt the end of the Jacobins, and many felt the end of the revolution. Rowan saw the coup as a victory for the Royalists and observed that 'from that period on everything bore a new face. Marat's bust and the bonnet of liberty were torn down and trampled upon in the theatres and other public places'.[300] The mere wearing of the characteristic long coat and short hair of a Jacobin resulted in several people being murdered in the street by La Jeunesse Parisienne, a right-wing death squad.

When news of the fall of Robespierre and the Jacobins reached Dublin in early August, William Drennan worried that Rowan himself might soon be guillotined.[301] Two circumstances aided his survival. Firstly, he was by this time living on his own resources and was not a dependent of the regime. Secondly, he had been in jail under the Jacobins.

He moved into his mother's old house on the Rue Mousseau, where his first son had been born. A locksmith who had once worked at Versailles now occupied the house. Rowan was disgusted by the way this man and his fellow citizens were abused and blackmailed by 'the several inconveniences of revolutionary government'. The locksmith ordered to produce carriages for heavy guns, a task for which he had no qualifications or experience. An inspector who could not

---

300 *Ibid.*, p. 238.
301 Agnew, ii, p. 88.

even identify the faults that required rectification rejected the locksmith's multiple efforts. Rowan also details a number of scams involving house searches that had no security objective but were designed to squeeze money from the householders.[302] When 700 workmen were killed in an accidental explosion at a powder magazine, rather than learn from the accident the regime chose to blame Jacobin sabotage.

It was not at first clear to Rowan whether the Jacobins could stage a comeback. However, the murders of Jacobins spread from Paris to the provinces, and within a few months 2,000 had been killed in the south-east alone.[303] By the time it became clear that their defeat was permanent, he had become disillusioned with Paris.

---

302 Drummond, p. 236.
303 Gough (1998), p. 72.

12.

Rowan and Mary Wollstonecraft

The separation from his wife and family was taking its toll on Rowan's feelings. He awaited Sarah's letters eagerly and was alarmed if they failed to arrive. He felt that he had lost his wife's affections and blamed himself and his 'ill usage and neglect' of his family. Personal loneliness and political disillusionment weighed heavy on Rowan at this period. Just when he was most in need of a friend with whom to share his sorrows, fears and disappointments, he found one in the person of the remarkable Mary Wollstonecraft.

Rowan attended a post-Terror festival in Paris in honour of the moderate revolutionary leader Mirabeau, who had been a great hero of the Irish and English radicals before his death from natural causes in April 1791. Strolling among the crowd was a woman who spoke English, followed by a maid with an infant held in her arms. One of his friends told Rowan that the woman was Mary Wollstonecraft. Rowan was surprised and shocked:

What? … this is Mary Wollstonecraft, parading about with a child at her heels, with as little ceremony as if it were a watch she had just bought at the jeweller's. So much for the rights of women thought I.[304]

Wollstonecraft was 35, and by this time was one of the best-known English radicals of her generation. She had already established herself as a professional writer of distinction. Rowan had almost certainly read most of her better-known political works, some of which had been reprinted in the *Northern Star*, the newspaper of the Belfast United Irishmen. When Edmund Burke had attacked Wollstonecraft's old friend Richard Price in his *Reflections on the Revolution in France*, Mary Wollstonecraft was the first into print with *A Vindication of the Rights of Men* in defence of Price in 1790.

Barbara Taylor tells us of Mary's rapid rise to literary fame:

Her defence [of Dr Price] was well received and she began to get a reputation. Two years later she followed up with *A Vindication of the Rights of Woman*. Her name was bracketed with Tom Paine's whose own *Rights of Man* appeared in 1791; she was commended in France and America, and fêted by fellow radicals in England.[305]

Wollstonecraft's publisher, Joseph Johnson, had his home and bookshop at 72 St Paul's Churchyard in London. In 1787 Johnson had brought the novice female writer into a formidable circle of Unitarian intellectuals, writers and artists

---

304 Gordon (2005), p. 248.
305 Taylor (2002), p. 7.

including Dr Price, Dr Joseph Priestley, Thomas Christie and Erasmus Darwin. All were, like Johnson, committed Unitarians who combined a theology they referred to as 'Rational Dissent' with a social radicalism that led them to be great supporters of the American and later the French Revolutions. Rowan's old teacher, John Jebb, had been a leading light in the circle, but he had passed away in 1786, the year before Wollstonecraft came among them. William Godwin the philosopher (Wollstonecraft's future husband) and Tom Paine, the great propagandist of the American Revolution, were also part of Johnson's circle. William Blake was semi-detached from the circle, for although he shared their radical politics his mysticism kept him at a distance from these scientific, rationalist thinkers.

Wollstonecraft had come to Paris in 1792 to observe the progress of the French Revolution at first hand. Johnson had agreed that she could write her impressions of the situation in France for his magazine, the *Analytical Review,* which he had founded with Thomas Christie. Christie had joined the battle against Burke on behalf of Price when he published *Letters on the Revolution in France* in 1791. He had relocated to Paris, and Wollstonecraft lodged in his house and was on very friendly terms with his wife. Among the English-speaking bohemians who frequented Christie's house was an American adventurer, Gilbert Imlay.

In her *Vindication of the Rights of Woman*, Wollstonecraft had suggested that marriage, which denied women independence, was a form of prostitution. She seemed to put her radical theory of sexual politics into action when she fell in love with Imlay. Mary could barely support herself in Paris, while Imlay was a wealthy businessman. Mary would not marry him because she did not want him to become responsible for her debts. When she realized that she was pregnant with Imlay's child, however, she changed her name to Mary Imlay and moved into his house.

Rowan believed that Mary had contracted this 'republican marriage' to avoid the internment that was introduced for English citizens in France in October 1793. Certainly some of Mary's English friends were arrested, including Tom Paine, Helena Williams and her lover, John Hurtford Stone. Paine was held for nearly two years, missing the guillotine by a whisker. Williams and Hurtford Stone were released after a short time.

Hurtford Stone is the same man who was once a member of Price's congregation at Newington Green. He was a dear and close friend to Lord Edward Fitzgerald, and had played a leading role in the Jackson mission, which was the source of Rowan's current difficulties.

Rowan never mentions John Hurtford Stone, although he may well have met him at this point. Neither can we know whether they knew each other earlier, although they had many close friends in common such as Priestley and Edward Fitzgerald, and others in Joe Johnson's London-based circle. In fact, Rowan tells us almost nothing of the Irish or English people he mixed with in France at this time with the exception of Mr Sullivan, the prison inspector, Madgett the spymaster and Mary Wollstonecraft. Both of the former were French citizens, and Mary was dead by the time the memoir was written. Although his French experiences may have cooled his ardour for revolution, Rowan never let down a friend or lost his loyalty to his comrades, whose physical safety and reputations he protected to the end of his days.

Mary's daughter, Fanny Imlay, was born in Le Havre on 10 May 1794, just about the time Rowan was sampling the delights of his bed of straw at Roscoff. Fanny's father did not display much enthusiasm for the joys of family life. By the time Rowan first caught sight of mother and baby, Wollstonecraft was beginning to suspect that Imlay's frequent and prolonged absences on business were a prelude to his total abandonment of her and their baby. Mary tried to take her own life the following year when her republican experiment in free love ended in disillusionment and despair. Drummond, Rowan's biographer, probably spoke for many when he observed that while Mary had been 'barbarously betrayed and deserted' he could not resist remarking that her experiment 'should never be repeated by any woman who places the slightest value on her honour'.[306]

Rowan, however, was of more generous heart. When he got over his initial shock at Mary's flouting of convention, they became dear friends. He was delighted to visit Mary, and over a cup of tea they would have 'an hour's rational conversation'. Both talked longingly of their absent partners, and when Mary said that no man and wife should stay together when love was dead, Rowan was deeply wounded. He felt that he had treated his wife and family so neglectfully that he might have lost Sarah's affections. Mary knew about this from experience, and assured Rowan that 'when a person we love is absent, all the faults he might have are diminished and his virtues augmented in proportion'.[307] If Mary still loved Imlay, no doubt Sarah still loved Rowan.

Mary and Rowan had been delighted by the early stages of the French Revolution. Both had admired Mirabeau and the Girondists, and both had been sickened by the onset of the Terror and the sight of blood that flowed in torrents at the foot of the guillotine. However, Rowan appears to have been sympathetic to Robespierre while Mary regarded him as a 'monster'.[308]

---

306 Drummond, p. 256.
307 Gordon, p. 249.
308 *Ibid.*, p. 267.

Rowan's letters to his wife seem to indicate that he had become disillusioned with 'reform and the other word that begins with r'. Although there may be an element of Rowan telling Sarah what he knew she wanted to hear, his disgust at the bloody execution of Robespierre's adherents by their erstwhile comrades is patently genuine, as was his disillusionment with the petty tyrannies of revolutionary government. Mary could see beyond the immediate difficulties to better times ahead:

> These evils are passing away, a new spirit has gone forth, to organize the body politic … Reason has at last shown her captivating face, beaming with benevolence; and it will be impossible for the dark hand of despotism again to obscure its radiance, or the lurking dagger of subordinate tyrants to reach her bosom.[309]

Mary was fortunate to have Rowan's company and friendship at this point, for most of her English friends had left Paris and poor Tom Paine was still languishing in prison. Even the climate served to chill Mary's worried and lonely heart. Taylor records:

> The winter of 1794–95 was one of the coldest on record. The Seine froze; so did the fountains. The Convention had abolished more price controls, the cost of bread rose, and the freezing of harbours like Le Havre on the Normandy coast prevented the import of emergency grain. People died of starvation; wolves howled at the gates of Paris. Coal was scarce and queues lengthened.[310]

---

309 Taylor, p. 152.
310 *Ibid.*, p. 243.

Much as she wished to stay, Mary left Paris for Imlay's house at Le Havre in the spring. Imlay was still in London on business, and eventually Mary departed to join him there in April 1795.

Rowan had been getting letters from Sarah urging him to leave France for America. When he agreed and made his plans known to Mary, she readied the house in Le Havre for him to stay while he awaited his transatlantic passage. Mary Wollstonecraft left for England and never saw Rowan again.

On reaching London she found that Imlay had been living with a young actress. She was distraught and tried to drown herself in the Thames. She slowly recovered and wrote to Rowan on a number of occasions. Her letters are frank and affectionate and make it clear that she regarded Rowan as a beloved friend and confidant. She eventually got over Imlay and married William Godwin in March 1797. In August Mary gave birth to a daughter, Mary Shelley, who became even more famous than her mother. Ten days later Mary Wollstonecraft was dead.

Godwin consoled himself by writing Mary's life story in such frank terms that he ruined her reputation for a few generations. When he acknowledged that Mary took particular 'gratification' in her relationship with Rowan, some reviewers chose to believe that this was code for suggesting that Wollstonecraft and Rowan were lovers. These reviewers were not sympathetic to Mary's views, and it suited their purpose to portray her as a 'loose woman'. Unluckily for Mary's reputation, William Godwin never wrote in code. Even by Godwin's very open and honest account, Mary had only four loves in her life, Fanny Blood, Henry Fuseli, Gilbert Imlay and Godwin. There is no basis for believing that in the case of Blood and Fuseli there was any sexual consummation.

Mary Wollstonecraft may have 'loved not wisely but too well'. Whether Mary Wollstonecraft and Rowan ever shared a warm bed during that frozen Paris winter is not relevant to our story. Rather, it is significant that the greatest radical English female of the eighteenth century befriended Archibald Hamilton Rowan when their spirits were at a low ebb, and each helped to steady the other's emotional and political nerves.

The End of Jackson

Sarah Rowan wrote to her husband regularly. Her letters gave him some satisfaction in that she reassured him that her earnest desire was that they should be reunited as a family. What she absolutely refused to do was give him any information regarding political affairs in Ireland, or the fate of Reverend Jackson, or his erstwhile comrades in the United Irishmen.

Jackson had languished in prison for over a year before being brought to trial. He had busied himself with writing a 'tedious' tract in defence of Christianity and in opposition to Thomas Paine's *Age of Reason*.[311] Tone had refused to testify against him, but Jackson was convicted mainly on the evidence of his friend, Cockayne. The case was adjourned for sentence, and a gallows was constructed outside Parliament House.[312] Everyone knew that Lord Clonmell would sentence him to death. Jackson 'deceived the senate', however, by taking arsenic and falling dead in the dock before sentence could be pronounced. Jonah Barrington witnessed the scene:

> [Jackson] was conducted into the usual place where prisoners stand to receive sentence … His limbs

---

311 Agnew, ii, p. 149.
312 *loc. cit.*

seemed to totter, and large drops of perspiration ran down his face. He was supposed to fear death and be in great terror. The judge began to announce sentence: the prisoner seemed to regard it but little appearing abstracted by internal agony. ... The sheriff on examination announced that the prisoner was too ill to hear his sentence. Meanwhile the wretched culprit continued to droop at length, his limbs gave way and he fell. Jackson had eluded his denouncers and was no more.[313]

Jackson, who came to Dublin as a secret agent, and was not, therefore, well known in the city, was given a splendid funeral, attended by several thousand people, including some Members of Parliament and barristers. Whether this was because Dublin was a cauldron of revolutionary and pro-French sentiment is impossible to say. It may have been that the drama of one man facing execution due to the treachery of an old friend had invoked public sympathy for Jackson.

Sarah felt no obligation to keep Rowan informed about Jackson, but she could not resist making disparaging reference to that wretch and arch-deceiver 'Mr T---'. She clearly believed that Wolfe Tone had led her husband and the family into misfortune, and he did not appear to be suffering any consequences himself. He had remained in Dublin for some time and had not been arrested or prosecuted. Sarah suspected that Tone had done a deal to save himself, probably to the detriment of her husband. William Drennan also suspected that a deal had been done, but saw it as an honourable triumph for Tone:

313 Barrington, p. 237.

Tone walks the streets I find, and therefore I suppose has secured himself by some negotiation of which I know nothing, but which I doubt not is honourable on his part, for I believe he would have suffered himself rather than be evidence against any poor unfortunate man, and as he stays here notwithstanding, he has certainly triumphed.[314]

Sarah did not believe that Tone was an honourable man. She did not want to know that it was her husband who had embroiled Tone in the affair and not the other way round. Tone's deal involved him and his family emigrating to America once the Jackson trial was over. Sarah had already embarked on a campaign to save her property, and her eventual success led her to seek to have her husband pardoned. She probably believed that their correspondence was being monitored, and at least she knew that she might choose to show copies of her own letters to those she was petitioning, particularly the Chancellor, Lord Clare. She was anxious to paint her husband as a reformed man who had been misled by bad companions, the chief of whom was Tone.

Tone's name had been mentioned in the indictment against Jackson and he was referred to frequently in the testimony.[315] Once the trial was over he could not long delay his departure for America. He left Dublin on 20 May for Belfast and took ship for America three weeks later. He and his family were 'treated royally' by the Belfast United Irishmen with excursions to the countryside and social gatherings involving much conviviality. Tone had decided

---

314 Agnew, ii, p. 148.
315 Bartlett (1998), p. xxix.

that he would not stay long in America, and confided his real destination to the Dublin and Belfast United Irishmen. A Belfast-based government spy told his employers that 'there is now here a Councillor Tone pretending to go to America ... his real design is to go to France'.[316]

By the spring of 1795 Rowan was 'much discontented with the distracted state of Paris'. He concluded that the French would be of no help to Ireland or any other country, and decided that he would try to escape to America. This was no straightforward matter as all ships travelling from France to the 'Asylum of Liberty' could expect to be searched and have both their cargo manifest and their passenger lists examined by the Royal Navy at sea. There was scarcely a British Naval officer who would not instantly recognize the name of Archibald Hamilton Rowan. The only question for an officer who would confront Rowan in such circumstances would be whether to bring him back to England or Ireland for trial and execution or to hang him from the yardarm as a rebel and a traitor.

With the help of Madgett, Rowan was given a false passport in the name of James Thompson. Rowan was also helped by James Monroe (1758-1831), a man whom George Washington had appointed as American ambassador to Paris the previous year. Monroe later became the fifth president of the United States of America. Washington felt that Monroe's well-known republicanism and support for the French Revolution would help to develop good relations between the countries. More recent scholarship suggests that Washington wanted Monroe out of the way so that he could conclude a treaty with the British in the absence of a staunch ally of the French.[317]

---

316 *Ibid.*
317 O'Brien (2009), p. 129.

Monroe and Rowan became close friends. The ambassador had recently secured Tom Paine's release from prison and was, at this point, nursing the very ill Paine back to health in the official residence. Monroe was anxious to help Rowan and gave him a message to deliver to Mr Randolph, the Secretary of State in Philadelphia. Randolph had only recently filled the position vacated by Thomas Jefferson. Monroe's message was designed to help Rowan with American allies he would meet on the way and to facilitate his acceptance into American society on his arrival. Monroe may have recommended the boarding house in Philadelphia, which Rowan used as a forwarding address. When Rowan landed in America, among the guests in his new abode were other future presidents: John Adams and Andrew Jackson.

Travelling through France at this time and crossing the Atlantic would be fraught with danger. In order to avoid meeting people in a 'diligence' where he would be asked questions about his destination and business, he decided to get to the coast on a sailing craft that he had recently bought in an auction of the effects of Philippé Égalité, who had been sent to the guillotine. Using the boat to get to the coast was a mistake. He was still within the city limits when an enthusiastic sans-culotte levelled a musket at him and forced him ashore. The drunken musketeer tried to grab hold of Rowan but staggered and fell into the Seine. Almost a hundred people surrounded Rowan, who insisted on him being brought to a nearby guard post to have his papers examined. The officer of the guard was happy to let him proceed, but the crowd was not, and they hauled him off to the mayor. The mayor decided that Rowan's papers were in order. When he returned to his craft he was astounded to see that none of his valuables had been touched, even though this was a time of food shortages and other hardships for the poor of Paris. He soon found that his mode of transport was creating suspicion among all who observed him from the riverbank, so he abandoned his boat and opted for a diligence. He visited some old friends at Rouen and stopped there for a few days, later arriving at Le Havre after a further day's journey.

The *Columbus* was the only ship in port that was bound for America. The captain, one John Dillon from Baltimore, told Rowan that his ship was full and that he had neither cabin nor berth to spare. Perhaps it was the captain's Irish name, or perhaps Rowan was desperate to depart France, but he revealed his real identity. Dillon immediately agreed to help, but warned Rowan that they would be stopped and questioned at sea by the British Navy. Dillon concocted some new bills under Rowan's assumed name of Thompson in order to reinforce the identity of an American merchant returning home.

They had only been at sea for two days when, as Dillon had predicted, they were confronted by a British frigate, the *Melampus*. The officer who led the boarding party, after examining the cargo, took a particular interest in 'Mr Thompson', and accosted him, saying 'Your name is Thompson, Sir. I understand this cargo belongs to you'. Rowan answered 'Only a part'.

When questioned about where he came from, Rowan said Charleston, of which he had some knowledge having visited that city during his student days. The officer then proceeded to ask general questions about the situation in France. When Rowan realized that the commander of the British vessel was his old chum from Cambridge, Sir John Borlase Warren, he prudently decided to retire to a cabin, staying there until the British allowed them to proceed.

The *Columbus* steered a northerly course to avoid Algerian pirates, whom they believed were being encouraged by the British to prey on American shipping. The voyage was long and tedious, and the lumbering *Columbus* made very slow progress, beset as it was by 'foul winds or calms'.[318]

Rowan often fretted, and had grown thin and suffered terribly with lumbago. He amused himself by translating pamphlets that he had brought with him from French into English. He wrote several letters to his wife, which, since he could not send them to her until he arrived at his destination, served as a memoir of a frustrating and discouraging voyage. He translated Madame Roland's speech before the Revolutionary Tribunal for Sarah. Madame Roland had been a committed republican who had sided with the Girondists and had gone to the guillotine in November 1793. On her way to execution as she passed a statue of the Goddess of Liberty she uttered the immortal words, 'Oh Liberty, what crimes are committed in Thy name'.

Rowan told Sarah that those twelve months in France had convinced him that neither reform nor revolution should be achieved by force. He told her:

> I have seen one faction rising over another and overturning it; each of them in their turn making a stalking-horse of the supreme power of the people, to cover public and private massacre and plunder; while every man of virtue and humanity shuddered in a disgraceful silence.[319]

On 28 June they happened upon a floundering whaler that had been abandoned by its crew. There was no sign of the crew or any lifeboats. As the whaler began to go under all the passengers went up on deck to observe the scene. Rowan

---

318 Drummond, p. 268.
319 Nicolson, p. 159.

was much affected as he was convinced that the crew had not survived. He went below deck to pray to his 'Omnipotent Being', and he resolved there and then that whatever the future held for him and his family he would never ask them to face the dangers of crossing the Atlantic Ocean.

As they came closer to their destination, the threat from the Algerians receded only to be replaced with a fear of pirates from Bermuda under the British flag, or even British privateers. They met a vessel that warned them that a ship under the British flag and British protection had plundered a brig out of Charleston. Rowan wondered:

> When will nations learn better conduct? Or when will the same morality which is the guide of individuals become the rule of nations?[320]

On 15 July they met a pilot boat at the mouth of the Delaware River, and with a fair wind and land on both sides of them they proceeded towards Philadelphia. On 17 July 1795 Archibald Hamilton Rowan stepped ashore in America.

---

320 Drummond, p. 279.

13.
Party Rage in the Land of Liberty

When he reached his boarding house in Philadelphia, Rowan was delighted to find that a parcel sent by Sarah from Ireland had arrived before him. He immediately wrote to thank her and to inform her of his safe arrival. He was particularly pleased that Sarah's picture had survived, though the glass was slightly damaged. However, he made an embarrassing faux pas when he thanked her for enclosing a lock of grey hair that he supposed to be that of his father. In Sarah's next letter she wrote, with understandable irritation, that 'a few days after we parted several hairs whiter than age almost ever makes them appeared on my forehead ... occasioned by sorrow'.[321] It was her hair that had gone grey.

Rowan was received in Philadelphia with 'great kindnesses'. The 'references and recommendations' provided by James Monroe helped him to gain acceptance into society. Mathew Carey, an Irish journalist based in Philadelphia, told

---

321 *Ibid.*, p. 288.

a friend in Dublin that 'there are in this country thousands of kindly souls who sympathize in his suffering'.[322]

The boarding house where he lodged was a haunt of Philadelphia's and America's political elite. It was also the haunt of British agents, but it took some time for this to become obvious to Rowan. John Adams (then serving vice president and future president) and Andrew Jackson (another future president) were not the only notables whom Rowan got to know quickly after his arrival. He dined with members of Congress, such as Carlow-born Major Butler from Carolina, and went hunting with the State Governor, Thomas Mifflin. Rowan was particularly pleased to make the acquaintance of Senator John Dickson, whose 'political character is well known and the sacrifices he has made in the cause of liberty have been very great'.[323] Dickson was a Quaker from Delaware who had fought in the Revolutionary War and had freed his slaves on a point of principle.

Caesar Augustus Rodney, a young republican lawyer, later to be Attorney General of the United States, became a close friend. Rodney's uncle, who died in 1784, had signed the Declaration of Independence. Many of the men and their families whom Rowan was now befriending had, a few years earlier, played their part in the defeat of the British and had established the first republic in the modern world.

It has been claimed that Rowan received a letter of welcome from President George Washington. The president was said to have complimented Rowan 'on his arrival in an asylum in which the Rights of Man created no alarm but were practically enforced and supported by the government'.[324]

This is unlikely for two reasons. Firstly, Rowan records that he thought about waiting on the president but changed

---

322 Bric (2008), p. 219.
323 *loc. cit.*
324 *Ibid.*, p. 217.

his mind when he heard that Washington had declined to meet Tallyrand.[325] Secondly, Washington had recently sponsored a deal with the British that became known as Jay's Treaty. The terms of the treaty became public knowledge and caused a furore just as Rowan arrived in Philadelphia. This treaty was regarded by its opponents as a sell-out to British monarchism and a stab in the back to republican France. While Washington was courting the British and annoying the French he was unlikely to go out of his way to welcome a high-profile pro-French fugitive from British justice such as Archibald Hamilton Rowan.

Federalists and Republicans

Jay's Treaty was just the most recent manifestation of a dispute between Washington and his allies, such as John Adams and Alexander Hamilton, and their more radical republican colleagues, Thomas Jefferson, John Madison and James Monroe. What was at stake was the future direction of the nation they had so recently brought into existence. Washington and his partisans believed that the new republic should be ruled by an educated political elite who should be above the vagaries of shifting public opinion. The Jefferson republicans believed that politicians should be elected by the people and do what the people demanded. This infant democracy had not yet settled questions such as whether the opposition had a right to criticize an elected administration or whether such criticism was treason or free speech, sedition or good democratic practice.

The federalist–republican divide appeared to Rowan as 'the rage of party' he had witnessed in France and which left him so disillusioned with the French Revolution. He

---

325 Drummond, p. 279.

accepted that the (American) Revolution had done amazing good, but was dismayed at the level of abuse of reformers.[326] Almost nobody realized at the time that what America was experiencing was the birth of the political party system that would eventually come to be seen as an essential, if regrettable, element of parliamentary democracy.

One aspect of this conflict was to pose serious difficulties for Rowan throughout his time in America. Washington and his party, who became known as 'federalists', were quickly becoming hostile to republican exiles from Europe. The federalists were convinced that these malcontents would throw their considerable skills of agitation and revolutionary energies behind Jefferson and the American republicans. As events unfolded the federalists were proven right: many of the United Irishmen who fled Ireland before and after the 1798 rebellion became hugely influential in Jefferson's republican faction, which eventually developed into the Democratic Party. Even before Rowan's arrival the laws had been changed to make it difficult for refugees from Europe to gain citizenship of the United States.

The Jay's Treaty contest was a gloves-off affair, and Rowan knew well that he would be caught up in it at his peril. He tried to keep his mouth shut on all except the most general of topics. He feared that as an alien fugitive he might fall victim to the ever-growing body of repressive laws introduced by the federalists to weaken their republican opponents.

Within two weeks of his arrival Rowan had a reunion with his three old friends 'and brother exiles', Theobald Wolfe Tone, James Napper Tandy and Dr James Reynolds. Wolfe Tone had arrived with his family in Philadelphia in early

---

326 *Ibid.*, p. 296.

August and moved into the boarding house.[327] Reynolds
had lived in Rowan's Dublin house after his release from
Kilmainham in 1794; the last time the pair had met was in
Rowan's cell at Newgate. Reynolds had sailed from Belfast
on the *Swift* (Belfast to Newcastle and New York) at about
the time when Rowan fled Ireland.[328] Reynolds had been
about to be arrested for treason having been implicated in
the Jackson plot. William Cobbett (1753–1835), who wrote
under the pseudonym 'Peter Porcupine', a pro-federalist
journalist who had no great regard for truth, claimed that
Reynolds had got his revenge on the British government by
'assisting at the hanging of George III in effigy from the
yardarm' of the *Swift*.

Reynolds was already well established in Philadelphia
and very active in the anti-federalist camp and the agitation
against Jay's Treaty. Rowan observed that Reynolds was as
busy, as sincere and as zealous as he was in Kilmainham.[329]
Tandy was resident in the lodging house when Rowan
arrived, having jumped bail in Ireland in 1793. Tandy had
avoided any public comment on the Jay's Treaty dispute
because he felt that 'as an alien it would be ungrateful in me
to take any active part in politics' in the country that had
given him refuge.[330]

Tone remembers the reunion as a 'singular encounter ...
our several escapes from an ignominious death seemed little
short of a miracle'.[331] Fourteen months after they had first
discussed the Jackson plot in a prison cell at Newgate, Tone,
Reynolds and Rowan renewed their discussion of a French
invasion of Ireland in the Philadelphia boarding house. It was

327 Nicolson, p. 160.
328 Bric, p. 219.
329 Drummond, p. 283.
330 Wilson, p. 38.
331 *Ibid.*, p. 37.

not long before news of the reunion filtered back to Ireland. It may be that Tandy mentioned the meeting in correspondence to his son, but Leonard McNally, the informer, told the Chief Secretary:

> A kind of seditious convention is now forming in America, composed of Hamilton Rowan, Napper Tandy, Doctor Reynolds and other fugitives from Ireland. These men have in their power and it is no doubt their wish to give every possible assistance and information to France.[332]

When Sarah Rowan became aware that Tone was on his way to America she had written to her husband warning him 'to avoid all connection with the arch deceiver'. However, within a few short weeks she had softened somewhat, and advised him that while he need not totally shun Tone, he should not make him a constant companion.[333] Perhaps the reason for her change of heart was that until Jackson came to trial she believed that Tone had betrayed her husband. Once the trial was over, though, it was clear to everyone that Tone was not the sort of man who would betray a friend to save himself, even if that friend had gambled recklessly with both of their lives.

It is obvious that Tone was influenced by Reynolds's attitude to Jay's Treaty, for within a short time he was writing to his dear friend Thomas Russell in Ireland, giving this assessment of the dispute:

> We are splitting here fast into two great parties, the rich and the poor. I mean poor relatively, for as to

---

332 *Ibid.*, p. 154.
333 Drummond, p. 287.

absolute poverty, there seems to me to be no such thing in America. The treaty with England is the question on which they are now at issue, but in fact it is but a text. The real state is Aristocracy against Democracy … against the weight of property and government influence Democracy is daily making ground.[334]

Unlike Reynolds, however, Tone had no intention of becoming directly involved in American politics; he did not intend to stay in the country any longer than was absolutely necessary.

Tone was anxious to get to France, and Rowan was to prove very useful in this regard. Both men were aware that Philadelphia was thronged with British agents and that they kept their public contact to a minimum. Tone feared that someone would tell the British; no doubt Rowan feared that someone would tell Sarah. Rowan was well known to Adet, the French ambassador, but Tone 'firmly quashed the suggestion they should make a joint approach to the French minister'.[335] Nonetheless, when Tone approached Adet as a vouched friend of Rowan, he could be sure of getting a hearing. Rowan also provided Tone with introductions to James Monroe and Nicolas Madgett in Paris. Madgett kept in contact with Rowan and wrote to him in January 1796, suggesting that Tone should come over to Paris instantly to confer with the French government.[336] The following month Tone arrived in France and met Madgett and Monroe, both of whom made a point of asking warmly after Rowan.

---

334 Moody, et al, (2001), p. 12.
335 Bartlett (1998), p. xxxi.
336 *loc. cit.*.

William Cobbett and Joseph Priestley

Philadelphia had become 'irksome' to Rowan. The house he was living in was 'crowded by captains of ships and English riders, each more impertinently inquisitive than the other'. A short time after his arrival he went to a town meeting held in the garden of the courthouse. The purpose of the meeting was to discuss Jay's Treaty. He was curious to see 'a popular assembly in the New World'. Wilson described what happened:

> One of the speakers was Blair McClenachan, a populist democrat and a wealthy merchant from Londonderry who had made his fortune in the flaxseed trade, and who had been described back in 1788 as 'the most violent anti-foederalist [*sic*] in America'. [He] whipped up anti-British emotions by requesting 'three cheers for the persecuted patriot Hamilton Rowan' throwing a copy of the treaty into the crowd and recommending that they 'kick the damned treaty to hell'.[337]

This incident was widely reported in the papers. William Cobbett took particular notice, and ensured that the matter would come back to haunt Rowan nearly three years later.

William Cobbett was a very dangerous, vindictive and unscrupulous journalist. He was born in Surrey and had been a sergeant major in the British Army. He arrived in America in 1792, and quickly made a name for himself as an advocate of the British Tory and American Federalist causes. One writer has said of him:

337 Wilson, p. 41.

Cobbett was in the flesh a bare-knuckled go for broke political gladiator, perennially struggling to change the mass beliefs of humankind. He was the type of man whose emotions fattened until they became intolerable.[338]

Cobbett was devoid of fear, and did not care who he offended. In Philadelphia, the birthplace of American republican democracy, Cobbett 'opened a print shop decorated with portraits of George III'. 'Peter Porcupine' derided the notion of democracy as 'the despotism of the many over the few' and described the recently deceased secular saint of Philadelphia, Benjamin Franklin, as 'a hypocrite, a whore-master and an infidel'.[339]

In early 1798 Cobbett suggested that Rowan, rather than being grateful to the government of the United States for allowing him to remain in their country as a fugitive, was prepared to allow himself to be used by the enemies of the government in its attacks on the administration. He went further, suggesting that, as a United Irishman, Rowan was a member of an oath-bound society that was in league with the French to overturn the government of the United States.

However, back in 1795, Cobbett had bigger fish to fry than Rowan. He therefore bided his time. The target of Cobbett's spleen and invective in 1795 was none other than Dr Joseph Priestley. Priestley had sailed from England on 8 April 1794 and arrived in America to a rapturous reception from Philadelphia republicans in early June. Cobbett published a series of vitriolic attacks branding the inoffensive, scholarly clergyman as a traitor, a republican

---

338 Nelson (2006), p. 2.
339 *Ibid.*, p. 5.

and a pro-French revolutionary extremist. He was anxious to refute the claims of Priestley's admirers that the doctor had been forced to leave England as a result of being persecuted by the government.

On Bastille Day 1791, a Birmingham mob had rioted for three days. They had burnt Priestley's home, laboratory and two Unitarian meeting houses. Their real target was Priestley himself, and they would have murdered him had he not made his escape. His crime was to infuriate this so-called 'Church and King Mob' by allegedly holding a dinner to celebrate the fall of the Bastille.

England had become a very dangerous place for Priestley in the three years since the riots. He had initially gone to London, but the Tory press continued to hound him. Throughout 1792 he and Tom Paine were being burnt in effigy by 'Church and King' mobs in several English cities. As the pressure mounted on both men, Paine was first to flee. In September, after dinner at Joseph Johnson's, William Blake warned Paine: 'You must not go home or you are a dead man'.[340] Paine left England for France that very night, never to return.

Priestley was now the most high-profile of the government's targets remaining in England. In early 1793, as war broke out between England and France, his position was becoming intolerable. When his plans to leave for America became widely known, William Drennan observed:

> the emigration will be a historical fact that will tell against England the longest day it has to live and I question if he could do so much service to the cause for which he suffers in any way by this action. Indeed if there is an invasion of England he would

---

340 *Ibid.*, p. 5.

probably be murdered and it is therefore the highest prudence to go off in time.[341]

It is unlikely that William Drennan had an inkling of what the British government knew. Just as Drennan was sympathizing with Priestley's plight, Jackson, the French agent, was flitting around London accompanied by Cockayne, the government spy. Jackson's handlers had instructed him to interview Priestley, among others, and he was in possession of a letter of introduction from Priestley's disciple, John Hurtford Stone. A number of Priestley's known associates had been compromised, including Benjamin Vaughan MP.

Just three weeks after he set sail the government began a round-up of democrats in London, and Thomas Hardy, John Horne Tooke and John Thelwall were dragged to the Tower. Although the three had not been involved with Jackson, the government felt that the climate was such that they could hang them on charges of treason. If Priestley had remained in England he would almost certainly have joined them in the Tower and in the dock.

When Priestly arrived in America he was offered a post at the University of Pennsylvania, but decided to move to Northumberland, a remote region of the state. He chose Pennsylvania because it was free from the curse of slavery. Living quietly in the backwoods did not save Priestley from Cobbett's invective. Cobbett published a pamphlet, *Observations on the Emigration of Dr Joseph Priestley*, which accused the doctor of treason against Britain and attempted to undermine his scientific credibility. Cobbett ridiculed Priestley's claim that he had not been protected by the British government. Had not two of the rioters who burnt

---

341 Agnew, ii, p. 33.

down Priestley home, laboratory, library and chapel been hanged?

> Would nothing satisfy him but the blood of the whole mob? Did he wish to see the town of Birmingham … razed and all its industries and inhabitants butchered; because some of them had been carried to commit unlawful excesses from their detestation of his wicked projects?[342]

Cobbett never disagreed without being disagreeable. Indeed, he took pleasure in gratuitous abuse. He declared:

> I hope to see the malignant old Tartuffe [charlatan] of Northumberland begging his bread through the streets of Philadelphia, and ending his days in a poorhouse, without a friend to close his eyes.[343]

We shall see later that Cobbett was prone to wishing a lonely and miserable death in poverty for those he chose to make his targets. When Sarah Rowan was hesitating about joining her husband in America she regarded the prospect of living near Priestley to be an inducement, highly respecting his 'Christian doctrine and scientific knowledge'. She doubted, however, that she would 'go to a country where a paragraph so vulgar and inhuman [as Cobbett's] could be tolerated'.[344]

Cobbett succeeded in making Priestley's first few years in America very uncomfortable. It was not until Priestley's good friend and admirer Thomas Jefferson became president in 1800 that Priestley felt welcome and safe in the United States.

---

342 Ingrams (2005), p. 25.
343 Drummond, p. 347.
344 *loc. cit.*

Despite the curse of Cobbett, Priestley did not die friendless in a poorhouse in Philadelphia. He died in peaceful comfort in Northumberland in 1804 surrounded by his family and friends. His eyes were closed by the friendly hand of John Binns, the Dublin-born United Irishman and one-time leader of the London Corresponding Society.

Avoiding Politics in America

Back in the winter of 1795, much to Rowan's discomfort, rumours were circulated about him, with 'some malignant spirits' claiming that he was agitating politics. These rumours reached the ears of Governor Mifflin. On one occasion Rowan heard two gentlemen talking about him giving different versions of the reception he received in France and both claiming to have received their information from other persons who had first heard it from Archibald Hamilton Rowan himself. Numerous accounts of his sayings and doings in America were published both by 'his enemies and his mistaken friends'.[345] When Rowan asked Sarah to pass on a letter of his to Samuel Neilson, the editor of the *Northern Star*, she refused because she surmised that Neilson would publish it in the paper. This was the last sort of publicity that Rowan needed either in Ireland or America.

Sarah was fighting a campaign to protect the family property from confiscation, and she needed to be able to portray her husband as a man who had been misled by others and who had now learnt the error of his ways. She strongly advised him that nature did not intend him to be a public character and that it would be highly improper for him to be one in his current circumstances. She suggested to him that

---

345 Drummond, p. 306.

he would be better off with Priestley in Northumberland than in Philadelphia with Tone and Reynolds. She upbraided him for not using his own understanding sufficiently and suggested that he caught his opinions and ideas from those immediately about him.[346] This charge wounded him; much as he tried to avoid any conflict with Sarah, he felt obliged to refute that criticism. He told her in his next letter:

> As to my sentiments they have been always nearly the same, as far as I can remember. The fact is that from education and principle I was led to assert and to attempt to support a reform of Parliament and the equal liberty of all religious sects. [My] Association[s] may have, and certainly did lead me more into active life than I wished, was fit for or will ever, in any case this side of eternity, fall into again.[347]

In the years that followed, Rowan was prepared to apologize for his actions, but he never disowned his opinions or sought to shift the blame for his actions onto his friends.

Some of the stories that appeared in America reached the ears of his family, and Rowan was anxious that Sarah would not think he was undermining their chances of retaining their property. He felt that the involvement in American politics of some of his fellow United Irish fugitives was imprudent and had the potential to damage both him and themselves.[348] He moved to Wilmington, Delaware, thirty miles outside Philadelphia, in an attempt to escape the limelight and the unwanted attention. A schoolteacher forged a document in Rowan's name urging British sailors to desert in American ports. Some thirty or forty people who

---

346 *Ibid.*, p. 289.
347 *Ibid.*, p. 290.
348 *Ibid.*, p. 306.

claimed to have deserted were alleged to carry certificates in Rowan's handwriting.[349] Luckily, a gentleman from Maryland who was familiar with Rowan's handwriting was able to expose the plot.

Some of his friends had urged him to stay in Philadelphia, others encouraged him to settle on a farm or plantation. Major Butler made him an offer of 2,000 acres of unsettled land on very generous terms.[350] None of these options appealed to him, and he told Sarah:

> I will go into the woods, but I will not kill Indians or keep slaves. Good God! If you heard some of the Georgians or Kentucky people talk of killing the natives! Cortes and all that followed him were not more sanguinary in the South than they would be in North America.[351]

Meanwhile, the controversy over Jay's Treaty continued to inflame passions, and Federalists were becoming increasingly hostile to exiles such as Priestley and Rowan. As increasing numbers of United Irishmen were arriving in America, Cobbett and other Federalist journalists began to turn their invective on them. One commentator said of the new Irish arrivals that 'they are United Irishmen, Freemasons and the most God-provoking Democrats this side of hell'.[352] If the references to God-provoking and hell are a bit over the top, the rest is fair comment as most United Irishmen, including Rowan, were democrats and had long associations with Freemasonry. Cobbett claimed that the United Irishmen were plotting with the French and that 'the name Irishman

349 *Ibid.*, p. 299.
350 *Ibid.*, p. 291.
351 *Ibid.*, p. 291.
352 Bric, p. 229.

is become, and not without reason, detestable in the ears of Americans'.[353]

In Wilmington, Rowan found the youth 'ill-behaved and ill-natured', and observed that 'they do not improve when they come to be men'.[354] He resented the way in which they would intrude into another person's business without having any intention of helping them or being of service. He indulged in his old boating passion by buying a craft, but complained that he had a very long hike from his new home to the river. He was also much annoyed by the way everyone used his boat as if it were their own. On one occasion a neighbour asked to borrow the boat but thought that Rowan should clean it out for him first.

Sarah and Lord Clare

When Rowan settled in Wilmington in early 1796 he was in a very precarious financial position. At the time of his escape from Newgate his income was £8,000 per year. However, a sentence of outlawry had been passed on him that entitled the government to confiscate his entire fortune. Sarah and the children could have been cast out of Rathcoffey and their house in Dominick Street. It seems, though, that from the beginning the Chancellor, Lord Clare, pitied Sarah. William Drennan had labelled Clare a bouncing bully, and Rowan had challenged the chancellor on behalf of Simon Butler. Even so, Clare must have had a generous side to his nature. He had allowed Tone to go to America rather than stand trial for treason over the Jackson affair. He seems also to have regarded Rowan as being 'trepanned at the time of the

---

353 Bric, p. 231.
354 *Ibid.*, p. 294.

Jackson episode' and to have been 'more sinned against than sinning'.[355]

Sarah and her children were a well-known and respected family in Dublin, and to have reduced them to penury for the sins of the father would have seemed very harsh. However, the passions that flared up in Ireland as the country slid into rebellion and retribution in 1798 were such that Lord Clare must be given credit for protecting Sarah and her children. For his part, Rowan always acknowledged that his conduct had given the administration all the excuse it needed to destroy his family. Lord Clare always forbore from doing so. Sarah would work long and hard on the better side of Lord Clare's nature, and in due course he would play a significant role in her husband's eventual pardon and return to Killyleagh.

For the present, Lord Clare allowed Sarah to collect whatever rents she could extract from her tenants. It was some considerable time before the family had their property re-granted to them, but Sarah could give the children the best education Dublin could afford. She could also send small sums from time to time to her husband at Wilmington.

Rowan was determined not to live off his friends, and at first did the most menial forms of manual labour to earn his keep. He lodged for a while with Mr Armour and worked in his garden for the wages of a day labourer.[356] He then tried his hand at brewing beer. Sarah was acutely embarrassed and complained that every captain of a ship from Philadelphia and Wilmington fills Dublin 'with accounts of you drawing beer, flour etc. which gives fresh food for scandal against me'.[357] Rowan replied 'in abject dependence I will not live while I can clean boots in an alley'.[358]

---

355 Nicolson, p. 165.
356 *Ibid.*, p. 167.
357 Drummond, p. 337.
358 Nicolson, p. 166.

However difficult his financial affairs were, and however lonely he was for his family, Rowan did not lack friends at Wilmington. His friend John Dickson had his residence there. Dr Logan, a cousin of Dickson, was an influential man among the republicans and he and Caesar Rodney also lived in or near Wilmington. Rowan was anxious not to associate only with the Jefferson republicans, and a Mr Bayard, a Federalist member of Congress, and Dr Tilton, an eminent physician, also formed part of his circle.

John Adams, the Federalist candidate, narrowly beat Thomas Jefferson in the presidential election of 1797. Among several pieces of legislation introduced to weaken the republicans and intimidate their foreign-born supporters was the Alien Friends Act. This Act authorized the president to deport any non-citizen suspected of plotting against the government, whether during wartime or peacetime. This law could have resulted in the mass expulsion of new immigrants. The Act was limited to two years, and no alien was ever deported under it, but it was a cause of great concern to Rowan. He knew that if he were deported to Ireland in the deteriorating climate leading to the 1798 rebellion he would have faced execution. Sarah Rowan felt that even if her husband departed America voluntarily at this point, the American government would tip off the English or their allies and he would be taken at sea with consequences 'too horrid to rest on'.[359] Rowan wrote to Timothy Pickering, the Secretary of State, anxiously enquiring about the destination of anyone who might be deported. He received no reply.[360] Rowan feared that the Federalist government would prove to be even more ruthless than the British, telling Sarah:

359 Drummond, p. 336.
360 Wilson, p. 51.

Over and over again do I say, if I am to live under
the lash of arbitrary power, at least let the whip be
the hands of those accustomed to use it, not picked
by a foot passenger who, unaccustomed to ride,
keeps flogging every post and rail he comes near,
pleased to hear how he can smack the whip. O
upstart aristocracy, what a fiend art thou![361]

Rowan was very disappointed with the contrast between the
theory of republican liberty that he and his fellow United
Irishmen espoused and the reality of life in the new America.
He was bemused that the great republicans of Virginia such
as Jefferson insisted on keeping their slaves. Rather than the
selfless pursuit of virtue, public good and happiness, Rowan
felt that Americans were in relentless pursuit of the dollar. He
bemoaned the 'pride of wealth and ignorance' that pervaded
American society. Wolfe Tone had very similar views. Both
recognized that the miserable poverty they had seen at home
was not known in America.

Tone described Americans as 'a churlish, unsocial race,
totally absorbed in making money'. Rowan saw America as
'a heaven for the poor and industrious; but a hell compared
to any other part of Europe for any other rank of society'.[362]
The great republican thinkers had believed that free citizens
of the republic would practise virtue and give selfless public
service to their societies. They would be paragons of culture,
promote scientific knowledge and show benevolence and
tolerance to their fellow man. The self-interested pursuit
of commercial gain came as a very unwelcome surprise
to Rowan, and he worried that it would sharpen class
antagonism.[363]

361 *loc. cit.*
362 *Ibid.*, p. 292.
363 Wilson, p. 6.

Rowan concluded that revolutions:

> Are effected by a cooperation of the benevolent and
> ambitious against the rich and the corrupt. As soon
> as the revolution is consolidated, those who were
> benevolent become corrupt from power and the
> ambitious make them their prey, and in their turn
> fall before a new collation.[364]

Rowan also felt that the struggle for democracy was
bedevilled by the fact that:

> Many who enlist under its banners are in fact
> aristocrats – many have no principles – many who
> wish only to lead dissolute lives, free from censure,
> and these commonly making the greatest noise, they
> obstruct the progress of truth and bring shame and
> trouble on those who are virtuous and sincere.[365]

Rowan was determined to keep a low profile in Wilmington.
However, his deep sympathy for suffering people was so
strong that he could not always restrain himself. Bric tells us:

> In August 1796 … he was so touched by the fact
> that forty passengers had died on the ship *Harriot*
> en route from Ireland to America, that thirty-six
> had been impressed, and that several others had
> arrived 'sick' that he used the upmost exertions in
> procuring accommodations for the relief of those
> distressed Irish emigrants.[366]

---

364 Drummond, p. 342.
365 *Ibid.*, p. 363.
366 Bric, p. 219.

He was also deeply concerned for the 'swarms of Irish' who were arriving in Philadelphia as indentured servants and 'bemoaned the brisk trade in Irish slaves'.[367]

> He was surprised that many members of the newly formed Society for the Abolition of the Slave Trade have not the least objection to buying an Irishman or a Dutchman, and will chaffer with himself or the captain to get him indented at about the eight part of the wages they would have to pay a country born. But to tell the truth they who are thus purchased generally do themselves justice and run away before half their time is up.[368]

On 10 February 1797 Rowan received a letter from Thomas Muir, whom he had last seen in the Tollbooth in Edinburgh in October 1794. Muir had some distressing news of the other Scottish democrats who had entertained Rowan and Simon Butler on that visit to Scotland. Muir told Rowan, 'I left Gerald in his last agonies; Palmer will not live; you would not know Skirving: and the state of Margarot's health is far from being firm'. Muir described his escape from the penal colonies of New South Wales and how after 'danger extreme' he arrived in New Spain and across the continent to Vera Cruz. From there he reached Havana, from where he wrote to Rowan on 3 December. He begged Rowan to write to his father, Thomas Muir, at Glasgow, and Rowan asked Sarah to arrange for someone to do so. At Havana Muir was made a prisoner by the Spanish. The French government convinced the Spanish to release Muir into their custody, but he was horribly wounded by a British cannonball onboard the ship

---

367 *loc. cit.*
368 Drummond, p. 318.

taking him to France. His jaw was shattered and he lost most of the sight in both eyes. Thomas Muir never recovered from his wounds and he died in Paris on 26 January 1799.

Muir's pessimistic assessment of the prospects of his comrades proved for the most part to be justified, for only Margarot made it back to Britain alive. In 1813 Margarot wrote to Rowan, twenty years after their one brief meeting in Edinburgh. He was in penury while Rowan was by now comfortably settled in Killyleagh. Rowan immediately sent 'his fellow sufferer in a common cause' the sum of £100.

Just as Muir's letter arrived in early 1797, Rowan took up an opportunity to go into business. Two Englishmen by the name of Jordan had emigrated from Manchester and set up a calico printing works on the Brandywine River about half a mile from Wilmington. When they became bankrupt they were left with a very well-equipped plant lying idle. William Poole, a wealthy Delaware Quaker and anti-slavery activist, urged Rowan to take over the business with the words: 'Friend Archibald, thou sayest that thou shouldest wish to settle among us, and have something to do: why shouldest thou not purchase these works?' Rowan was reluctant to ask Sarah to part with so much money when things were hard at home, but Poole was, among other occupations, a banker, and he agreed to extend credit until the works turned a profit. Rowan informed his prospective customers

It was once Hamilton Rowan Esquire,
Now it's a calico printer and dyer.

The business never really took off, however, due to the yellow fever epidemic that raged in Philadelphia and because of unfair business practices by the competition, who imported calicoes from Britain. In time, Rowan was forced to close it down at a considerable loss, his life as an entrepreneur having lasted for only two years. It is not clear how much in total this venture cost him, but he lost $500 when he sold his excess stock alone. He advertised the auction of the business with typical integrity:

> Any person inclined to sacrifice his property by carrying on the manufactory in America may have the whole for one half the sum they cost and immediate possession given.[369]

---

369 Drummond, p. 314.

14.

The Needle of Peter Porcupine

As he tried to make a living in America, Rowan was very conscious of the deteriorating political situation in Ireland. He believed that the suppression of the United Irishmen might lead Ireland into leaderless and bloody rebellion. He wrote to Sarah, saying:

> I wish you out of Ireland; I dread the moment when ignorance and despair, without anyone to appease or keep down the storm, may burst from their shackles.[370]

In December 1796, Wolfe Tone and a French fleet were enduring hurricane-force winds in Bantry Bay on the west Cork coast. Rumours abounded that Archibald Hamilton Rowan was on board. Sarah was in England on business, and she arrived in Chester on 31 December 1796. The mayor and some officials went to her lodging house and asked if she knew the French were at Bantry and if her husband was with them. She replied

---

370 Drummond, p. 292.

that she could prove that her husband was in America, but they demanded to examine her correspondence for evidence of treason nonetheless. She denied that she had any treasonable papers, but insisted that some of her letters were private and she would not allow the mayor to see them. She was prepared to show them to General Johnston, the commander of the Chester Garrison. When General Johnston saw Sarah's letters he apologized for all the trouble she had been given and Sarah was allowed to go on her way without further molestation.[371]

This incident had a fortunate consequence when Sarah reported it to Richard Griffith, a family friend and neighbour. Griffith lived at Millicent, about five miles from Rathcoffey. He was a liberal supporter of Catholic emancipation and had been a close friend to Rowan before Rowan's departure from Ireland. Griffith was an advocate of political reform, but as Ireland moved closer to rebellion he took command of the Kildare yeomanry and helped to put down the rebellion in Kildare in June 1798. However, his loyalty and commitment to Rowan was in no way altered by his stance on the rebellion.

Griffith called on Lord Clare in Dublin. He provided the chancellor with a copy of a letter Rowan had sent to Sarah, dated 14 August 1796. Griffith later advised that it would be very helpful if Rowan could get a sworn document by a noted magistrate to the effect that he was in America on Christmas Day 1796. Rowan said that he would try to get such a document, but the people with whom he was associating at this time were Quakers and disliked oath-taking. He said, 'Mr Dickson, the first character in the State is of the Society of Friends. I wish there was a society of rational Quakers and I would join them'.[372]

---

371 *loc. cit.*
372 *Ibid.*, p. 305.

The chancellor suggested to Griffith that Rowan should sign a petition addressed to his Majesty that might be the means of obtaining a free pardon once peace was made. Griffith immediately sent a draft urging Rowan to lose no time in signing and returning it.

Had Rowan signed the petition he would have accepted that his behaviour in Ireland had been 'misguided'. He would have admitted that he had been 'abashed and confounded' when he fled from the justice of his country, but claimed that his time in France had fully convinced him of the errors of his ways. In America he had reflected on 'the folly and turpitude of his conduct and was prepared to publicly confess his guilt'. He would have:

> humbly implored his Majesty to accept the deep contrition of a heart truly penitent for past errors and fraught with the warmest attachment to the British constitution and to your Majesty's person and government.[373]

Rowan knew that Sarah would be furious with him for not grasping this opportunity, so he went some length to explain his position to her:

> I never will sign any petition or declaration in favour of the British constitution in Ireland which embraces such flagrant abuses as I have witnessed, and of which I have been in some measure the victim; ... I would have promised a perfect quiescence under the present government, and should have been sincerely grateful to those who had it in their power to crush my family through me, yet forbore. But my opinions were not

---

373 *loc. cit.*

hastily adopted; they were neither the result of pride, nor of ambition, nor of vanity; they were the result of the most mature reflection of which I was capable: they cannot alter; and though I might desist from acting on them I never will disown them ... [If I] may be enabled to make over my fortune to you and the children, you should consult your friends upon what mode would be best for you to pursue, for I am determined.[374]

Although for the present Sarah's hopes of a free pardon were shelved, significant progress had been made. The chancellor was becoming convinced that Rowan was no longer involved in politics. 'He evinced a cordial sympathy' for Sarah and began advising her on how to handle matters in such a way which would eventually lead to 'the accomplishment of her wishes'.[375]

Twelve months later, however, things took a major turn for the worse thanks to William Cobbett. The public meeting at which McClenachan made the outburst that attracted Cobbett's ire took place shortly after Rowan arrived in Philadelphia, which implies that the meeting was in the latter part of 1795. Cobbett revived memories of the incident when he attacked Rowan in an article dated 17 February 1798. The *Baltimore Federal Gazette* had a few days previously contained the following item:

> On Sunday here arrived from Wilmington, on a short visit, that persecuted patriot and warm assertor of the civil and religious rights of mankind, Mr Archibald Hamilton Rowan.

Rowan claims that he visited Baltimore for the purpose of meeting his 'worthy and esteemed friend H. J.'[376] This

---

374 Drummond, p. 354.
375 *loc. cit.*
376 Drummond, p. 326.

is likely a reference to Henry Jackson, his fellow United Irishman. Jackson was a wealthy iron-founder who had been at the heart of the United Irish conspiracy in Dublin along with his son-in-law, Oliver 'Cromwell' Bond. If 'H. J.' does refer to Henry Jackson, however, then Rowan is confused about his dates. Henry Jackson did not escape to Baltimore until 1799.[377] His son-in-law, Oliver Bond, had died in mysterious circumstances in his cell at Kilmainham in July of the previous year.[378]

One way or another, Cobbett responded to the *Gazette*'s tribute to Rowan in his usual scurrilous terms:

What could ... any sans-culotte scoundrel say more? This Rowan is known to have escaped from the hands of justice in his own country, and to have fled to France; he is known to have been one of those men who have caused the convulsions in Ireland, with all their fatal consequences; he is known to be an apostle of those abominable principles which have deluged Europe with blood and which it is every man's object to keep far from this country. [...] He is known to have joined the Jacobin anti-federal faction here from the moment of his landing. It is notorious he was introduced to and welcomed at an anti-federal meeting who gave three cheers for Rowan and another three for kicking the treaty to hell. And it is notorious that all his friends and associates are men who act as if they had bound themselves by an oath to overthrow and destroy the federal government.[379]

---

377 Wilson, p. 60.
378 Whelan, p. 243.
379 Drummond, p. 327.

Cobbett is here accusing Rowan of associating with an oath-bound group attempting to overthrow the American government. Even if this accusation were untrue, it remained dangerous to Rowan. More than the fact that this was calculated to make his position as an alien precarious, he feared that the British newspapers might pick it up and that Sarah would be furious with him.

Rowan wrote to Cobbett on 20 February 1798:

> Sir,
> Soon after my arrival in America, whither I had fled confinement inflicted for entertaining political opinions flowing from feelings over which I could have no control, I retired to a distance from Philadelphia. I entered into no party, and not being a citizen, I studiously avoided mingling in the politics of this country. Thus retired, offending neither government nor individuals, I expected to live unmolested; yet during my residence in the United States, I have been the unnecessary subject of frequent paragraphs in your paper. I wished to believe that you had seen the indelicacy and impropriety of such a procedure; but a publication in your paper of Saturday destroys that expectation. As you have received no injury from me, I request of you to explain to me what are your motives for repeatedly wounding my feelings and breaking into the peace of my family, by whom your paper may be read possibly, in Europe.
> I am, Sir &c,
> A. H. Rowan.[380]

---

380 Drummond, p. 329.

Cobbett responded by putting a notice in his paper to the effect that 'the person who requests to know my motives for publishing certain material' could, if they wished, send a letter for publication, which would be fully answered, but he 'would not respond to a secret inquisition'.[381] A furious Rowan asked for an interview with Cobbett, and, accompanied by his friend, a Mr Stafford, they met at Cobbett's office on 23 February. Cobbett was accompanied by a Mr White. There followed a robust exchange of views in which Cobbett defended his every action and said that he had held off attacking Rowan for a long time until he read the *Baltimore Gazette* item and received an anonymous letter from Wilmington. At one point Cobbett said that when he wrote the item he thought he was doing the right thing, but was now better informed as to Rowan's character. He said, 'at this moment he was convinced he had misrepresented a very worthy man ... but he would not apologize'. Rowan snapped that if he wanted an apology he would have asked for one; all he wanted was to be left alone.

Rowan achieved his objective. Cobbett never mentioned Rowan again, but he continued his career as a public defamer of democrats until he had to flee the United States in 1800. The reason for his flight was that he had ended up at the wrong end of a lawsuit from the eminent physician and politician Dr Benjamin Rush, whom he had mocked as the 'Pennsylvanian Hippocrates'.

Back in William Cobbett's soldiering days in the 1780s he had hated the officer class of the British Army, regarding them as 'an epaulet gentry of profound and surprising ignorance'.[382] He had great respect for his commanding officer, however, who was none other than Rowan's United Irish comrade Lord Edward Fitzgerald. Fitzgerald was

---

381 *loc. cit.*
382 Ingrams (2005), p. 13.

probably the only person Cobbett ever respected in his first forty years of life. In his memoirs he did not even declare any respect for his father or mother.[383] If FitzGerald's evolution from dashing British officer to leading Irish revolutionary amounts to an extraordinary transformation, then the evolution of Cobbett in his later life from Tory libeller, defamer and scandal-monger to a champion of reform and the oppressed peasantry of England is equally remarkable.

Cobbett eventually developed a huge respect and admiration for Tom Paine, the man at whom some of his most cruel invective had been directed. Paine was once a hero of the American Revolution, but after his publication of *The Age of Reason* and his attack on George Washington for alleged betrayal he cut a lonely and isolated figure in an America that had rejected him. Cobbett, who loved to kick a man when he was down, wrote:

How Tom gets a living now or what brothel he inhabits I know not. Whether his carcass is at last to be suffered to rot on the earth or to be dried in the air is of very little consequence. Whenever and wherever he breathes his last, he will excite neither sorrow nor compassion; no friendly hand will close his eyes, not a groan will be uttered, not a tear will be shed. Like Judas he will be remembered by posterity; men will learn to express all that is base, malignant, treacherous, unnatural and blasphemous by a single monosyllable, PAINE[384]

The man responsible for this scabrous prose would one night sneak, under cover of darkness, into a graveyard in the French

383 *loc. cit.*
384 Nelson, p. 7.

Protestant refuge of New Rochelle, twenty-two miles north of New York City, and proceed to dig up Tom Paine's bones in order to smuggle them back to his native England. Cobbett intended to raise a public subscription to erect a mausoleum in central London for his newfound hero, having changed his mind about Tom Paine. The man on whom he had heaped the most scathing and cruel abuse in life he was to honour to the point of necromancy in death. If anything could be more ironic than Cobbett's change of heart about Tom Paine it is the fact that he lost the bones on the journey home; instead of a hero's grave, Tom Paine has no grave. Cobbett's antics achieved little more than the inspiration of a Tory nursery rhyme:

> *Poor Tom Paine now there he lies,*
> *Nobody laughs and nobody cries,*
> *Where he is gone or how he fares,*
> *Nobody knows and nobody cares.*

A twenty-first-century folk singer, in an audacious distortion of sentiment worthy of Cobbett, turned this into a tribute to Tom Paine by adding:

> *I will dance to Tom Paine's bones,*
> *Dance to Tom Paine's bones,*
> *I will dance in the oldest boots I own,*
> *To the rhythm of Tom Paine's bones.*[385]

---

385 'Tom Paine's Bones', a song by Graham Moore.

15.

The Prospect of Union

In the spring of 1798 the political tension in Dublin was rising to fever pitch. The Sham Squire warned Edward Cooke at the Castle that Councillor Tone had sent word from Paris that the United Irishmen should be in a state of preparation as the French would be there by 17 March, St Patrick's Day.[386] The Sham informed Cooke that 'the leading people in Belfast and the other towns of the north are to be consulted whether they are prepared to have arms, pikes etc'.[387]

In a pre-emptive strike, the government swooped on a meeting at Oliver Bond's house on Bridgefoot Street on 12 March, capturing most of the Leinster Directory. Any of the known leaders who were still at large went underground, including Samuel Neilson and Lord Edward Fitzgerald.

According to William Drennan, about a week after the arrests the chancellor rode up to Sarah Rowan's carriage in a Dublin Street and:

---

386 Bartlett (2004), p. 223.
387 *loc. cit.*

congratulated her on the behaviour of Mr [Rowan]
for some time past so opposite to that of his former
political companions, and assured her that at the
conclusion of the war such conduct must facilitate
his return to his country, his wife and his property.[388]

Before this incident the chancellor's and Sarah's regular points
of contact were in private or by correspondence. Lord Clare's
decision to go public and to make sure he was overheard
was an overt political message that would not be lost on his
listeners. We do not know where this exchange took place,
however, if it were outside the Presbyterian meeting house
at Strand Street that Sarah attended, then Lord Clare would
have assured himself of the audience he desired. Drennan,
the Emmet family, Oliver Bond and Henry Jackson's family
were being reminded that they were playing for very high
stakes, and of the awful consequences of losing.

Within days of this incident The Sham Squire suggested
that the chancellor should be advised against:

> Going abroad in the street or riding by himself for
> in this paroxysm of treason, some of these hardy
> villains are sworn to do him some act of bodily
> injury.[389]

The rebellion that finally broke out in Ireland that summer
is scarcely mentioned in Rowan's or Sarah's correspondence.
Many of Rowan's intimate friends lost their lives, and many
more spent long terms in prison or were banished from
Ireland forever. Lord Edward Fitzgerald died in great agony
in Newgate in June 1798. He had been badly wounded

---

388 Agnew, ii, p. 383.
389 Bartlett (2004), p. 234.

when he resisted arrest in Thomas Street, Dublin a few days previously. Oliver Bond died in custody the following month. It is likely that he was murdered on the order of the authorities.[390] Thomas Bacon, who had supplied the uniforms to Rowan's Volunteers back in 1792, was hanged from a lamp post in central Dublin during the rebellion. Wolfe Tone died on 19 November of self-inflicted wounds to his throat. He had been captured in the uniform of a French officer after a naval battle off the Donegal coast. When his request to be shot was denied, he decided that suicide was a more honourable death than the gallows.

In a letter dated May 1799, Rowan remembers how he and 'poor Tone' had admired America from afar. This is the only mention Rowan makes of any of his dead comrades in his correspondence while in America. He was anxious to make it clear to all that he was not involved in any way with the rebellion, although he never criticized those who were. Whenever in later life he had occasion to mention them it was to defend their characters, motives and integrity. It should also be noted that there is no record that any of his surviving comrades ever felt that his subsequent action in pleading for a pardon and saving his family from ruin was in any way dishonourable.

The rebellion had made it much more difficult for the chancellor to help Sarah in the restoration of their property. Sarah sounded a despondent note in a letter dated 1 May 1799, the fifth anniversary of their parting:

> I am satisfied let them say what they will that your property will never be re-granted. I do believe that it was once the intention of government to give it to me, but the circumstances which have occurred in

---

390 Whelan (2010), p. 243.

Ireland since that time have prevented them. From this conviction I have given up all idea of remaining in this country.[391]

With this letter she enclosed several newspapers and pamphlets dealing with the proposed Act of Union between Britain and Ireland. The British government was determined to abolish the Irish Houses of Parliament and institute a complete transfer of powers to Westminster. The chancellor and Lord Castlereagh knew that getting the Irish Upper and Lower Houses to vote for their own extinction would be difficult: it would require even more bribes than usual to get the members to put personal gain before principle.

Sarah expressed her fear that the Union would pass into law, but she warned Rowan that if this happened 'it will be no reason for your being permitted to return to this country, quite the contrary'.

Rowan, however, was delighted by the prospect of Union, writing to his father:

I congratulate you upon the report that spreads here that Union is intended. In that I see the downfall of one of the most corrupt assemblies that ever existed ... [It will be] the wreck of feudal aristocracy.

Rowan's view was not popular among his fellow Irish exiles, and he was 'sent to Coventry' by many of them. However, he remained, in his own words, 'as obstinate as a pig'. He hoped that the Union would be of great advantage to the poor. He advocated 'a Union which would throw work into the cabin and take a third of taxes and a tenth of income etc.

---

391 Drummond, p. 337.

out of the rich man's house'.[392] This idea of taxing the rich for the advantage of the poor was very much ahead of its time. It would appear that Rowan was very much influenced in this idea by Tom Paine, and particularly Part II of *Rights of Man.*

Rowan suggested that Union would 'take a feather out of the rich man's cap ... but will put many a guinea in the poor man's pocket'.[393] Why he was so optimistic about the prospects of Union for the Irish poor is hard to fathom at this remove. However, his hopes were somewhat realized. While Dublin and most of Ireland went into massive decline after 1800, Belfast and Ulster prospered, and Belfast changed from being a modest if thriving town before the Union to becoming Ireland's pre-eminent industrial city with a skilled working class at the middle of the nineteenth century.

Having concluded that she would not get the property returned in the short term, Sarah wrote to Lord Clare on 9 August asking that her husband be allowed to come to Europe. She asked that if her husband were to be intercepted by British frigates while crossing the Atlantic he should not be arrested and returned to Ireland to be hanged, but 'would be suffered to continue his journey to the Continent'.

Departing America

On 9 September the Chief Secretary Lord Castlereagh wrote to Sarah assuring her that 'her husband might reside in Europe without molestation so long as he continues to demean himself in a manner as not to give offence'.[394]

---

392 *Ibid.*, p. 341.
393 *loc. cit.*
394 Nicolson, p. 170.

Castlereagh made it clear in this letter that the decision was made on the basis of the favourable reports of Rowan's behaviour made by the Lord Chancellor.

On 9 July 1800, after a stay of five years in America, Hamilton Rowan stepped on board the brig *Sally* out of Newcastle, Delaware, bound for the German port of Cuxhaven, near the free German city of Hamburg. Hamburg might seem a strange choice of destination for a man who wished to be seen as having opted out of politics and public controversy: Napper Tandy was kidnapped there by the British, and it was a city seething with French, British and United Irish espionage and intrigue. Tandy had been released because the British knew the kidnapping was a breach of international law. He returned to a hero's welcome in France, where he died in 1803. Rowan probably chose Hamburg because it was closer to Ireland and England than other places he had considered. Most importantly of all, communications with England were relatively good, and that would be vital for his campaign for a free pardon, the restoration of his property and permission to return to Ireland.

The ship's captain had insisted that Rowan should have a passport, but he accepted that Castlereagh's letter to Sarah would suffice. Rowan brought on board with him an opossum, a dog, a red bird and a dozen potatoes. He had twenty guineas in his pocket. Neither the opossum nor the bird survived the six-week voyage.

After a few days at sea they were brought to by a British armed cruiser of twenty-two guns, a privateer. The British boarding party carefully examined Rowan's papers. They chose not to believe that Rowan was who he said he was, and hoped that they could prove he was a Frenchman or a Dutchman and that he owned some of the cargo. The British tried to bribe one of the *Sally*'s crew to say that the cargo was foreign owned so that they could seize it. They came upon a box of Rowan's correspondence, which included letters from the late Benjamin Franklin as well as letters from Thomas Jefferson and Caesar Rodney. Jefferson was soon to be president of the United States, and in 1807 would appoint Rodney as his Attorney General. As the British 'rigidly' examined these letters they forced the *Sally* off its course and obliged it to follow them for two days.[395]

The privateer eventually released the *Sally* and allowed her to proceed. This delay maddened the captain, who blamed Rowan. After a blazing row Rowan attempted to pacify the captain by throwing the box of correspondence overboard. He would afterwards regret the loss of these mementos.

On 13 August the *Sally* sailed around the north coast of Scotland, passed the Fair Isle, the most southerly of the Shetlands, into the North Sea, then headed due south for Cuxhaven. Although Rowan knew that Sarah would not be there to meet him, his heart was 'beating with a high throb of affection and anxiety' for he knew that Sarah would join him as soon as she could.[396] When Sarah heard of his safe arrival in Hamburg she asked Lord Clare to help to organize passports for her and the children. She crossed to England and sailed from London to Cuxhaven. She wrote ahead to Rowan, asking him to come and meet her and her children, William, Jane and Bess, at Cuxhaven.

Rowan called on Sir James Crawford, the British minister at Hamburg, and showed him Castlereagh's letter. He was naïve if he thought that he would be made welcome. Crawford was instrumental in the Tandy kidnapping and had spent much of his time in Hamburg monitoring various United Irish exiles and their contacts with the French.

---

395 Drummond, p. 365.
396 *loc. cit.*

He rebuffed Rowan's advances coldly, pointing out that Castlereagh's letter did not authorize Rowan 'to expect those attentions usually reciprocal between British subjects and their minister'.

Rowan did not stay in Hamburg for long as he was 'surrounded and tormented by fools and knaves … and he quit that emporium of mischief'.[397] He hoped to settle in Lubec, but as he could not rent suitable accommodation he eventually settled at Altona, a city contiguous to Hamburg. There he rented a handsome house, and he and his family found themselves in 'the midst of a pleasant society'.

His many influential friends in England and Ireland continued to lobby on his behalf. These included Richard Griffith in Ireland and Lord Pelham and Thomas Steele, the British Paymaster General, in England. In late December 1801 Lord Clare wrote to Griffith advising him to tell Rowan to be patient and that the best time to petition the Crown would be when 'a definitive treaty of peace is settled', and when that time came 'his friends will be enabled to support his petition with effect'.[398] The Treaty of Amiens was signed in March 1802, but Lord Clare had died the previous January. Nonetheless, Rowan followed the late chancellor's advice. Having refused to sign Griffith's draft petition in 1796 because of its reference to the British constitution in Ireland, by July 1802 Rowan was prepared to sign a plea for pardon. He began by profusely thanking the King and his government for the protection of his wife and family, and continued:

> conscious of the excellence of the British constitution, in which your petitioner sees with heartfelt

---

397 Drummond, p. 366.
398 *Ibid.*, p. 368.

satisfaction his native country participating under the late happy union, effected by your Majesty's paternal wisdom and affection; and assured that his conduct will not belie these sentiments, your petitioner approaches your Majesty's throne at this auspicious moment, praying that your Majesty will condescend to extend your royal clemency to your petitioner in such manner as your Majesty in your wisdom may think proper.[399]

This was passed on to through Thomas Steele, who was an old school friend from Westminster and Cambridge, but almost a year went by before Rowan heard any response.

Meanwhile, Rowan's financial affairs were most precarious as he still had no access to his property or personal fortune. All the family had to live on was the rents that their tenants were disposed to pay, as they had no way of enforcing arrears. There were certain tensions between Sarah and her husband as neither was inclined to limit themselves to an annual budget of £600. Rowan was under pressure when he declared:

The fact is I have always lived in too high a style and my family do not like to give up indulgence. But what is to become of the children? Have we the wherewithal to put them in any decent line of profession? No. And we are too fond of our rank in life to make them tradesmen. My God I would rather dig and delve if anyone would hire my body than thus be eternally on thorns.[400]

---

399 *Ibid.*, p. 368.
400 Nicolson, p. 176.

Such were his financial problems that he even seriously considered going back to Ireland and giving himself up. He decided, however, that this course would be too risky; they might neither pardon nor hang him, but send him to Botany Bay.[401]

The State Prisoners in Hamburg

In summer 1802 some of the state prisoners who had been interned in Fort George in Scotland were released following the Treaty of Amiens, and they arrived in Hamburg on or about 6 July. Rowan's petition for pardon was at this point under consideration at the highest level, and much rested on the credibility of his claims that he would be of good behaviour in the future. He never claimed to have broken his links with these unrepentant rebels. The conservative elements resisting the pardon could, however, have used news of any contacts Rowan had with his old friends as evidence that he was still a dangerous man. Nonetheless, he wrote immediately to them offering to be of any service he could.

He received a warm reply from Thomas Addis Emmet:

My Dear Friend,
I received your letter yesterday ... I have shown it to Dowling, Chambers and some others with whom you were formally connected in intimacy. They all desire me to assure you of their affection and esteem. We were in some measure appraised of your situation and by the injury you might possibly sustain by holding intercourse with us; we therefore voluntarily deprived ourselves of the pleasure we

---

401 *loc. cit.*

should enjoy in your society, and declined calling on you directly on our arrival. For my part it would give me the upmost pain if your friendship towards me were to lead you into any embarrassment, or subject you to any misrepresentation on a point of such material importance to yourself and your family.[402]

Emmet went on to say that he needed no assistance and would shortly go to America.

Samuel Neilson, who was also bound for America, wrote too, thanking Rowan and stressing that, though he had endured eight years of hardship, his property destroyed and his family reduced to a forlorn state, he remained committed to the cause of his country and general liberty. Neilson's letter finishes in such a way as to make clear that whatever about Rowan's decision to avoid radical political activity he was not averse to the spread of radical, revolutionary and democratic ideas. Neilson concluded:

> As to your friendly offer of books, send me any you have to spare (except Jefferson's Notes, which I am already in possession of), Reynolds' Trial, Priestley's Letters, Cooper's Essays and Trial, Paine's Letters etc., are all new and interesting to me. I lodge at Jacob Heuserman's Little Fisher-street No. 248 and will ever remain your sincere friend,
> SAMUEL NEILSON.

There is a sad irony in Neilson mentioning Thomas Cooper in his last letter to Rowan. Cooper was an English-born Unitarian who had been attacked by Edmund Burke because

---

402 Drummond, p. 468.

of his support for the French Revolution. Cooper went to America in 1793 and settled in Northumberland, where he was joined by Priestley the following year. Yellow fever hit Wilmington in 1796. Rowan's friend, the Quaker Poole, was stricken with this highly contagious and deadly disease. As his family were too afraid to nurse him, Rowan moved in to his house. Rowan believed that vapours developed and given to him by Thomas Cooper had protected him from contagion. Samuel Neilson died of yellow fever in Poughkeepsie, New York, on 29 August 1803.

Eventually, Rowan's plea for pardon began to yield results. In April 1803 Thomas Steele wrote, informing him that he could come and live in England provided that he agreed that he would not set foot in Ireland. When Rowan indicated his acceptance of this condition Steele wrote to him again, informing him that he was now free to come to England and that 'the officers of the port have been instructed to let you pass without molestation'.[403]

London and William Godwin

Rowan reached London on 16 June 1803 and went immediately to Thomas Steele's office, where he was shown the King's warrant for pardon. He was required, however, to give two sureties of £10,000 not to go to Ireland. Richard Griffith was on hand and agreed to pledge these sureties. As Rowan was now free to settle in London he rented a house at 58 Sloane Street where he and the family lived for the next three years. Sloane Street was named after Hans Sloane, one of the great scholars who graduated from the Killyleagh Academy.

Although Rowan's dearest desire was to return to Ireland, he made the best of his time in London. Almost

---

403 Drummond, p. 373.

immediately he renewed his acquaintance with the remnants of Joseph Johnston's publisher's circle of rational Dissenters. Many of the earlier members of the group were now dead, including Jebb, Price and Mary Wollstonecraft. Priestley was in America, where he died on 6 February 1804. Tom Paine was also in America, living in obscurity and poverty.

Joseph Johnston, however, was still very much alive. He had been chastened somewhat by imprisonment for sedition in 1798, and was now more interested in publishing educational books than controversial political works. William Godwin had remarried, and he and his new wife, Mary Jane, were busy establishing a juvenile library to stimulate young minds and young imaginations.

In 1793 Godwin had published *Enquiry Concerning Political Justice and its Influence on Morals and Happiness*, a work that had 'an enormous effect'. Godwin must have been greatly influenced by the writing of Francis Hutcheson earlier in the century, for A. C. Grayling tells us:

> Godwin said the American and French Revolutions between them were a harbinger of a new era of peace and progress. He painted an optimistic and idyllic picture of the realization of Enlightenment, envisioning rational autonomous people enhancing each other's well-being in a spirit of mutuality. Each of us is the arbiter of how he should act ... our action should aim at creating the greatest good all round ... intellectual pursuits and feelings of kindness towards others are the chief source of happiness.[404]

Godwin was now at the centre of a group of old radicals, emerging writers and poets that included William Hazlitt

---

404 Grayling (2007), p. 150.

(junior) and Charles and Mary Lamb. Rowan could now enjoy the company of men and women of intellect, original thinkers and philosophers. This was just the sort of polite and cultured society he had craved and missed in America.

Within a few days of his arrival in London, Rowan called to Godwin's home at Hanway Street. The two had met at least once before in 1794. Rowan had admired Godwin's groundbreaking novel *Caleb Williams*, which had caused a sensation when it was first published in 1794. Rowan and Godwin had been associated with many of the prominent radicals of the previous decade, and Rowan considered himself a dear friend of Mary Wollstonecraft, Godwin's much-lamented wife.

The two men quickly became close friends and constant companions, and for the next three years Godwin, Rowan and their families saw a great deal of each other. They dined at each other's houses, which were close by, and entertained political and literary guests. Rowan seems more often than not to have been the host. They also went to the theatre and other public events together.

Godwin records in his diary on 23 July 1803 that Rowan called on him in the company of Thomas Holcroft (1745–1809), the well-known playwright and novelist. Holcroft had first published Thomas Paine's *Rights of Man* in 1791, and had been charged with high treason in 1794. When the trials of Horne Tooke and Thomas Hardy collapsed, Holcroft had been released without ever getting the chance to vindicate his character. He was branded thereafter by the hostile Tory press as 'the acquitted felon Holcroft'.[405]

In the same entry Godwin records the death of Lord Kilwarden, who had been killed that very night by pike-wielding rebels in Dublin. Godwin must have added the

---

405 *Ibid.* p. 156.

record of Kilwarden's death later, as the news could not
have reached London from Dublin so quickly. It did not
emerge until later in the year that the leader of the rebellion
in which Kilwarden was killed was Robert Emmet, the
younger brother of Rowan's friend Thomas Addis Emmet.
Within a few weeks Robert Emmet would be captured,
tried and executed. Thomas Russell, another friend of
Rowan's and dearest comrade of Wolfe Tone, was executed
at Downpatrick in October, having been convicted of
involvement in the Emmet conspiracy.

John Philpot Curran, who was now a member of the
British House of Commons, was also part of Godwin's London
circle. He had defended Rowan in 1794, and would have
been expected to defend Robert Emmet. However, he was
embarrassed by the fact of his daughter Sarah Curran being
romantically involved with young Emmet prior to the rebellion,
and he refused the brief. The informer Leonard McNally (yet
another acquaintance of Rowan) defended, or rather betrayed,
Emmet by disclosing his defence to the prosecution.

On 27 September, a week after the execution of Emmet,
Rowan wrote a note to Godwin mentioning 'poor Emmet'.
Obviously the rise of tensions in Ireland following Emmet's
rebellion did nothing to help Rowan's campaign to return
home. What is more surprising is that he does not appear to
have been harmed by the fact that one of the centres of the
Emmet conspiracy was Rathcoffey in Kildare, the townland
where Rowan had his mansion.

One of Emmet's most trusted staff officers was the
bricklayer and veteran of the 1798 rebellion Michael
Quigley. He had been employed by Rowan on the building
of Rathcoffey, and had been so impressed by Rowan's politics
that he had joined the United Irishmen a few years later.[406]

---

406 Whelan (2010), p. 156.

Quigley had broken his banishment order by returning from France to help Emmet. The authorities knew that Quigley had been visiting other Kildare-based veterans of 1798, promising large amounts of firearms and brandishing large sums in gold to impress them that Emmet had the backing of men of substance. Rowan's enemies in Ireland might have liked to believe that he was involved, but it does not appear that the government thought so.

On 31 January 1804 Rowan dined at Godwin's in the presence of Samuel Taylor Coleridge and John Foulkes, a lawyer whom Godwin had known at least since 1793. Foulkes had been an associate of Thomas Holcroft, John Thelwall and Horne Tooke, and had helped in their defence at the treason trials in 1794. He had also defended James Quigley, the United Irishman who was executed at Maidstone in Kent after being convicted of treason in 1798. Quigley stood trial with John Binns and Arthur O'Connor, but they had been acquitted.

Foulkes had also defended Colonel Edward Marcus Despard, a friend of Godwin, who had been executed in February a few months before Rowan arrived in London. Despard was a United Irishman, a one-time hero of the British Empire and an old comrade of England's greatest living idol of the time, Horatio Nelson. Despard had been convicted of plotting with working-class radicals in London to kill King George III. In fact he had been trying to forestall the London radicals in order that they might rise in support of Robert Emmet's Dublin rebellion and a hoped-for French landing in Ireland.

At Godwin's house, Rowan met Fanny Imlay, whom he had last seen as an infant in the arms of Mary Wollstonecraft in Paris. She was now 9 years old and living with her 5-year-old sister, Mary Godwin, later Mary Shelley. Mary Jane, Godwin's new wife, had two children of her own from previous relationships, so the couple had four young children in their care. Godwin's home was like a laboratory for testing his revolutionary theories on the education of children. Godwin felt that rather than coercing children and inculcating them with the beliefs of their parents or society at large, they should be encouraged to read, to think for themselves and to use their imaginations.

Rowan would have very much approved of Godwin's view that young children should, through the development of their imaginations, learn empathy with their fellow human beings rather than pursue their more narrow self-interest. Eventually, when he had his personal and family fortune restored, Rowan made a very generous donation of £450 to support Godwin's work. A modern historian, Philip Orr, has pointed out that, by his support of Godwin, Rowan was:

> Making a contribution to a pedagogy to which Francis Hutcheson had earlier contributed, with his belief in the experimental vigour, and benign character of children ... [Godwin's juvenile library] with its selection of schoolbooks, copybooks, quills, slates and maps marked a new respect for children's education. It is a journey which places Rowan, Hutcheson and the Scots-Irish dissenting culture at a key place in the evolution of the modern belief in widespread education, conducted in large degree through the encouragement of imagination and creativity rather than arid instruction.[407]

Another insight provided by Godwin's diary is that Reverend Benjamin Beresford and Rowan's sister, Sidney, seem often

---

407 Orr, p. 227.

to have dined with the Rowans and the Godwins at this point, and that when the ageing and ailing Gawin Hamilton came over to London to visit his son in 1805 he also dined at Godwin's.

On 9 January, Godwin and Rowan attended the elaborate state funeral of Lord Nelson at Saint Paul's Cathedral. Nelson had been killed at the Battle of Trafalgar the previous October. Perhaps they had gone to pay tribute to a great commander who had for a time mentored Rowan's eldest son. Perhaps they were there because Nelson had tried but failed to save the life of the United Irishman Colonel Edward Marcus Despard by giving character evidence at his trial to the effect that Despard had been a loyal and a brave soldier and was not the sort of man who would engage in treason.

Of course, to mourn England's greatest hero publicly would also have helped Rowan's campaign to go home to Killyleagh.

16.

The Londonderry Lordling

One of the first people Rowan called to see when he returned to London was Lord Castlereagh. Castlereagh had worked hard to get him a pardon in England, however Castlereagh explained that to get a pardon under the great seal of Ireland was more problematical as 'it would give great offence, especially to the [Irish] aristocracy'.[408] He intimated that nothing more could be done for Rowan as long as the current administration, under Prime Minister Henry Addington, was in office.

Castlereagh had left the government with his mentor, William Pitt, in 1801, because they had promised that once they had abolished the Irish Parliament and delivered the Union the way would be cleared for Catholic emancipation. When George III refused to countenance the measure, Pitt resigned and Castlereagh followed him out of office. By the time Rowan and Castlereagh had their first meeting in July 1803, however, Castlereagh had rejoined the Addington administration, refusing the office of Home Secretary 'because of his scruples over the way Ireland was been

---

408 Nicolson, p. 177.

run under Lord Hardwicke', the first post-Union Lord Lieutenant.[409]

Castlereagh and Hardwicke disagreed over many issues. Whether Rowan should be allowed to return Ireland was, perhaps, not the most important. However, recent Castlereagh recent biographer John Bew tells us:

> In Lord Hardwicke's view, which was probably justified, the type of favouritism which Castlereagh was showing to a reprobate Protestant landlord would not play well in the rest of Ireland. Most former radicals had not benefited from the personal intervention of a minister of state; hundreds had been hanged or exiled. Not only would this 'give the greatest offence to the loyal', complained Hardwicke, it would also, 'compared with the treatment of the disaffected who are less well connected ... look like a flagrant piece of class distinction.[410]

Nor was Hardwicke the only senior politician opposed to any leniency towards Rowan. William Sampson, a lawyer and United Irishman who was himself unsuccessfully pressing to be allowed to return to Ireland, tells us in his memoir, 'Lord Chancellor Redesdale did not think Hamilton Rowan safe and his return would be deprecated by the loyal inhabitants of that country'.[411]

Addington was forced out of office in May 1804, and Castlereagh and Pitt came back into power. Rowan again called to see Castlereagh, carrying with him a new memorial seeking to be allowed return to Ireland. Castlereagh greeted him warmly and made a suggestion that solved a problem

---

409 Bew (2011), p. 194.
410 *loc. cit.*
411 Sampson (2002), p. 22.

which had long troubled Rowan. His lordship suggested that a military career would be available to Gawin William, Rowan's eldest son, either in the East Indies or at the military academy at Woolwich. Rowan told Castlereagh that he needed time to think about this offer as William had been encouraged to become a merchant and he would be reluctant to try to change the young man's mind. However, William Drennan recorded six years earlier that William was by that time 'a complete convert to maternal opinion and the leniency of government and is eager to serve in the army or navy against the common enemy'[412]

One way or another, Captain Gawin William Hamilton Rowan went on to have an illustrious career in the navy for over thirty years, at one point serving under Lord Nelson and seeing action in China, Egypt, the West Indies and South America. He retired to Killyleagh in 1834 due to ill health. Shortly after his arrival home he was thrown from a jaunting cart. He died at Rathcoffey while visiting his father that same year, aged 51.

Why did Lord Castlereagh help Archibald Hamilton Rowan?

Lord Castlereagh has the distinction of being regarded as the apostate villain who is credited with playing the most prominent role 'in extinguishing the dreams of the founding fathers of Irish republicanism in 1798'.[413] R. R. Madden asserted that Castlereagh's 'memory had the smell of hot blood about it'. 'The Robespierre of Ireland' is regarded as having provoked and then suppressed the rebellion, and to have bribed the Irish Parliament to

---

412 Drummond, p. 383.
413 Bew, p. 3.

bring about the Act of Union in 1800. He went on then, with the Duke of Wellington excepted, to be the most successful Irishman in British politics yet. As his most recent biographer observed, 'his native country never saw him as one of her sons'.[414]

Rowan and Castlereagh were regarded by their contemporaries, as they have been by posterity, as being on the opposite sides of the great political divide that rent Ireland asunder at the end of the eighteenth century. One was a leader of the United Irishmen, the other had overseen the destruction of that organization. Yet after the death of Lord Clare, Castlereagh became Rowan's greatest champion within the administration. Moreover, he became both an advisor and a benefactor to the Rowan family. How could these men be reconciled after the bloody events of 1798, without one or other of them sacrificing their principles?

Rowan and Castlereagh had much more in common than divided them, at least in terms of background and upbringing. The political and religious links between them and their families were strong and went back a very long way. Both were from wealthy landed families of Scottish extraction who settled in east County Down. Their ancestral homes are situated at opposite ends of Strangford Lough, about twelve miles apart as the crow flies. They could equally boast eminent ancestors who raised troops of horses to fight for William III in the Jacobite wars. Their families had a strong tradition of pro-reform politics and New Light Presbyterianism.

Both men and their fathers had been prominent in the Volunteers. Castlereagh was only 15 years old when Rowan joined the ranks on coming to Ireland in 1784. Two years

---

414 Bew, p. 4.

earlier Robert had taken part in a Volunteer mock battle outside Belfast, and a witness described how the then 13-year-old had performed:

> [He] commanded the light infantry of the Ards independents, of which his father was colonel. His company consisted mostly of boys a few years older than himself. Their appearance attracted universal notice and excited the most pleasing emotions as it promised a succession of patriot soldiers under whose banner Ireland would recline in safety. The conduct of young Stewart ... displayed such germs of spirit and judgement as excited admiration, extorted applause, and laid the foundation of that popularity which he afterwards obtained.[415]

Sixteen years later, in July 1798, the United Irishmen of Ards rose and captured the towns of Donaghadee, Newtownards and Scrabo, and marched to ultimate defeat at the battle of Ballinahinch. One can only wonder how many of Castlereagh's boy soldiers of 1782 were in the rebel ranks in 1798. It is also reasonable to suggest that many of Rowan's Killyleagh Volunteers may have fought at Ballinahinch in 1798.

Castlereagh's family had links to the radical strand of Protestant Dissent that had connections to the philosophy school at Killyleagh established by Rowan's ancestor, the University of Glasgow and the Dublin Unitarians of Cromwellian descent. Alexander Stewart, Castlereagh's grandfather and 'a stout republican', had been a friend of Francis Hutcheson the philosopher, William Bruce the publisher and William Drennan's father, Reverend Thomas

---

415 Clifford (1991), p. 17.

Drennan. Hutcheson, Bruce and Drennan were graduates of Glasgow.[416] Stewart had been an elder of First Presbyterian, Rosemary Street, Belfast in the 1720s. William Drennan was born in the Rosemary Street manse in 1754. Sometime in the 1740s Alexander Stewart acquired an elegant and beautifully furnished townhouse at 28 Henry Street, Dublin where Castlereagh was born in 1769. The library in this house was a repository of republican radical literature, and:

> there were many editions of Hutcheson's works, along with Edmund Ludlow's *Memoirs*, James Harrington's *Commonwealth of Oceana* and Robert Molesworth's *An Account of Denmark* – all formative texts in the classical republican seventeenth-century tradition of the Commonwealth man.[417]

The library also contained such heterodox religious works as the sermons of Benjamin Hoadley, an Anglican bishop who denied that the scriptures gave any justification for the Church hierarchy. The library also contained an unbound copy of the memoirs of Thomas Emlyn, who had been imprisoned in Dublin in 1703 for expressing his Unitarian opinions and denying the divinity of Jesus Christ.[418] Most of these titles were also in Rowan's library at Rathcoffey, which he had inherited from his maternal grandfather, William Rowan.

Alexander Stewart became involved with the Dissenting congregation based at Wood Street, Dublin. This congregation moved to a new meeting house at Great Strand Street in 1763. Castlereagh was baptized at Great Strand Street in 1769, and his father continued to pay a pew rent there up to the mid

---

416 Agnew, ii, p. 477.
417 Bew, p. 10.
418 Stewart (1993), p. 116.

1790s. Archibald Hamilton Rowan and William Drennan also paid a pew rent to the Great Strand Street Meeting House in the 1790s.

In 1789, Castlereagh's father was ennobled as Lord Londonderry. There was some bemusement in Ireland as to the reasons for the Londonderry elevation, and one wag observed that he was 'almost the only Irishman to receive his Majesty's favour without rendering service'.[419] Londonderry was, in fact, rewarded for marrying into a powerful English Whig family. Castlereagh's mother had died when he was just one year old. A few years later his father married the sister of the First Earl of Camden. Such an entry into the aristocracy was often a first step for materially successful Protestant Dissenters towards membership of the Established Church, and a breach with their Dissenting religion and politics. At first it was by no means clear that Londonderry and his son were heading in this direction, yet it was not long before the signs began to appear.

Lord Londonderry's elevation gave rise to an election in County Down in 1790. Castlereagh was the candidate on the reform and anti-government ticket. His opponent was from the conservative and pro-government Downshire family. The election was a 'very bitter affair', with many people who would emerge as leading United Irishmen in the next few years very active on Castlereagh's side. Samuel Neilson was his election agent and Reverend William Steel Dickson of Portaferry, an admirer of Alexander Stewart, was very active in encouraging support for the grandson of his old friend. It is likely that Gawin Hamilton and his tenants voted for Castlereagh, who won the election with a large majority.

William Sampson, a lawyer and United Irishman, later claimed that the pro-reform pledge made by Castlereagh

---

419 Allen, p. 28.

at the hustings was not very different from the oath of the United Irishmen. Sampson also bitterly observed, however, that 'he that remained true to his test was hanged and he that was forsworn hanged him'.[420]

The Northern Whig Club was formed in 1790, and Rowan, Gawin Hamilton, Castlereagh and Londonderry became members. Castlereagh was young and handsome – in fact he was underage when he began his canvass in 1789. William Drennan saw him in Dublin shortly after his election and thought him 'certainly a most promising young man and one of the handsomest in the House perhaps to become one day the most able'.[421] However, it was not long before Drennan and many of the other reformers became disillusioned with their new MP. Once in the House, he started to vote with the majority. Much against the wishes of his County Down constituents, he railed against the Catholic convention of 1793 and 'lashed himself into a passion' over the issue. Drennan concluded that he was nothing more than 'a proud aristocrat under the garb of great mildness and complaisance'.[422] It was not long before another erstwhile supporter, Drennan's brother-in-law, Sam McTier, was referring disparagingly to Castlereagh as 'The Londonderry Lordling'.[423] Sam McTier was an elder of the Rosemary Street congregation, as Castlereagh's grandfather once had been.

Castlereagh's first few years in Parliament were marked by a very obvious cooling between the Stewarts and their former supporters. It was not until 1795, though, that the breach became permanent and Castlereagh joined the government and began to use his considerable energy and

---

420 Sampson, p. 238.
421 Agnew, ii, p. 356.
422 *Ibid.*, p. 469.
423 *Ibid.*, p. 505.

abilities to crush the reform movement and the United Irishmen. It is significant that Castlereagh did not formally cross the floor and join the government until his uncle, Lord Camden, replaced the Earl of Fitzwilliam as Viceroy of Ireland in February 1795. By this time Rowan was somewhat cut off from events in Ireland as he had been a fugitive in France for several months.

When Fitzwilliam was sworn in as Viceroy of Ireland in December 1794, the Protestant Dissenters of Dublin were delighted as it seemed to herald a new dawn: he was known to be a supporter of reform and Catholic emancipation. In January 1795 Reverend William Bruce (nephew of the publisher of the same name) led a delegation of Dissenting ministers and elders to Dublin Castle to welcome Fitzwilliam warmly. Bruce was one-time minister at Great Strand Street, Dublin, but by this time was based at Rosemary Street, Belfast. A manuscript copy of Bruce's address and Fitzwilliam's loquacious reply can been seen in the records of the Dublin Unitarian Church held in the Royal Irish Academy.[424] Bruce asked William Drennan to accompany the delegation. Drennan had no objection, but did not go because he doubted that anyone would let him travel in their coach.[425] He had been acquitted of charges of seditious libel a few months previously.

Fitzwilliam was recalled in March, giving rise to a surge of discontent in Ireland. He was replaced as Lord Lieutenant by none other than Lord Camden, Castlereagh's uncle.

The Roman Catholics, the Protestant Dissenters and the Dublin mob were outraged. With all hope of constitutional reform now gone the mood of the radicals hardened, and a revolution with French support began to appear

---

424 Ria Duceus.
425 Agnew, ii, p.118.

to be the only viable alternative. The night-time seizures of the weapons of the gentry by the Defenders increased significantly. Castlereagh, however, saw his uncle's elevation as an opportunity to advance his considerable political ambitions. Even before the formal announcement of Camden's appointment, Castlereagh began to 'assume [the] airs of a future secretary'. [426]

When the Great Strand Street Vestry Committee decided unanimously that this time there should be no address of welcome to the new Lord Lieutenant, Londonderry did not bother attending the meeting. Many now realized that the Stewart family had given in to the lure of ambition and were turning their backs on the radical republican heritage bequeathed to them by Alexander Stewart.

In recruiting Castlereagh to office, the British and Irish governments were gaining the skills of a very able man who knew radical Protestant Dissent from the inside. He was not at all reluctant to hang former supporters to please his new masters if he believed the constitution was under threat. His father Londonderry's bloodlust when dealing with former friends appears at least on some occasions to have been motivated by personal spite. He had his former supporter Reverend James Porter of Greyabbey hanged in front of his congregation because the Unitarian clergyman had lampooned him in a humorous satire *Billy Bluff and the Squire*. However, Castlereagh was motivated only by wishing to do the bidding of his masters. As long as the emergency lasted he would be as cruel and ruthless as he believed was necessary, and when Pitt or Lord Cornwallis favoured a less barbarous approach Castlereagh could be relied on to try to moderate the terror.

Out of sympathy for Sarah, Lord Clare had wished to make an exception of Rowan, and Castlereagh had no

---

426 *Ibid.*, p. 134.

difficulty in indulging Clare. Most of the former friends whom he hanged had been engaged in a rebellion that Castlereagh was determined to extinguish. Rowan was not even in Ireland during the emergency and so, apparently, posed no threat to the government. Presumably Castlereagh had no knowledge of the helpful advice Rowan had given to the Committee of Public Safety in Paris. Also, Castlereagh knew that, at some time in the future, he would have to stand for election in County Down and the support of Gawin Hamilton and his tenants would be vital in this regard. In fact, by the time this election came about in August 1805 Gawin was dead and the tenants who were now Rowan's were all for Castlereagh.[427] However, Rowan never sought to use his influence to guide his tenants in how they should vote. The conservatives hated Castlereagh because of the Union and the radicals hated him because of what went before. Much to the delight of radicals and conservatives alike, Castlereagh lost the 1805 election.

Both Castlereagh and Rowan had been to France after the revolution. Both saw at first hand that the revolution had unleashed volatile and violent forces that challenged the notions of enlightenment, humanity and democracy that were believed to have driven the revolution in its early stages. The experience had turned Castlereagh into a reactionary, or at least had hardened his already reactionary instincts. Rowan retained his radicalism but realized that revolutions are liable to be sidetracked by ambitious factions, and that good and enlightened men such as Lafayette or Mirabeau often lose control to ambitious factions that claim to act in the name of the people, but in fact serve only their own interests.

No other man did more to bring about the Act of Union between Britain and Ireland than Lord Castlereagh.

---

427 Agnew, iii, p. 351.

Whether he acted out of the conviction that the Union would bring about better times in Ireland, or because he knew that the Union was what William Pitt wanted, can be debated. Rowan, as we have seen, fully supported the Union and saw it as a defeat for the aristocratic faction that had controlled Ireland for so long. The same element, having lost their Parliament and House of Lords, fought a rearguard action to prevent the promised implementation of Catholic emancipation. This faction was very opposed to allowing Rowan to return to Ireland.

When faced with choices in terms of strategy and policy throughout his career, Castlereagh always put his own interests first. Helping Rowan to return to Ireland on a promise of good behaviour had few disadvantages for Castlereagh. A publicly repentant rebel, who was happy to live with privacy and contentment under the new constitutional Union with Britain, might help to reconcile the radical Presbyterians to the new political paradigm. In the event, the Ulster Presbyterians seemed quickly to become reconciled to the Union that Castlereagh had foisted on them: over the next century they became the Union's greatest supporters and defenders.

17.

Return to Killyleagh

Rowan was enjoying his social and intellectual life in London, although he fretted in Sloane Street and continued to press his requests for permission to return home. He received regular reports from his land agent, by coincidence also Archibald Hamilton. The news from Killyleagh was worrying. The 75-year-old Gawin Hamilton had apparently fallen under the domination of his mistress, Ursula Carlyle, with whom he had had a son. Hamilton informed his employer that:

> Ursula is a woman of uncommon violence of temper and that violence is considerably inflamed by intoxication; when in that state she is outrageous even to desperation. The servants in the house partake of her good cheer, the humbler neighbours also partake, and the consequence is she is supported in all her designs by those around her.[428]

When Gawin crossed over to London on a visit to Sloane Street in early 1805 it was clear that he did not have long

---

428 Nicolson, p. 177.

to live. Rowan was anxious that if his father died when Ursula was in possession of the castle and its contents she might try to seize possession of the title deeds for herself and her son.[429] He instructed his land agent to take all steps necessary to prevent this from happening. Hamilton went to the castle and put many of the valuables under lock and key and out of Ursula's reach. Gawin Hamilton died on 9 April and the land agent rushed from Belfast to secure Killyleagh for his employer. Hamilton claimed that when he broke the news of Gawin's death to Ursula she became deranged. He described how:

> She shrieked, tore her hair, and beat her head against the wall and threw herself down the grand staircase heaping abuse in a most horrid manner. Rather than let that 'infamous son of a bitch' Hamilton Rowan inherit the castle, Ursula vowed she would set fire to the powder magazine 'and blow herself and the castle to hell'.[430]

Whether the land agent's account of the events is true or not, Ursula was forcibly removed to her sister's house in the town and her possessions sent after her.[431]

It then became vital for Rowan to secure his pardon in Ireland. Fortunately, the application following his father's death coincided with a change in the ministry, and the Duke of Portland agreed to an alteration to the terms of the pardon to allow him to return to Ireland.

Rowan crossed the Irish Sea, arriving in Dublin on Thursday 13 June 1805. As he sailed into Dublin Bay he would have had a clear view of Howth Head and the

---

429 *loc. cit.*
430 *loc. cit.*
431 *loc. cit.*

graveyard at Kilbarrack. His old protagonist, the Sham Squire of the *Freeman's Journal*, was now two years dead, and buried at Kilbarrack, a few feet from where Rowan had launched Sweetman's small craft on a May night more than a decade earlier.

Hamilton, the land agent, was on hand at the Pigeon House and drove Rowan by carriage to Dominick Street. Here he waited a few days before presenting himself at the Court of King's Bench to plead the King's pardon. A much-changed man had returned to a much-changed country. Rowan was now 53 years of age. His sense of obligation to 'explore ... political truth and having found it avow it with firmness' had been replaced by an acute sense of duty to his wife and growing family. He now had ten children, the last two born in Hamburg. He had not renounced his most cherished principles of freedom of conscience, liberty of expression and universal emancipation; he had merely promised not to act on them. His promises to the government were easy for him to make; he had, after all, already made these promises to Sarah, and probably intended to keep them.

There was no reform movement or revolutionary movement extant in Ireland to tempt Rowan back to political activism. Many of the friends he had left behind in 1794 were dead, and many more had been banished on pain of death if they returned. The Society of United Irishmen and the hopes for reform were no more. The much-vaunted unity of Catholic, Protestant and Dissenter, if it ever existed outside of the imaginations of Rowan, Tone and the leading United Irishmen, was now forgotten. The last public manifestation of revolution had ended two years earlier with Rowan's comrade Thomas Russell hanged at Downpatrick. The headless corpses of Robert Emmet and twenty working men were dumped in a mass grave at Bully's

Acre in Dublin. For the first time is his life, Rowan felt free to put the interests of his wife and family before his public duty. He was in a position to enjoy his considerable wealth without feeling an obligation to risk life, fortune and family in a cause that had been vanquished, perhaps forever.

However, before he could begin the next chapter in his life he had to appear before the Court of King's Bench in Dublin. On Monday 1 July 1805 Rowan was obliged to plead the King's pardon. The court was packed with spectators as members of the Bar crowded the courtroom and the public gallery was filled to capacity. Rowan was technically in custody. The first order of business was to have the sentence of outlawry annulled because of errors in the writ. The first error seems somewhat contrived as Rowan claimed that the writ referred to him as 'Esquire' when at the time he was, in fact, 'Yeoman'.[432] The second error was of more substance as the writ declared that he was within the realm at a time when he was, in fact, 'in Philadelphia in the Province of Pennsylvania in North America'. The writ of outlawry was duly annulled. When asked why he should not face death by execution for treason, Rowan had to go down on his knees and plead for pardon. His plea was granted. He could have left it at that, but begged to be allowed to address the court to express 'his heartfelt gratitude for the clemency of his sovereign'. He was particularly grateful that while he was in a foreign country his wife and family had 'not only been unmolested but cherished and protected' during his absence. He continued: 'All are liable to error. The consequences have taught me deeply to regret some of the violent measures which I then pursued'.[433] The ambivalence of this expression of remorse was lost on Lord

---

432 *Freeman's Journal*, July 1805.
433 Drummond, p. 377.

Justice Downes. The judge released him with the words, 'Mr Rowan, from the sentiments which you have expressed I have hope that your future conduct will prove that his Majesty's pardon has not been unworthily granted'.[434]

Rowan then left the court a free man. There was a slight hitch, however, when the jailer, Dowell, whom Rowan had either tricked or bribed in 1794 to facilitate his escape, tried to arrest him. Dowell believed that although Rowan had been pardoned for treason he was still liable to serve the rest of the sentence from which he had escaped in 1794. Another generous bribe resolved the impasse, and Rowan was free to go back to England to put his financial affairs in order and bring his family home, at last, to Killyleagh.

Rowan went back to England a very wealthy man. He now had his father's fortune along with his own, which had been restored to him. William Drennan reckoned that Rowan was now 'worth £4,000 a year and has advertised to set lands in several different counties'.[435] Gone forever were the days of hardship and penury, waiting for small remittances on the banks of the Seine, the Brandywine and the Elbe. He bought a magnificent carriage and four elegant bay horses. He hired a chef-butler, a footman and a lady's maid.

He did not forget his obligations to others: John Sweetman was paid for his boat, and the Sheridans and Murray were rewarded for their role in his escape. He made generous provision for Ursula Carlyle and her son,[436] and gave £450 to William Godwin.

In July 1806, Rowan, with his family, servants, coach and horses, landed at Donaghadee in County Down and travelled around Strangford Lough toward Killyleagh. As they entered

---

434 *loc. cit.*
435 Agnew, iii, p. 348.
436 Nicolson, p. 180.

the town they were greeted by a great multitude, cheering and shouting for joy. The traditional honour of un-harnessing the horses and the crowd pulling the carriage annoyed Sarah, who declared that she would not be drawn by human creatures who could debase themselves to the rank of beasts.[437] Rowan and the rest of the family appeared to enjoy their stylish return. That night bonfires blazed, fireworks cracked, and the town was brilliantly illuminated. Over the next few days all the 'genteel people' in the neighbourhood called to welcome back Killyleagh's most famous son. Maybe it was the incident involving the horses that created a bad first impression, but Martha McTier reported that many thought Sarah Rowan proud and high-handed.[438]

In October the family moved to Dublin for the winter, and Rowan rented the Bishop of Derry's house in Dawson Street at a rent of £300 for half a year. William Drennan thought the place a palace, but Rowan was determined to be seen to live the life of a respectable and prosperous member of the community. Drummond claims that 'most if not all [of] Rowan's former political opponents were well pleased that he should be restored to his country and his family'.[439] Jonah Barrington recalls seeing Rowan and his family splendidly dressed in the castle drawing rooms, and added:

> They were well received by the Viceroy and by many of the nobility and gentry; and people should consider that His Majesty's free pardon for political offences is always meant to wipe away every injurious feeling from his subjects' recollection.[440]

---

437 *Ibid.*, p. 181.
438 Agnew, iii, p. 531.
439 Drummond, p. 379.
440 Barrington, p. 236.

However, a public row that ended up in the courts took the fairytale sheen from the homecoming. Archibald Hamilton, the land agent, went bankrupt and claimed that many of the debts he had contracted were on behalf of Rowan. He also claimed that he had neglected his own legal practice in order to better serve Rowan during the time he was prevented from coming to Ireland. Archibald Hamilton and his wife, Sarah Hutton, had been great admirers of Rowan before they fell out. The Hutton family were Dublin's pre-eminent Unitarian family, whose ancestor had come to the city as an officer in the Cromwellian army. Sarah gave birth to a son in August 1805, and William Drennan attended the birth. Sarah named her child William Rowan in honour of her husband's employer. William Rowan Hamilton grew to be Ireland's greatest mathematician, and famously carved the theory of quaternions with a penknife on Broom Bridge, Cabra, in 1843. Back when the young genius was an infant, the courts held that Rowan's offer 'to compound for the sum £1,500 was equitable and sufficient'.[441] However, for some years Rowan had no agent to help administer the affairs of his widely scattered lands and properties.

In February 1806, William Pitt died, and a new administration, known as 'the Ministry of all the Talents', was formed, which included Charles Fox. Rowan's friend and fellow political exile William Sampson was in Hamburg at this point, hoping for permission to return home. Hamburg was in danger of being invaded by Prussian troops. Sampson, his wife and family took ship for England, and he immediately presented himself at Charles Fox's London office. He did not get to meet Fox, and when the next day he went to the office of Lord Spencer he was arrested and told

---

441 Nicolson, p. 175.

that he was not welcome in England or Ireland and that he must take ship for America immediately. His wife appealed to Fox, who saw to it that the deportation was delayed for a few weeks. She then appealed to some of Sampson's old friends from Ireland, well placed in Westminster, to help him. Lord Moira, Henry Grattan and John Philpot Curran either ignored Mrs Sampson's letters or refused to help. This was particularly disgraceful in the case of Curran, who had worked together with Sampson in many famous trials in Ireland in the 1790s. When the Sampsons had a son in 1794 they named him John Philpot Curran Sampson. Sampson's Irish friends were afraid of appearing to be in sympathy with treason.

There was one Irishman who was not afraid to stand by an old friend. Rowan wrote to him 'with every offer of service pecuniary or otherwise. He made an application for permission to visit Sampson, which was granted'.[442] Sampson went to America in April. His wife returned to Belfast for a short time. When Martha McTier called on her in July she gave her full details of the shabbiness of Moira, Grattan and Curran, and the generosity, not to say courage, of Rowan.

Rowan bought a house in Leinster Street in Dublin with a garden adjoining the Irish Royal Society. He had laboratories installed at Killyleagh, Rathcoffey and his Dublin home. He dabbled in chemistry and studied printing and lithography. He attempted to make Killyleagh a centre for the linen trade, and he built two new streets in the town to house the working people.[443] He was a benevolent and fair landlord who exhibited a real concern for the well-being of his tenants. In times of distress he

442 Agnew, iii, p. 506.
443 Nicolson, p. 184.

would reduce rents. His tenants at Killyleagh wrote to him in 1814 telling him:

> Our best thanks are due, and are hereby given to Archibald Hamilton Rowan Esquire, not so much for his unsolicited reduction of our rents as for the patriotic liberality which induced him to meet and share the distress of the day with his tenantry.[444]

Rowan always maintained the reputation of being the poor man's friend. He was very involved in charitable work with the Great Strand Street Unitarians, and was unique among upper-class philanthropists of his era in that he gave public support to trade unions, which were regarded as illegal combinations at the time. Among the unions that thanked him for his support in times of distress or during industrial disputes were the Silk Manufacturers of Dublin, the Working Ribbon Weavers, the Dublin Lamplighters, the Operative Broad Silk Manufacturers and the Glovers and Skinners.

John Hancock, a Quaker friend from Lisburn, shared many of Rowan's political and social opinions.[445] Like Rowan he was an outspoken critic of slavery and the slave trade. He wrote to Rowan to congratulate him for supporting the silk weavers:

> I am completely with thee in thy reasonings in their favour; I am pleased to see thee stand forward as the tribune of the people on this occasion. The common calamity affecting all classes of the community necessarily leads to disputes between the employers and the employed, in the struggle of each class trying to shift the back-breaking load off themselves; but I

---

444 Drummond, p. 382.
445 *loc. cit.*

fear all will be in vain, without a total change of the system.[446]

A Dalliance with Treason?

He had promised Sarah and the government that he would have no more involvement in treason, but he did not promise that would not continue to fight for religious liberty through constitutional means. From the moment of his return he associated with those Roman Catholics who were still demanding religious emancipation. He joined the Catholic Committee. In 1811, King George III, the greatest opponent of Roman Catholic rights, relapsed into mental illness for the last time and his son, also George, became Prince Regent. Catholic hopes were revived as it was expected that the Tories would lose power to the Whigs, who favoured emancipation. The new Regent reappointed the Tories, however, much to the dismay of the Roman Catholics and their liberal Protestant supporters.

In December 1811 Rowan attended a meeting in Fishamble Street, which was called to send a pro-emancipation petition to the Prince Regent. The meeting was declared illegal and broken up by the magistrate. Rowan assisted in reconvening the meeting in another venue. This meeting was also broken up, and it was clear to Rowan that the government of the day had no intention of allowing even constitutional activity in pursuit of Roman Catholic rights. The realization that constitutional methods were unlikely to deliver Catholic emancipation may have caused Rowan to waver in his determination never again to risk flirting with treason.

Catholic leaders were concerned that disaffection was spreading. In an attempt to convince the government of

---

446 Drummond, p. 392.

their loyalty they cast suspicion on their own supporters by informing the Castle that:

> The old system of United Men [is reviving], consisting of brewers, bakers, butchers, grocers, shoemakers and the like, but looking to higher leaders like the Catholic delegates, or former United Irishmen; and one to the 'conspirators' claimed to have been told that it was a 'new business ... similar to the plan of Robert Emmet in 1803 ... that an Ambassador ... had arrived from France stating that the French would soon invade England or Ireland.'[447]

Fortunately for Rowan, the government did not take this information seriously. A French agent had visited Dublin, and Rowan was one of the few people he had consulted. Luke Lawless was sent as an agent by Napoleon to 'discover the dispositions of the Irish people and the identity of any leaders of any party still seeking independence from Britain'.[448] Rowan was taking a great risk in not only meeting Lawless but, according to Lawless, encouraging the French to invade and assuring Lawless that the County Down Presbyterians would support an invasion. Elliott tells us that:

> Rowan also assured Lawless that despite the government's campaign to separate the Presbyterians from the Catholics, their love of independence remained strong and they would join again with the Catholics if another rising occurred. The decline of the linen industry, the closure of the American and continental

---

447 Elliott. p. 356.
448 *Ibid*, p. 358.

markets, and the competition from English cotton
had intensified the northern Presbyterians' distrust
of England, and he had been assured by the County
Down people that they would welcome another
opportunity to overturn English rule in Ireland.[449]

If Rowan actually said these things to Lawless he was either
'living in a fool's paradise' or he was telling the agent what he
thought he wanted to hear. Rowan's personal disillusionment
with the French Revolution began during his imprisonment
in Brest during the Terror of 1795, and only increased after
the fall of Robespierre. Most of the surviving United Irishmen
had long before come to despise Napoleon, not so much for
his cynical betrayal of Ireland but because of his imperial and
anti-democratic usurpation of the principles of the revolution.
Rowan must have known that in 1812 very few County
Down people would have welcomed a French invasion force.

As Napoleon did not press ahead with his invasion plans,
the account of the disposition of the northern Presbyterians
attributed to Rowan was never tested. If Lawless reported
Rowan accurately this was, as far as we know, Rowan's last
brush with treason. Perhaps Lawless was urging a Napoleonic
invasion, and it is possible that he fabricated, or at least
embellished, Rowan's views.

Shortly after Lawless's visit Rowan received a letter
from the poet Percy Bysshe Shelley, who was 19 years old
at this time. Shelley had come to Dublin to distribute his
pamphlet, *An Address to the Irish People*. Shelley was at the
time a disciple of Rowan's old friend William Godwin. In a
letter dated 25 February 1812 Shelley enclosed some copies
of his pamphlet and promised to send copies of a new one
on which he was still working.

---

449 *Ibid.*, p. 360.

Rowan's previous biographers disagree as to whether Rowan either answered the letter or met the young poet. Drummond, who had the advantage of knowing Rowan personally, said that 'it cannot be doubted that Mr Hamilton Rowan treated the young enthusiast with his wonted courtesy and hospitality'. Nicolson claimed that Drummond had no basis for this assertion and that Rowan did not answer Shelley's letter, doubting whether Rowan's 'esteem for Godwin was wholly unmixed.'[450] With gratuitous nastiness, Nicolson referred to Godwin as 'a greedy old man'. Nicolson's doubts about Rowan's feelings towards Godwin probably arose from his abiding enmity towards both his subject, Rowan, and the much-respected old philosopher.

All the evidence suggests that Rowan and Godwin were dear and sincere friends. Godwin's diary records the pair in regular, if not in daily, contact during Rowan's London years between 1803 and 1806. Nicolson notes that Rowan had made a generous financial donation to Godwin 'when he could ill afford it'. However, he cannot bring himself to believe that this was a gesture from a decent wealthy man to a friend in need. It is clear from the invective that pervades Nicolson's book that generous gestures, or indeed any expression of sympathy or benevolence towards fellow human beings, were to Nicolson at best indications of eccentricity and at worst indicated egomaniacal insanity.

Shelley was in lodgings in Sackville Street, Dublin, and Rowan kept the letter in Killyleagh, so it is likely that it was addressed to him there.[451] Had he been in Dublin at the time he would almost certainly have reacted as Drummond suggests.

---

450 Nicolson, p. 186.
451 *loc. cit.*.

Within a few days of his arrival in Dublin on 28 February, Shelley addressed a meeting called in favour of Catholic emancipation. He got a mixed reception. Shelley 'desired the emancipation of Catholics from their legal disabilities, but he avowedly desired still more their emancipation from Catholicism'.[452] It is not surprising therefore that 'some of his references to the Catholic religion were received by his audience with strong signs of disapproval'.[453]

Shelley was deeply disappointed by what he found in Ireland. He told his friend Miss Hitchener:

> One class was bigoted, another lost in petty party aims, another blankly apathetic, [and] only in the remnant of the United Irishmen did he find spirits who seemed capable of being anything but merely oppositionist or ministerial.[454]

His favourable reference to the remnant of the United Irishmen suggests that he did indeed meet Rowan. There is absolutely no doubt that Rowan would have gone out of his way to meet any friend of Godwin had it been possible. It is also very likely that if Rowan was in Dublin on 28 February 1812 he would have attended the meeting at which Shelley spoke.

The booksellers of Dublin were afraid to stock Shelley's pamphlet and the poet had to hire an Irish servant to distribute it in the street. Passers-by in Sackville Street were surprised when copies of a pamphlet were dropped at their feet. They could not know, of course, that the youth at the window overhead who was raining down sedition, literally on their heads, would one day be recognized as one of England's greatest poets.

---

452 Wise (1890), p. 19.
453 *Ibid.*, p. 20.
454 *loc. cit.*

Shelley's pamphlet was an attempt to put into simple language the benevolent, tolerant and enlightened philosophy originally pioneered by Francis Hutcheson and later espoused with vigour by the United Irishmen. In 1812, however, benevolence and tolerance were in some ways a beaten docket in Ireland. The alliance of oppressed Catholics and democratic Protestants and Dissenters that was the very essence of the United Irish Society had broken down. William Drenann feared that the Catholic community were beginning 'to pursue their own community interests while ignoring the greater goal of creating a common civil society'.[455] In the years ahead Roman Catholics would pursue emancipation supported by the old United Irishmen such as Drennan and Rowan, but when they went on to campaign for repeal of the Union the liberal Protestants preferred to seek the reform of society in alliance with their fellow reformers in Britain.

455 Hall (2011), p. 62.

18.

New Light on Presbyterian Loyalty

If the disposition of the northern Presbyterians was as Rowan allegedly described it to Lawless in 1812, it was to alter dramatically within a few years. Most of the northern leadership of the United Irishmen who had survived the rebellion had either welcomed, or eventually became reconciled to, the Union. It is true that, unlike Rowan, they did not become reconciled to its architect, Castlereagh. Some, including Reverend William Steel Dickson, did all they could to ensure that Castlereagh was defeated in the 1805 election. Dickson's antipathy to Castlereagh was not about the Union; it was about his betrayal of the cause of reform and his support for the execution, imprisonment and banishing of his former supporters.

Most Ulster Presbyterians saw the 1798 rebellion as a disaster for the common people of Ireland, both Catholic and Protestant. It was also a significant setback for the Unitarians, although the scale of damage did not become apparent for a number of years afterwards. Two factors served to obscure the extent to which contemporaries believed that the Unitarian theology and liberal politics of Rowan and his fellows had ushered in the calamitous events of 1798. There is a very old saying to the effect that success has many fathers but failure is an orphan. In 1799 the Synod of Ulster was anxious to play down the involvement of Presbyterian ministers in the rebellion, claiming that only a very small number of clergy were involved on the rebel side. The Synod minute of 1799 records:

> The Synod has the satisfaction of finding, that the general conduct of its members and probationers has been conformable to order and good government, in the late afflicting circumstances of the country. It appears that of the comparatively small numbers implicated in treasonable or seditious practices, two only, one a Minister, the other a Probationer, have been executed; two are still in confinement – some have expressed their sincere contrition – others are no longer connected to the Synod – and the remainder have either voluntarily or with the permission of government removed from the kingdom.[456]

Those who drafted this minute were being disingenuous. They knew well that 'three [ministers] had been executed, eighteen more were incarcerated ... Twenty had fled or were transported to the United States'.[457] In spite of this the Synod maintained the fiction that the Presbyterian clergy had been, with a few exceptions, supporters of the government.

The involvement of some prominent New Light ministers on the government side and some Old Lights on the side of the rebels served to mislead historians, if not

---

456 Clifford (1991), p. 111.
457 McBride (1993), p. 207.

well-informed contemporaries, about the true nature of the Presbyterian rebellion.

New Light ministers such as Reverends Robert Black, William Bruce and Vance sided with the government while Old Lights such as John Glendy and Reverends Thomas Ledlie Birch and Henry Henry fought with the rebels. This served to suggest that the matter of whether one was Old Light or New Light was irrelevant to which side one was on. A modern historian, Reverend William McMillen, has identified that of thirty ministers and probationers who had some association with the rebels, twenty-seven were New Light.[458] The rebellion in Antrim and Down involved a broad section of the Ulster Presbyterian people, but it was driven by the enlightenment and democratic principles of the New Light Presbyterian clergy and elders.

Castlereagh knew well what the real situation was, and made particular use of those New Light Ministers who had sided with the government. In the aftermath of the rebellion he initiated a dialogue with Reverends Black and Bruce to use the *regium donum*, a government grant to help to pay ministers, to strengthen the Loyalists and weaken the democrats within the Synod.

After the rebellion, his father, Lord Londonderry (the murderer of Reverend James Porter of Greyabbey), had used his financial leverage on some congregations to force them to remove the ministers he believed were sympathetic to the rebellion.[459] Castlereagh now had access to the deeper pockets of the state, and followed his father's strategy, but on a grander scale.

Reverend Robert Black had written to Castlereagh in 1800 assuring him that he could appeal to the fund of good

---

458 McMillen in Swords (1997), p.85.
459 *Ibid.,* p. 94.

sense in the Synod to impress on them the importance of loyalty to the government. In the minute of the 1799 Synod quoted above, Black tried to ingratiate himself with Castlereagh by denouncing the imprisoned Reverend William Steel Dickson, in his absence, for involvement in treason and sedition. He did not name Dickson, but it was clear to all that he was one of the two ministers in confinement that the minute suggested was implicated in treason. When Dickson was released from internment in Fort George in Scotland in 1802, he fought for more than a decade with Black and the Synod to force them to reverse their arbitrary verdict.

Under the new *regium donum* scheme only ministers of 'good character', that is those who were loyal, would benefit from Castlereagh's and the government's new benevolence. McBride suggests that:

> Castlereagh wanted to reward those who have committed themselves in support of the State against a democratic party in the Synod, several of whom, if not engaged in the Rebellion, were deeply infected with its principles. It was only 'a considerable fermentation' in the body, perhaps even a schism, which would change its temper.[460]

Black and Bruce were Unitarians, but Bruce, in William Drennan's words, was now 'walking hand in hand with Castlereagh in a new alliance of Church and State'. However, the two ministers, whether they knew it or not, were being used by Castlereagh to ferment a split in Irish Presbyterianism. Castlereagh's use of the *regium donum* did not achieve his ambition of a schism at this point. He was

---

460 McBride (1998), p. 217.

accused of trying to develop a hierarchy in Presbyterian Church governance, which had the effect of uniting New and Old Lights against what they saw as an 'attempt to make the Synod a creature of the State'.[461] The tension Castlereagh fostered continued, albeit under the surface, for many years before the eventual schism that saw the exit of the democrats from the Synod.

One issue of contention was the disgraceful treatment of Steel Dickson, who continued to be ostracized by the Loyalists and supported by the Democratic Party. However, the central, if unspoken, fault lines were between those who saw the United Irishmen and rebels of 1798 as heroes and those who regarded them as infatuated fools and traitors. The other issue of division was the question of what the relationship between Presbyterians and Roman Catholics should be. Would emancipation help Roman Catholics to shake off priestly superstition and enjoy civil religious liberty as tolerant free citizens, or would emancipation be a step in the onward march of Popery and pose a threat to the very existence of Protestantism in Ireland? Rowan and his fellow Unitarians inclined towards the former view. Their prestige and influence took a hammering in 1798. As one historian observed, 'the insurrection was the beginning of the end for liberals in politics and theology and the reaction told in favour of Toryism and Orangemen.'[462] When the battle lines were drawn again, Rowan in old age made a courageous stand for the old Unitarian values. He might have won or drawn the argument if the question put were 'should Roman Catholics be treated with toleration?', but that was not how the question was posed. He and fellow Unitarians were not asked about their attitude to Catholics,

461 *Ibid.*, p. 218.
462 Swords, p. 87.

but about whether they believed Jesus Christ to be God or the son of God. It would have been difficult to win an argument anywhere in Christian Europe in the early nineteenth century if the only answer you could give to that question with a clear conscience were 'no'. It appears that many Ulster Presbyterians who felt they had followed the Unitarians into a futile and calamitous rebellion were not prepared to follow them to hell and eternal damnation.

For the first decade or so after the rebellion, however, things carried on much as they had done among the Ulster Presbyterians throughout the preceding century. New Lights and Old Lights tolerated each other and members of congregations followed their individual consciences and tried to avoid theological disputes within the Synod and elsewhere. The dispute between Reverend Black and William Steel Dickson was an embarrassment to most moderate Presbyterian clergy, who just wanted to get on with tending to the spiritual needs of their congregations.

For Rowan, religious opinions were always a matter of private conviction. In his early manhood and middle age, when his religious beliefs lay lightly on his shoulders, he never felt he needed to defend his opinions publicly. In his seventieth year, though, as he entered old age, a climate of uncharacteristic intolerance began to be asserted within Irish Presbyterianism, and the days when Unitarians such as Rowan would be tolerated within the Synod of Ulster were coming to an end. In the coming battle Rowan would be in the heart of the fray, not in order to attack any other person's religious opinions but simply to assert his right to his own opinions without being branded a heretic.

When he had settled in Ireland back in 1784 he found the rational and liberal religion available to him there to be very congenial. In Dublin, at Great Strand Street, Reverend John Moody was long-time minister, and William Bruce was his assistant from 1782. William Bruce was still in his pro-reform and liberal phase, and would have expounded on the need for parliamentary reform and civil and religious liberty, the causes so dear to Rowan's heart. Bruce had worn his Volunteer uniform when he preached at the great Volunteer conventions of the era.

Rowan and Bruce had both attended Warrington Academy, where Bruce had studied under Dr Joseph Priestley. When Bruce moved on to Rosemary Street, Belfast, in 1790, Rowan could still attend the sermons of that other old Warringtonian and pupil of Priestley's, Reverend John Moody. Moody was held in great esteem by the Roman Catholics of Dublin as a result of his efforts on their behalf.[463] Reverend Boyle Moody, minister at Newry, a brother of John Moody, was imprisoned after the rebellion and died as a result of his persecution in 1799.[464] If Rowan attended the other Unitarian meeting house at Eustace Street, Dublin, he would have listened to Reverend Philip Taylor, who had studied at Warrington under John Aikin, the father of Anna Barbauld, whom Rowan regarded as the first love of his life.

Moody ministered for fifty years in Dublin, and when Rowan returned from exile in 1806 he could again attend Moody's sermons. Moody had presided at the baptism of Castlereagh in 1769, the marriage of Mary Anne Emmet, witnessed by her younger brother, Robert, in 1799, and the funerals of Mary Anne Emmet and her son, Hugh Emmet, in 1805.

When Rowan was resident at Killyleagh he was just as well served in terms of Unitarian theology for 'the presbytery at Killyleagh had long been the most heterodox connected

---

463 Armstrong (1829), p. 75.
464 Swords, p. 113.

with the Synod of Ulster'.[465] Heterodox, in this context, means that Unitarians predominated or were at least very welcome in the congregation. The minister at Killyleagh from 1813 to 1817 was Reverend William McEwen, a very learned man who, when he left Killyleagh, took up the position of professor of elocution at the Belfast Academical Institution. In 1824 McEwen became the first editor of the *Northern Whig*, a liberal newspaper that Rowan had a hand in establishing. Such was McEwen's admiration for Rowan that he penned a poem in his honour:

> And there was one with master mind
> Each feeling of his heart refined
> When flashed his eye t'was sweet to trace
> The eagle daring of his race!
> And he who wakes the minstrel shell
> His virtues knew and loved them well
> A mind with classic lore imbued
> A heart that prized his country's good
> The first to raise the patriot band
> When rose the valiant of the land
> Fair freedom traced his name on history page
> Her bravest knight in youth, her steadiest friend in age.

The Academical Institute and the Blackman

In 1814, a number of Rowan's former United Irish and Unitarian associates came together to found the Belfast Academical Institute, which is to this day a highly regarded centre of learning in Belfast. Directly in front of the elegant Georgian edifice stands a statue of Reverend Henry Cooke DD, which is colloquially known as 'The Blackman'. The

---

465 *Ibid.*, p. 88.

Blackman has his back turned to the institute, which he regarded from its foundation as a cauldron of heresy and democratic liberalism.

The institute's founders included William Drennan (resettled in his native Belfast since 1807), William Tennant, Robert Caldwell and Robert Simms. The latter three had been proprietors of the *Northern Star*. Also among the founders was Reverend Henry Henry, an Old Light minister who had been imprisoned as a rebel in 1798. Drennan explained that the object of the new institution was to 'offer a useful and liberal education to the young of the province without distinction to sect or profession'.[466] He hoped to 'diffuse knowledge among the middling orders, to stimulate the study of the Irish language, and to inculcate love of country'.

Castlereagh and the Irish Secretary, Robert Peel, were concerned by the influence that 'democrats' such as Drennan wielded in the management of the institute. Castlereagh's main concern was that if Drennan's new institution could train Presbyterian ministers and grant certificates of qualification, then it amounted to 'a deep laid scheme to bring the Presbyterian Synod into the ranks of democracy'.[467]

So now, fourteen years on from his original interference in the affairs of the Synod, Castlereagh was again exerting influence in the same old conservative cause. A close eye would be kept on the proceedings at the Belfast Academical Institute.

The democrats made a major error of judgement when they held a Saint Patrick's Eve dinner in 1816. There must have been a great deal of alcohol consumed for the event turned into something like a United Irish reunion. Robert

---

466 McBride (1998), p. 212.
467 *loc. cit.*

Tennent, the chairman and former United Irishman, told the assembly that the institute would pass on the spirit of 1782 and 1792 to a new generation. Toasts were drunk to the American and French Revolutions and the old United Irish call for 'A Radical Reform in the Representation of the people in Parliament' was heard in public for the first time in many years.[468] Robert Tennent had to resign as chairman, and Castlereagh was able to use the affair as a pretext for increasing the government's control over appointments to the institute.

In the last quarter of the previous century, Presbyterians had sought to 'contain doctrinal differences which had earlier disturbed the peace'.[469] In the second decade of the nineteenth century, however, two developments added fuel to the fire that Castlereagh had been trying to fan for more than a decade. In 1813 the law was changed, and it ceased to be a criminal offence to call oneself a Unitarian. With the change, many who had lived in a tradition of circumspection were now for the first time free and proud to declare their theological positions. Some of them boasted about the progress of Unitarianism, much to the disquiet of their orthodox colleagues. On the other hand, orthodox Presbyterianism began to be infected by a spirit of evangelism and the 'missionary impulse which had begun to revitalize the British Churches in the wake of the French Revolution'.[470] Conservative Presbyterians began to challenge others on questions of orthodoxy. It was probably inevitable that the compromise which had held the Presbyterians together for so long could not endure in the changing circumstances.

It is a sad irony that Archibald Hamilton Rowan, who had given the best years of his life to advocating a

468 *Ibid.*, p. 212.
469 *Ibid.*, p. 219.
470 *loc. cit.*

brotherhood of all the sects, played a pivotal, though wholly unintentional, role in bringing the tensions between the orthodox and the liberals to the surface.

When Reverend McEwen, the minister at Killyleagh, resigned his position to take up his new post at the Belfast Academical Institute in April of 1817, Rowan attempted to recruit a replacement for his friend. His first choice was Reverend Henry Montgomery, who was at that time ministering to a congregation at Dunmurray, near Belfast. Rowan knew that Montgomery was a Unitarian and would have been very impressed by his spirited defence of William Steel Dickson at the Synod in 1813. Dickson had laboured for years to reverse Black's and the Synod's condemnation of him. In that year, Montgomery finally succeeded in having the condemnation overturned.

Montgomery turned down the invitation to Killyleagh, however, because he too was expecting to be offered a post at the Academical Institute. In fact, he was offered and accepted the post of headmaster of English just ten days after he had received Rowan's letter inviting him to Killyleagh.[471]

McEwen then suggested that Rowan invite 29-year-old Reverend Henry Cooke, who was at the time minister to a congregation at Donegore, near Templepatrick, to preach at Killyleagh. This was usually a prelude to appointment as a minister if the congregation liked what they heard.

Cooke was only 10 years old when in 1798 the minister who had baptized him, Reverend John Glendy, had to flee his burning meeting house because of his involvement in the rebellion. Cooke watched as two elders of his congregation were hanged. Cooke blamed Glendy for turning Maghera into a hotbed of rebellion, and believed that Glendy had inculcated his congregation with 'his revolutionary principles

---

471 Boyd (2006), p. 16.

without opportunity or power of reply'.[472] J. L. Porter, Cooke's biographer, observed that 'atheism and infidelity were boldly avowed by the leaders of the United Irishmen while the Loyalists were generally orthodox'.[473] Very much later, Cooke claimed that this formative experience turned him into a great respecter of the status quo and law and order.

Cooke came highly recommended by McEwen, who told the elders at Killyleagh:

> By rendering every service in your power to Mr Cooke you will secure to yourself the society of a well-informed man, and to the congregation a useful and popular preacher. He is by no means bigoted in his opinions, and has too much good sense not to be charitable toward those who differ from him in sentiment … he possesses great general information, and you will find him a good scholar, an able preacher and an honourable man.[474]

McEwen was right to suggest that Cooke was a good preacher. He impressed the Killyleagh congregation and was given the position. McEwen was wrong about Cooke, though, in almost every other respect, for Cooke was a zealous bigot who never displayed any charity towards those who differed from him in sentiment, and did not think that personal honour was important when he was engaged in what became his life's work. Within a few years Cooke would embark on a crusade of heresy hunting, hounding Unitarians out of the Presbyterian Church in Ireland.

---

472 Porter (1871), p. 10.
473 *Ibid.*, p. 13.
474 *Ibid.*, p. 17.

Cooke was a conservative in politics and a supporter of the great Ulster landowners and the Orange societies, to which most Presbyterians of the day, including Rowan, had an aversion.

It is unlikely that Cooke would have lasted at Killyleagh if it were not for the fact that he had an important ally among the elders, one who shared his conservative politics and his antipathy towards Unitarianism. This was none other than Rowan's own son, Captain Sidney Hamilton Rowan. Sidney was apparently a man of:

> Ardent piety and undaunted courage ... animated by a love for evangelical truth and by the desire to eradicate Arianism [Unitarianism] from the Presbyterian Church in Ireland.[475]

Sidney's undaunted courage is no surprise given what we know of his parents and his older brother, William.

How or why Sidney developed his love of evangelical truth and his apparent religious intolerance is a mystery. His parents were Unitarians. How could he have wished to drive his parents, their friends and his own former minister at Killyleagh, Reverend McEwen, out of the Presbyterian Church? Unlike most other Protestants or Christians, Unitarians do not try to inculcate their children with the beliefs of their parents. If Rowan and Sarah thought that their children would of their own accord develop liberal and tolerant religious sentiments, they were very wrong in the case of Sidney.

Perhaps Sidney had an antipathy to his father because he had abandoned his children and risked the family's fortune and reputation in a cause that Sidney either did not understand or abhorred.

---

475 *Ibid.*, p. 17.

Heresy Confronted

It is not clear if Cooke and Rowan clashed over theology during the first few years of Cooke's ministry at Killyleagh. The matter did come to a head in the spring of 1821 when Rowan invited Reverend John Smethurst of Exeter to preach there. A short time earlier the Belfast newspapers carried an advertisement to the effect that Smethurst had been appointed:

> By the Unitarian fund in England to visit the Province of Ulster, and would shortly commence his mission by preaching in Belfast, Carrickfergus, Lisburn, Saintfield, Downpatrick, Killyleagh and adjoining districts.[476]

The invitation to Smethurst to come to Ulster may have emanated from the Presbytery of Antrim, which was and had always been Unitarian, or from the democrats in the Belfast Academical Institute. The fact that Killyleagh was mentioned in the original advertisement suggests that the initial invitation may have come from Archibald Hamilton Rowan. Perhaps he was wearying of the zealous Trinitarian orthodoxy that he had been forced to endure for nearly four years. Certainly the liberal and free theology of Smethurst, along with his democratic and radical social outlook, would have been like a breath of fresh air to Rowan at this point.

Smethurst's mission started well, and he attracted large numbers of people, 'particularly those who still remembered the heroic rebels of '98'.[477] However, a hostile witness, J. L. Porter, suggested that Smethurst overplayed his hand, and that:

---

476 Boyd, p. 19.
477 *loc. cit.*

> He assailed the doctrine of the Trinity, insulted the
> Trinitarians, told them they taught the supreme
> Deity of the saviour because they lived by it and
> generally concluded his address with a few political
> touches advocating advanced liberal views, which
> most thoughtful men would call revolutionary.[478]

Porter was Cooke's son-in-law and biographer and was
justifying his hero's later actions. It is highly unlikely that
Smethurst had assailed any doctrine or insulted anybody,
although it is very likely that he had expressed advanced
liberal political opinions. He almost certainly spoke about
the connection between the Presbyterian Church and the
State as fostered by Black, Bruce and Castlereagh, and may
have suggested that such connections are not good for the
development of true and liberal religion. It is unfortunate
that Porter does not record what Smethurst's political
comments were so we could assess whether or not they
were revolutionary. Most of the political controversy of the
time concerned reform of representation in Parliament.
For 'thoughtful' Tories of the day, anyone who supported
parliamentary reform, broadening of the franchise or Catholic
emancipation was considered a revolutionary. We know that
in 1821 Rowan was very publicly identified with the Catholic
Association's effort to keep the Catholic rights question on the
agenda. The English and Irish Unitarians would at this point
have been strong advocates of Catholic rights and very vocal
in favour of the abolition of slavery, which was still thriving
in the southern American states. It is likely, therefore, that
Smethurst's political comments addressed these matters.

Whether or not Porter's account of Smethurst's preaching
is fair or accurate, the mission seems to have gone very well

---

478 *loc. cit.*

until he came to Killyleagh, when it started to go terribly wrong. Cooke and Sidney Hamilton Rowan were there to tell him that he was heretical and that he and his friends would be fully answered the following week if they chose to come and listen. The following Sunday the Killyleagh Meeting House was filled to capacity, with many who could not gain entrance clustering about the windows and doors. Smethurst was not present as Cooke denounced him and 'expounded the true gospel of Jesus Christ'. Thereafter, Cooke and Sydney Hamilton Rowan followed and harassed Smethurst everywhere he went:

> Wherever Smethurst would be preaching, Saintfield, Downpatrick, Carrickfergus or any other place he was billed to be, Cooke interrupted Smethurst, put questions, contradicted the Arian theology, and expounded what he believed to be the truth. That continued until Smethurst decided that he had had 'enough of that gentleman from Killyleagh who appeared to be most dreadfully alarmed about Unitarianism'. He brought his mission to a close and returned to England.[479]

Cooke, however, had enjoyed 'the excitement of public controversy', and had no intention of stopping now. He next turned his attention on what Castlereagh regarded as the democratic faction within the Belfast Academical Institute. Ironically, the focus of Cooke's first formal attack was the appointment of William Bruce junior, the son of Castlereagh's old collaborator to the chair of Biblical languages Hebrew and Greek. Most of the Unitarians at the institute were not best pleased with the appointment

---

479 *Ibid.*, p. 20.

of Bruce junior, perhaps because of the well-known links between his father and Castlereagh. In spite of the young Bruce's loyalism and proven qualifications, Cooke pointed out the dangers of permitting a man professing Arian views to train Presbyterian ministers. A few years previously Castlereagh had feared not the theological but the political dangers posed by many of the Unitarian teachers at the Academical Institute.

Cooke raised the matter of the appointment of Bruce junior at the annual Synod held in Newry in 1822. Due to the passage of time Cooke was introducing an old political conflict to a new generation in the Synod, albeit in the guise of a new theological dispute. Many of the original protagonists had passed on or were so old and infirm that they had withdrawn from public affairs. Reverend Black was dead. He had controlled the Synod from 1798, but lost his influence when Reverend Montgomery succeeded in overturning Black's denunciation of Steel Dickson at the Synod of 1813. Black committed suicide by throwing himself off Derry Bridge into the River Foyle in 1817.[480] William Drennan had died in 1820 insisting that an equal number of Protestants and Catholics carry his coffin to his grave. Castlereagh had descended into melancholy paranoia and would cut his own throat in August 1822. Steel Dickson was 78 years of age, and was living on charity in the form of a weekly allowance from Reverend McEwen's second Belfast congregation.[481] When Dickson died two years later, McEwen and some eight to ten other people stood by a pauper's grave in honour of a man who had once been so well known and popular that he had been appointed adjutant general of the County Down rebels in 1798.

---

480 Clifford (1991), p. 154.
481 Shannon, (1900), p. 49.

Cooke's attack on Bruce and the Unitarians at Newry did not have much effect, but he had now embarked on a crusade, and raised the matter again at the Synod the following year, this time with even less success. The Presbyterian clergy had no stomach for a theological schism. Cooke brought his crusade to the people and took to the road, travelling long distances on foot or horseback, preaching at two and sometimes three meetings a week. Some regarded him as a destructive influence, and his application for appointment to a congregation in Armagh was rejected in 1823. However, his relentless campaigning energy began to tell, and the following year he was elected moderator of the Synod of Ulster. This not only gave him new prestige but entitled him to be invited to London that year for discussions with a newly appointed parliamentary commission, which had been set up to advise as to what might be done about Catholic rights.

The Defeat of the Heretics

The renewed struggle for Catholic emancipation, which resulted from revived parliamentary interest in the question, gave rise to Rowan's last ever visit to England, as well as the last occasion on which he might have had to fight a duel.

On 14 February 1825, Mr George Robert Dawson, MP for Londonderry, launched a strong attack on the Catholic Association. He informed the House that Mr Hamilton Rowan had recently been admitted into membership of the association, and continued:

> [Rowan's name] was received with thunderous applause. Hamilton Rowan it will be remembered was one of the body called United Irishmen. He had been implicated in seditious practices in 1793, for which he

was imprisoned. Previous to his trial he contrived to escape, and remained for many years in exile. He was attainted for high treason, but being afterwards, by the lenity of government, allowed to return to Ireland, the best return that he could make for the mercy which had been shown to him was by enlisting himself as a member of an association quite as dangerous as that of his own United Irishmen. The name of this convicted traitor was received with thunderous applause, and why? In order that this recollection of the disastrous period with which that name was connected might be revived in the minds of the deluded peasantry, and help the designs of this abominable association.[482]

Robert Peel also censured the Catholic Association for their indiscretion in passing a vote of thanks to Archibald Hamilton Rowan, an act he regarded as 'sufficient to excite suspicion and alarm'.[483]

Rowan was not without friends in the House of Commons, and Mr Hely Hutcheson and Mr Brougham rose to his defence. Hutcheson told the House that 'Ireland had not now a man more universally respected for the integrity of his public principles and the virtues of his private life' than Hamilton Rowan. He went on to say that 'the most enlightened and best men in Ireland in 1793 had been among the United Irishmen', and had they succeeded in getting the reforms they sought the rebellion of 1798 would never have happened. Brougham said that:

> The charge against the Catholic Association was that they spoke with respect of an attainted traitor ...

---

482 Drummond, p. 403.
483 *loc. cit.*

There was not a man more dearly beloved in Ireland. If to hold Mr Rowan as an object of respect and affection be a crime, then we are all guilty.[484]

Rowan was now 74 years of age. Drummond tells us that 'the lion had grown old but not so sick as to be kicked with impunity'. Rowan made arrangements to travel to London to offer challenge to Dawson. On his arrival in the city he immediately wrote to Dawson 'in terms of more strength than suavity'. Lord Hotham, a young officer in the Guards, intervened, telling Rowan that if he wished to receive an explanation from Dawson he would first have to withdraw his own offensive letter. Rowan agreed, and thereafter received the following from Dawson:

16 Upper Grosvenor Street, June 30th 1825

Sir,
The letter which you have addressed to Lord Hotham, bearing the date 26th June, enables me to assure you, that in introducing your name into the debate in the House of Commons, I was influenced solely by considerations of public duty, and that nothing was further from my wish than intentionally to wound your feelings or to offer you any premeditated insult.
I have the honour to be, &c.
G. R. Dawson[485]

Dawson was 35 years old, and probably did not relish the thought of fighting a duel with a 74-year-old man. This

---

484 *Ibid.*, p. 406.
485 *loc. cit.*

letter satisfied Rowan and was the end of the affair as far as he was concerned.

However, his son, Captain William Hamilton Rowan, read of Robert Peel's words while on duty in the Mediterranean. He had to be restrained by his commander from resigning his commission and travelling to London to call Peel to account. He wrote a scathing letter to Peel pointing out that, while he did not approve of his father's attendance at political meetings, Peel's attack should not have been made. He reminded Peel that his father had received the King's pardon for his actions, and that in any event:

> Their stain had been blotted out by the blood of his children, shed in their country's service: one had died of sickness and hardship; another fell in action on the coast of Spain and he had himself been severely wounded.[486]

The ministerial attacks on Rowan were regarded as unfair and unwarranted by many, and he received numerous letters of support, including one from Lord Cloncurry, the Catholic aristocrat and former United Irishman. Cloncurry took the opportunity when sending Rowan a donation to the Great Strand Street charity to express his admiration and respect for that part of Rowan's life 'which has provoked the everlasting malice of the enemies of your country and humanity'.[487]

When his old friend the Quaker Poole heard of the affair, he wrote from America describing Rowan's excursion into England as foolish. He concluded with friendly advice:

---

486 Drummond, p. 417.
487 *loc. cit.*.

To old men such as we are, it appears to me to be of much more importance to preserve the quietude of our minds than to take a very deep interest of any kind in the affairs of the world from which we are soon to pass away.[488]

As it turned out, Rowan still had nine years to live, and he did not, or possibly could not, take his old friend's advice, for the campaign for Catholic emancipation had still to be won and his minister back in Killyleagh was slowly but surely using his crusade against the Unitarians to place himself at the head of a pan-Protestant alliance to resist Catholic claims.

When Henry Cooke was first formally asked his views on the question of Catholic emancipation, his response to the parliamentary commission appeared moderate in that he told them that he was in favour of limited concessions although the majority of Protestants were not. Shortly thereafter, however, he published a pamphlet 'calling on all loyal and orthodox men to support him in his campaign against Arians, Radicals and Papists'.[489]

It appeared to Cooke that both houses of Parliament were well disposed towards granting Catholic emancipation. Unlike many Presbyterians, Cooke had always shared the Tory politics of the great landed families. He determined to build a grand alliance of the landed gentry and the Orange society, which until then tended to draw its membership from among Anglicans rather than Presbyterians. Cooke was very successful in this endeavour, for Montgomery admitted that:

The entire Orangemen of Ireland from the peer in his castle to the peasant in his hovel rallied around him;

---

488 *Ibid.*, p. 421.
489 Boyd, p. 27.

Orthodoxy in all its phases hailed him as its champion.
Thus uniting Evangelicalism with Orangeism, the
countenance of the aristocracy with the applause of
the multitude, in a few months ... he had acquired
extraordinary popularity and influence.[490]

His aristocratic friend Lord Mountcashel, who was more
extreme in his anti-Catholicism, lied to the British House of
Lords when he told them that 99 per cent of Irish Protestants
were opposed to equal rights for Roman Catholics.
Mountcashel now urged Cooke to use his newly acquired
popularity and influence to expel the Unitarians from the
synod.[491] As long as Unitarians retained any influence on
the Presbyterian community they would use it to support
Catholic emancipation.

The Synod of 1827 was held in June of that year in
the Orange stronghold of Strabane. Thirty-eight elders
and 130 ministers attended to conduct the Synod, but the
assembly also attracted a vast concourse of people of other
denominations who came to demonstrate their support for
Cooke, 'the redoubtable leader of Orthodoxy and opponent
of the Roman Catholic claims'. At first Cook's move to
dismiss Reverend William Porter from his post as clerk of
the Synod because of his avowal of Arian views appeared
to flounder, but by the end of an acrimonious three days
of wrangling 117 ministers and eighteen elders declared
their orthodoxy. Montgomery knew that many who were
Unitarians had declared themselves orthodox out of fear of
losing their jobs, and he recorded that, as their names were
called:

490 *loc. cit.*
491 *Ibid.*, p. 28.

Some of them look down in shame, others looked up in agony; but only two alternatives presented themselves to view – closed pulpits, starving children and destitute old age, or all those appalling evils avoided by uttering a solemn falsehood before God and the world.[492]

Archibald Hamilton Rowan was of course outraged by the events at Strabane, and he wrote to Cooke requesting a meeting of the Killyleagh congregation to discuss the matter:

The late discussions in the Synod of Ulster [have a] tendency to divide the Presbyterian interest, to restrict its liberty and compromise its independence. It is desirable to ascertain whether such proceedings meet with the unanimous concurrence of the body of Presbyterians.

I do therefore request a meeting of the Presbyterian inhabitants of Killyleagh to take the subject into consideration.

The contrariety of our political opinions would not alone have caused the proceedings which the enclosed notice announces ... but your conduct at the Synod proves to me that the same spirit of intolerance prevails in your religious conduct.[493]

Rowan was ill at the time, but made the long journey from Dublin expecting that Cooke would facilitate the meeting. Cooke, however, absolutely refused to hold such a meeting, claiming that the *Northern Whig* newspaper, which was associated with Rowan, had misrepresented his

492 *Ibid.*, p. 31.
493 Swords, p. 87.

views.[494] Cooke had all his life resented the fact that Glendy, the minster who had baptized him, could expound his revolutionary views from the pulpit to a congregation who were given no right to reply. He was now determined to deny that very right to the eldest and most venerable member of his own congregation.

On Sunday 27 August 1827, Rowan attended the service in Killyleagh. When the service was over he stood up and asked the congregation to remain for a few minutes as he had some resolutions he wished them to discuss. Cooke was furious. The protagonists were not evenly matched. Cooke was by now at the height of his reputation and oratorical powers. He was the popular and influential leader of conservative Protestantism. Rowan was 76 years of age, his once-formidable presence reduced by old age and infirmity. Now in poor health, his hearing was very impaired and he could hear only a buzz when two or more people were talking.[495]

Cooke ordered the congregation to leave the meeting house and 'Rowan was left behind on his own standing erect in the pew with the resolutions still unread in his hand'.[496]

J. L. Porter, when describing his hero's great triumph over a sick and elderly man, claims that Rowan had been advised by his Unitarian friends to confront Cooke in this way and that it was they rather than Cooke who were responsible for Rowan's humiliation. There is no evidence for this claim. When Rowan decided to make a stand on any issue he was not given to seeking or taking the advice of others. It is inconceivable that this episode was planned by anyone other than Rowan himself.

---

494 Porter, p. 112.
495 Drummond, p. 430.
496 Orr, p. 225.

The End of Rowan's Public Life

On Tuesday 20 January 1829 a great meeting of friends of civil and religious liberty was held in the Rotunda in Dublin. The Duke of Leinster was in the chair. The newspapers of the day described how those attending were 'of the first rank, wealth, influence, talent, public and private worth'. Rowan, in his eightieth year, addressed the gathering, telling them that:

> He remembered early in life, when the people of this country were armed and determined to preserve themselves against foreign invaders – then he became one of a body now called the Old Volunteers. He remembered a period when the object was to remove domestic dissension – then he became a United Irishman; and now he came forward at a period when if Irishmen were really united, they must be free (Loud Cheers).[497]

As Rowan left the meeting he had to be helped by two friends, one on either side. As they walked down Sackville Street they were surrounded by an immense crowd who cheered their venerable hero. When the three tried to escape in a coach the crowd took the horses from the carriage and drew Rowan in triumph to his home in Leinster Street. This was the last opportunity the ordinary people of Dublin had to show their affection and respect for a man who had been a popular hero since the Mary Neal affair more than forty years earlier.

Yet even now he was not prepared to take Quaker Poole's advice and live out his last years quietly. In October 1831 he wrote to the *Northern Whig*, the liberal newspaper he had

---

497 Drummond, p. 431.

helped to found, suggesting that the old test of the United Irishmen could be adopted by the reform movement of the day. He suggested that reformers should pledge to use all their abilities and influence for the:

> Attainment of an impartial representation of British subjects in Parliament under our most gracious monarch William the Fourth, in the spirit proposed by his highly esteemed Ministers Lord Grey, &c, ...
> Entering my 82nd year, frail in body as in mind, such as I am I am yours sincerely,
> A. H. Rowan.[498]

This should not be interpreted to mean that the old republican radical had become a monarchist in his dotage. The civic republicanism espoused by Rowan had its seed in the Cromwellian Commonwealth. It was revived by Francis Hutcheson, William Bruce and Thomas Drennan and blossomed during that circle's Dublin years among the old Protestant Dissenters at Wood Street. They had great reverence for William III and were enthusiastic supporters of the Hanovarian succession. They demanded civil and religious liberty and reform of representation in Parliament. It was only when George III opposed every measure of reform that the more radical elements such as the United Irishmen concluded that a brotherhood of affection between all the sects in Ireland would need to be forged if the cause of reform were to triumph. If Rowan's own generation 'of God-provoking democrats' added to the tapestry of this republican heritage it was by adopting the principle that every male citizen regardless of social rank should have an equal say in choosing their parliamentary representatives.

---

498 *loc. cit.*

Rowan urged people to support that great Reform Act sponsored by Lord Grey, which is sometimes regarded as the birth of modern British democracy. The Act came into force in 1832. William IV was cooperating with Lord Grey. Had George III and William Pitt behaved accordingly in the early 1790s it is likely that they would have had the full support of Archibald Hamilton Rowan and the United Irishmen.

In his beliefs, Rowan was totally consistent. He was an Irishman, a patriot and a republican, but he was never an Irish nationalist. He once observed that 'the votaries of liberty are of no country, or rather of every country'.[499] Rowan supported the Act of Union from the start. Most of his surviving United Irish and Unitarian comrades had no difficulty in seeing the significant economic benefits of the Union in Ulster. However, they continued to demand full civil and religious liberty under the British Crown and Parliament. It is hard to credit that Rowan was again prepared to collaborate with the French in 1811, but if it is true it was in the context where Catholic rights had again been denied and even constitutional protest was being suppressed.

Towards the end of 1831 Rowan again entered into public controversy, this time to save the reputation of Samuel Neilson, a long-dead but much-admired comrade. In that year Thomas Moore, a dear friend of Robert Emmet, published *The Life of Lord Edward FitzGerald*. Some interpreted certain passages in the book as accusing Neilson of betraying Lord Edward. The octogenarian Rowan was having none of it. He printed and circulated a robust defence of Neilson, which began as follows:

> Having had a long and sincere regard for Samuel Neilson and the strong conviction of his patriotism

499 Bric, p. 224.

and integrity I was extremely hurt to find that some unguarded expressions in a late publication concerning the death of Lord Edward Fitzgerald had been tortured by his enemies into a declaration that the capture of that unfortunate high-spirited young nobleman was to be attributed to information given by [Neilson] to the government.[500]

He also circulated the full text of the letter he had received from Neilson at Hamburg thirty years earlier. He asked Moore and the public 'to judge whether such sentiments as it contains could come from one so tainted'. Rowan's intervention totally vindicated Neilson, and Moore wrote a gracious and respectful letter to Rowan accepting the points he had made. Would that Rowan had known the true identity of the informer and his handler! The traitor who sold Lord Edward was a Catholic lawyer, Mangan, and his handler was none other than Rowan's incorrigible old persecutor, the Sham Squire.

Rowan's defence of Neilson was his last intervention in public affairs, and for the last two years of life he was cared for by two of his daughters, Miss Rowan and Mrs Fletcher. He pottered away with his experiments in his laboratory. In April 1834 his much-loved wife, Sarah, passed away. The woman whom he loved for nigh on fifty-five years and who had stood by him through the worst of times was now gone forever. Then on 17 August his eldest son, Captain William Hamilton, died at Rathcoffey following an accident. After this second blow Rowan went into a rapid decline, passing away on 1 November 1834.

The Unitarians of Great Strand Street, having no burial ground of their own, brought Rowan's body to the vault in

---

500 Drummond, p. 434.

Saint Mary's in what is now Wolfe Tone Street. There he was placed with his recently interred wife and son. Reverend James Armstrong read the service and Reverend William Drummond addressed the assembly.

Armstrong was born in Ballynahinch in County Down and received into the ministry in 1806. As a child he had likely witnessed the sack of that town by the military in 1798. Armstrong was an accomplished historian and his work on the origins of Protestant Dissent in Dublin did much to record for posterity its Cromwellian and New England connections.

Drummond had United Irish sympathies in his youth, and had some poetry published in the *Northern Star*. He had felt a cavalry officer's pistol to his head when he was threatened following the battle of Antrim. However, he was a changed man when he came to bury Rowan. His well-meaning eulogy of Rowan now reads as an embarrassing travesty, as does much of the biography of Rowan that Drummond published in Dublin in 1840. A modern historian, Philip Orr from County Down, had this to say about the Rowan portrayed in Drummond's funeral oration and his book:

> Instead of the young man who would have easily thrown the English out of Ireland as furniture out of a Cambridge window we meet a man eulogized ... for his Christian charity, his urbanity and courtesy. His patriotism we are told led him into excess and into unduly visionary projects, but now Rowan in death has gone to meet a God who sounds like an ideal cosmic landlord – his universal Father, friend and benefactor.[501]

---

501 Orr, p. 218.

If the choice of Drummond to contextualize the life of Archibald Rowan was particularly inappropriate, the choice of Saint Mary's as his final resting place was serendipitous: almost ninety years earlier Francis Hutcheson the philosopher and William Bruce his cousin and publisher had been interred there. In 1697 Rowan's paternal great-grandfather had founded the philosophy school at Killyleagh where Hutcheson and Bruce had first adopted their Dissenting Protestant principles.

In the document that might have propelled Rowan to the gallows in 1794, Wolfe Tone told the French that 'the Dissenters are much more numerous and are the most enlightened body of the nation ... they are enemies to English power from reason and reflection'. Hutcheson and Bruce had played a major part in developing those enlightened ideas.

At St Mary's, Rowan was laid to rest among his own.

19.

Conclusion

William Rowan and Gawin Hamilton, the grandfather and father of Archibald Hamilton Rowan, had bequeathed to him their radical Whig principles. In his early manhood Rowan had been exposed to the ideas of the most eminent political reformers in both England and Ireland. He was just 17 years old in 1768 when George III and his ministers initiated their campaign to silence John Wilkes. About this time the King began to alienate his American subjects, and Rowan heard at first hand the King's most articulate and able opponents tell the stories of how they had opposed arbitrary power and tyranny. Wilkes had been thrown into prison and Charles Lucas had escaped into exile. By the time Rowan met Lucas the good doctor had returned to Dublin in triumph, and as a member of the Irish House of Commons had earned a reputation on both sides of the Atlantic as a champion of civil liberty.

At Cambridge Rowan was mentored by Dr John Jebb, the most thoughtful and original revolutionary democrat of his era. In the year of his rustication Rowan attended Dr Priestley's Warrington academy, a cradle of liberal education and politics. If this were not enough to ensure that Rowan would spend his life fighting for radical and democratic causes, he was also profoundly influenced by Unitarianism.

As the modern world emerged in America and Europe, many of the leading radicals of the age refused to be bound by dogmas, superstition and ancient authority, whether civil or religious. For them, reason would be the guide of all human endeavours, both earthly and spiritual.

Rowan was associated with the Irish expression of Unitarianism, which thrived in Ulster and Dublin amongst the New Light Presbyterians. Rowan associated with the Great Strand Street Unitarian congregation in Dublin. Francis Hutcheson, William Bruce, John Abernethy and Tomas Drennan had once been associated with that congregation and had formed an influential circle of enlightened civic republicans. They demanded civil and religious liberty for all, including Roman Catholics. Many of Rowan's fellow Unitarians, including William Drennan, William Steele Dickson and Samuel Neilson, had been inspired by the work of Francis Hutcheson's group and became the leading lights of the new United Irish Society and helped determine its non-sectarian and democratic character.

Rowan possessed sympathy for the poor and downtrodden, which was sometimes expressed in charitable and philanthropic ways. On many occasions, however, such as the Mary Neal case and the shooting of the Dublin bull-baiters, he was prepared to fight an unforgiving ruling class in the pursuit of justice for the poor.

His two previous biographers suggest that he was motivated by a love of approbation and that he frequently sought the favourable opinion of others. Drummond implies that this was a form of immaturity or a character flaw. Nicolson views it as a sign of eccentricity, or even insanity. Francis Hutcheson believed that man's highest sense of worth is intimately tied up with selflessly giving to his community and being well thought of.[502] Rowan's supposed desire for approbation is explicable and perhaps even commendable in this context.

In truth, though, Rowan was not nearly so motivated by the need to be adored by others as these writers suggest. On the contrary, he was at the receiving end of the most scurrilous disparagement from two of the most obnoxious journalists of the age: Francis Higgins (the Sham Squire) and William Cobbett (Peter Porcupine). A man whose main concern was with popularity would never have championed such an unpopular cause as Rowan did when he supported the Act of Union against his America-based United Irish comrades, who were vehemently opposed to the measure. And that is not to mention that his political activities did not earn him much approbation from the person he loved most in the world, Sarah Hamilton Rowan.

It seems that it was the height of folly for Rowan to involve himself with the spy, Jackson. It is easier to understand when we realize that Jackson came recommended by a Unitarian network that Rowan trusted implicitly. The fact that Rowan's brother-in-law, Benjamin Beresford, was involved in the plot from the outset suggests that Rowan's involvement may have begun before he met Jackson in Newgate.

Rowan was appalled by what he witnessed in revolutionary France. His military escort to Brest boasted of their atrocities in the Vendée, and he watched from his cell window as many unfortunate men were dragged to the guillotine. After the fall of Robespierre, Rowan's boots were stained with the blood of revolutionaries murdered by their erstwhile comrades. He saw the rise of self-serving factions where he had expected the revolution to bring men to the fore

---

502 Dingley (2013), p 4.

who would give virtuous and selfless public service. He was moved to translate a speech of the great female republican, Roland, who cried out on her way to the guillotine, 'Oh Liberty, what crimes are committed in thy name!'

Rowan found the new republic in America to be motivated more by the pursuit of the dollar than the pursuit of happiness or virtue. While there was no Terror in America, the revolution descended into 'the rage of party', which eventually developed into the regulated conflict between rulers and opposition that is the very essence of parliamentary democracy. Much to his discomfort, he correctly foresaw that the new American capitalism would sharpen class divisions and antagonism.

When Rowan appeared before the King's Bench and went down on his knees to plead for pardon, was he betraying his principles in order to save his neck and his property? Certainly, none of the United Irishmen who survived the rebellion ever suggested any criticism of Rowan or his actions. Most survivors made the best arrangements they could with the government to get on with their lives after the defeat. Rowan's pardon did not involve him in implicating any of his old comrades. While he was prepared to express regret for the consequences of his own actions, he never criticized a fellow United Irishman, living or dead.

Rowan loved the company and conversation of intelligent men and women, but he was a man of action rather than an intellectual. It should be remembered that some of the greatest thinkers and writers of late eighteenth-century England admired Rowan and regarded him as a friend. Joseph Priestley, William Goodwin, Mary Wollstonecraft and Tom Paine were all proud to be associated with Archibald Hamilton Rowan.

When he was restored to Killyleagh he continued his charitable work and his fight on behalf of the lower orders and their trade unions. Like many of the surviving Belfast

United Irishmen, he promoted economic and industrial development and built houses for the workers in Killyleagh.

Rowan continued to support the right of Roman Catholics to equal citizenship. He always believed that once this was granted Catholics would shake off priestly influence and behave as enlightened men and free themselves from the influence of their Church. In that, he was sadly mistaken. After emancipation the influence of the Roman Catholic Church increased, and during the nineteenth century sectarian divisions in Ireland re-emerged with the ultras on both sides seizing the initiative and eclipsing the non-sectarian democratic liberalism that had been championed by the United Irishmen.

In spite of the total and utter defeat of the United Irishmen, Rowan must have felt some satisfaction in his old age as he saw how the world had changed. The United States of America had proven that Tom Paine's model of a democratic republic could be the sustainable basis for a modern state. It is true that slavery continued, but the slave trade had ended and the days of that accursed system were obviously numbered. Catholic emancipation had been achieved and, whilst universal suffrage had not yet been introduced, the 1832 Reform Act appeared to pave the way for further reform.

He did not live to see Daniel O'Connell's demand for the repeal of the Union increase sectarian divisions on the island, nor did he see his old protagonist, Reverend Henry Cooke, revel and prosper as he fanned the flames of increased intolerance.

His defeat at Killyleagh Meeting House at the hands of Cooke would not have concerned him unduly. While he would have deeply regretted the triumph of intolerance within the Presbyterian mainstream, he continued until the end of his days to worship with the staunch old Unitarians at Great Strand Street.

Archibald Hamilton Rowan was too much of an optimist to believe that reason and reflection would not eventually triumph over superstition and bigotry. He would have gone to his grave convinced that religious persecution would once again 'be compelled to abjure her tyranny over conscience'.

His optimism regarding the power of human reason, the capacity of humankind for selfless public virtue and the possibility of universal emancipation appears naïve in the light of subsequent history. Yet he deserves better than the judgement of his two previous biographers who infer that he was motivated by a foolish egoism and an incorrigible desire to please. They chose not to see that he was guided by the most profound and enlightened convictions regarding virtue, human freedom, democracy and freedom of conscience. Rowan risked his family, his fortune, his liberty and his life for his sacred principles of universal suffrage, religious toleration and a representative legislature.[503] Every citizen of a modern democratic state who enjoys these freedoms should salute 'those most God-provoking democrats this side of hell' who fought and suffered to secure them.

Nationalists in Ireland have turned many well-known United Irishmen into icons. Archibald Hamilton Rowan has escaped that fate. Perhaps this is because he survived the rebellion, or maybe it is due to what William Drennan saw as 'the Long Parliament in his countenance, some of the republican ferocity'.

Modern liberal Unionists may be embarrassed by their United Irish ancestors such as Archibald Hamilton Rowan. Some may have imbibed Harold Nicolson's description of Rowan and his fellow reformers as eccentric and dangerous egotists and traitors. Any such judgement would be a harsh injustice, just as Nicolson's book is a splenetic travesty.

---

503 Orr, p. 228.

It is beginning to be recognized that 'the evolutionary principles' of nascent liberalism derived from the Scottish Enlightenment (and Francis Hutcheson) allowed many Irish reformers to reconcile themselves to the Act of Union.[504] This was certainly the case with Rowan from the beginning. After some soul-searching and growing concern at the emergence of a 'Catholic Interest' that had little desire to forge an alliance with liberal Protestants, Rowan's friend William Drennan came around to the same point of view. The United Irishmen Rowan and Drennan have a strong claim to be the originators of modern liberal Unionism.

It is a great shame that Ulster Loyalists today know almost nothing of Archibald Hamilton Rowan, or of the contribution of their ancestors to modern democratic thought and human rights.

The one-time occupant of Killyleagh Castle should be an icon, not just for truly democratic Unionists, but for all those who hold that a modern state should be based on shared values of freedom, democracy and pluralism rather than the ethnic or religious affiliations of its citizens.

---

504 Hall, p. 64.

Primary sources

Dublin Unitarian Church Collection, Royal Irish Academy, Dublin.

Memorials, written in America in 1796, A. H. Rowan, Royal Irish Academy, Dublin.

Trial of Archibald Hamilton Rowan, 1794, Royal Irish Academy, Dublin.

The trial of Robert Edgworth, Esquire, Dublin 1778, Royal Irish Academy, Dublin.

Catalogue of the library of A. H. Rowan, Royal Irish Academy, Dublin.

Letter to A. H. Rowan, from Archibald Hamilton, 1807, Royal Irish Academy, Dublin.

Marriage and Baptismal register, 1750–1810, Unitarian Church, Dublin.

William Godwin's Diary, 1788–1836, Bodleian Library, Oxford.

Newspapers

Freeman's Journal, 1786–1803.
Dublin Evening Post, 1778–1805.
Northern Star, 1792–1797.
Northern Whig, 1823–1832.

Bibliography

Agnew, Jean, (ed.), (1998-1999) *The Drennan–McTier letters, 1776–1819*, 3 vols (The Women's History Project/Irish Manuscripts Commission).

Allen, Harry, (2004) *The Men of Ards* (Ballyhay Books).

Andrews, S., (2003) *Unitarian Radicalism, Political Rhetoric 1770–1814* (Palgrave).

Aptheker, Herbert, (1960) *The American Revolution*, (International Publishers).

Armstrong, Revd. James, (1829) 'Presbyterian Congregations in Dublin,' in *Ordination Service of James Martineau* (Goodwin).

Barrington, Jonah, (1997) *Personal Sketches and Recollections of His Own Time* (Ashfield Press).

Bartel, Roland, (ed.), (1965) *Liberty and Terror in England* (D.C. Heath).

Bartlett, Thomas (2004), *Revolutionary Dublin, 1795–1801: The Letters of Francis Higgins to Dublin Castle* (Four Courts Press).

- (2003) *1798: A Bicentenary Perspective* (Four Courts Press).

- (1998) *Theobald Wolfe Tone* (Lilliput Press).

Belsham, Thomas (1873), *Memoirs of the late Rev. Theophilus Lindsey, M.A.* (R. Hunter).

Benn, George (2008), *A History of the Town of Belfast* (Blackstaff Press).

Bew, John (2011), *Castlereagh: Enlightenment, War and Tyranny* (Quercus).

Beckett, J. C. (1976), *The Anglo-Irish Tradition* (Faber and Faber).

Binns, John (1854), *Recollection of a Life: Twenty Nine Years in Europe and Fifty Three Years in America* (Para McMillen).

Boylan, Henry (1981), *Wolfe Tone* (Gill and Macmillan).

Boyd, Andrew (2006), *Montgomery and the Black Man* (Columba Press).

Bric, Maurice J. (2008), *Ireland, Philadelphia and the Re-invention of America 1760–1800* (Four Courts Press).

Byrne, Patrick (1955), *Lord Edward Fitzgerald* (Talbot Press).

Campbell, Flann (1991), *The Dissenting Voice: Protestant Democracy in Ulster from Plantation to Partition* (Blackstaff Press).

Carroll, Denis (1998), *Unusual Suspects: Twelve Radical Clergy* (Columba Press).

Cash, Arthur, H. (1998), *John Wilkes, The Scandolous Father of Civil Liberty* (Yale University Press).

Chambers, Liam (1998), *The Rebellion in Kildare, 1790–1803* (Four Courts Press).

Clifford, Brendan (1989), *Belfast in the French Revolution* (Belfast Historical and Educational Society).

- (1991) *Scripture Politic: the Works of William Steel Dickson* (Athol Books).

Connolly, S. J. (2008), *Divived Kingdom Ierland 1630–1800* (Oxford University Press).

Cloncurry, Lord (1850), *Personal Recollections of Life and Times* (J. McGlashan).

Cullen, Seamus (2003), *The Emmet Rebellion in Kildare* (Gallery Press).

Curtin, Nancy (1998), *The United Irishmen: Popular Politics in Ulster and Dublin* (Clarendon Press).

Davis, M. T. (2004-2007), 'A Register of Vexations and Persecutions' in *Enlightenment and Dissent*, 23.

Dickson, David *et al* (eds.) (1994), *The United Irishmen: Republicanism, Radicalism and Rebellion*.

Dingley, James (2013), *Francis Hutcheson his Life and Work: An Introduction* (Belfast, 2013).

Disney, J. (1787), *The Work of John Jebb*.

Drummond, William (1840), *Autobiography of Archibald Hamilton Rowan* (T. Tegg and Co.).

Elliott, Marianne (1982), *Partners in Revolution: The United Irishmen and France* (Yale University Press).

Fitzpatrick, W. J. (1865), *The Sham Squire and the Informers of 1798* (M. H. Gill & Son.).

Fleming, D. A., and Malcomson, A. P. W. (2005), *A Volley of Execration: The Letters and Papers of John FitzGibbon, Earl of Clare 1772–1802* (Irish Manuscripts Commission).

Goodwin, Albert (1979), *The Friends of Liberty: The English Democratic Movement in the Age of Revolution* (Hutchinson).

Gordon, Lyndall (2005), *Mary Wollstonecraft: A New Genus* (Little, Brown & Company).

Gough, Hugh (1998), *The Terror in the French Revolution* (Palgrave Macmillan).

Grayling, A. C. (2007), *Towards the Light of Liberty* (Walker and Company).

Hall, Gerald R. (2011), *Ulster Liberalism, 1778–1876: The Middle Path* (Four Courts Press).

Hanna, W. A. (2000), *Intertwined Roots: An Ulster-Scot Perspective* (Columba Press).

Herlihy, Kevin, (ed.) (1996), *The Religion of Irish Dissent, 1850–1900* (Four Courts Press).

- (1997), *The Politics of Irish Dissent, 1650–1800*, (Four Courts Press).

- (1998) *Propagating the Word of Irish Dissent, 1650–1800* (Four Courts Press).

Hill, Jacqueline (1997), *From Patriots to Unionists: Dublin Civic Politics and Irish Protestant Patriotism, 1660–1840* (Clarendon Press).

Holmes, Finlay (2000), *The Presbyterian Church of Ireland* (Columba Press,).

Hume, David (1998), *To Right Some Things That We Thought Wrong: The Spirit of 1798 and Presbyterian Radicalism in Ulster* (The Ulster Society).

Ingrams, Richard (2005), *The Life and Adventures of William Cobbett* (Harper Collins).

Jacob, Rosamund (1937), *The Rise of the United Irishmen* (Harap).

Kronenberger, Louis (1974), *The Extraordinary Mr Wilkes* (Doubleday).

Larkin, John, (ed.) (1991), *The Trial of William Drennan* (Irish Academic Press).

Lloyd, Walter (1899), *The Story of Protestant Dissent and English Unitarianism* (Philip Green).

Madden, R. R. (1860), *United Irishmen Life and Times* (Lea and Blanchard).

Mansergh, Danny (2005), *Grattan's Failure, Parliamentary Opposition and the People of Ireland 1779–1800* (Irish Academic Press).

McBride, Ian (1993), 'William Drennan and the Dissenting Tradition', in Dickson, et al, *United Irishmen.*

Scripture Politics (2009), *Eighteenth Century Ireland* (Gill & Macmillan).

McDowell, R. B. (1940), 'The Personnel of the Dublin Society of United Irishmen, 1791–4', *Irish Historical Studies.*

(1998), *The Proceedings of the Dublin Society of United Irishmen* (Irish Manuscripts Commission).

McFarland, E. W. (1994), *Ireland and Scotland in the Age of Revolution* (Edinburgh University Press).

McMillan, William, 'Presbyterian Minister and the Ulster Rising' in Swords, Liam, (ed.) (1997), *Catholic Protestant and Dissenter: The Clergy and 1798* (The Columba Press).

Miller, Kerby A. (2003), et al, *Irish Immigrants in the Land of Canaan: Letters and Memoirs from Colonial and Revolutionary America, 1675–1815* (Oxford University Press).

McNeill, Mary (1960), *The Life And Time of Mary Ann McCracken, 1770–1866: A Belfast Panorama* (Blackstaff Press).

Moody, T. W., Vaughan, W.E. (1986), *Eighteenth-Century Ireland, 1691–1800* (Clarendon).

Moody, T. W., McDowell, Woods (2001), *The Writings of Theobald Wolfe Tone, 1763–98* (Oxford University Press).

Morley, Vincent (2002), *Irish Opinion and the American Revolution 1760–1783* (Cambridge University Press).

Namier, Sir Lewis and Brooke, John (eds.) (1964), *House of Commons, 1754–1790* (HMSO).

Nelson, Craig (2006), *Thomas Paine: Enlightenment, Revolution, and the Birth of Modern Nations* (Penguin).

Newsinger, John, (ed.) (1992), *The Autobiography of Jemmy Hope* (Merlin Press).

Nicolson, Harold (1943), *The Desire to Please: A Story of Hamilton Rowan and the United Irishmen* (Constable).

O'Brien, Conor Cruise (1993), *The Great Melody: A Thematic Biography of Edmund Burke* (University of Chicago Press).

- *(2009) First in Peace: How George Washington Set the Course for America* (Da Capo Press).

O'Donnell, Ruán (2003), *Robert Emmet and the Rebellion of 1798* (Irish Academic Press).

Orr, Phillip, 'Doing History', in Hill, Myrtle, Turner, Brian and Dawson, Kenneth, (eds.) (1998), *1798 Rebellion in County Down*.

Orr, Phillip, 'A Reinterpretation of the Life of Archibald Hamilton Rowan' in *1798 Rebellion in County Down*.

O'Toole, Fintan (2001), *A Traitor's Kiss: The Life of Richard Brinsley Sheridan* (Farrar, Straus and Groux).

Philip, Mark (1991), *The French Revolution and British Popular Politics* (Cambridge University Press).

Porter, J. L. (1871), *The Life and Times of Henry Cooke* (J. Murray).

Quinn, John (2002), *Soul on Fire: A Life of Thomas Russell* (Irish Academic Press).

Robbins, Caroline (1987), *The Eighteenth Century Commonwealthman* (University of Wisconsin Press).

Rodgers, Nini (2000), *Equiano and Anti-Slavery in Eighteenth-Century Belfast* (Ulster Historical Foundation).

Sampson, William (2002), *Memoirs of William Sampson* (Whittaker, Treacher and Arnott).

Small, Stephen (2002), *Political Thought in Ireland, 1776–1798* (Clarendon Press).

Smyth, Jim (1992), *Men of No Property: Irish Radical and Popular Politics in the late Eighteenth Century* (Gill and Macmillan).

Shannon, Millin (1900), *History of the Second Congregation of Protestant Dissenters in Belfast* (W. & G. Baird).

Stewart, A. T. Q. (1993), *A Deeper Silence: The Hidden Origins of the United Irishmen* (Faber and Faber).

- (1991), 'A Stable Unseen Power', in Larkin, J., *The Trial of William Drennan* (Irish Academic Press).

Tannahill, Reay (ed.) (1966), *Paris in the Revolution: A Collection of Eye-witness Accounts* (Folio Society).

Taylor, Barbara (2002), *Mary Wollstonecraft and the Feminist Imagination* (University of California Press).

Thompson, E. P. (1964), *The Making of the English Working Class* (Pantheon Books).

Tillyard, Stella (1997), *Citizen Lord, Edward Fitzgerald, 1763–1798* (Chatto & Windus).

Wade, Stephen (2008), *Foul Deeds and Suspicious Death in Dublin* (Barnsley).

Weber, Paul (1997), *The United Irishmen in Hamburg, 1796–1803* (Four Courts Press).

Wells, Roger (1986), *Insurrection: the British Experience, 1795–1803* (Sutton Publishing Ltd.).

Whelan, Fergus (2010), *Dissent into Treason: Unitarians, King-killers and the Society of United Irishmen* (Brandon).

Whelan, Kevin (1996), *The Tree of Liberty: Radicalism, Catholicism, and the Construction of Irish Identity* (Cork University Press).

Wichert, Sabine (2004), *From the United Irishmen to Twentieth-Century Unionism: A Festschrift for A.T.Q. Stewart* (Four Courts Press).

Williams, G. A. (1968), *Artisans and Sans-Cullotes* (Thompson).

Wilson, David A. (1998), *United Irishmen, United States* (Cornell University Press).

Wise, Thomas J., (ed.) (1980), *An Address to the People of Ireland by Percy Bysshe Shelley* (Clarendon Press).

Index